In Bushveld and Desert

A Game Ranger's Life

By the same author

Die lang pad van Stoffel Mathysen (1998)
Stoffel in die wildernis (2000)
Skuilplek (2002)
Stoffel by die afdraaipad (2004)
Stoffel se veldnotas (2007)

Christiaan Bakkes

In Bushveld and Desert

A Game Ranger's Life

Stories and photographs selected and arranged
by Suzette Kotzé-Myburgh
Stories translated by Elsa Silke

Human & Rousseau
Cape Town Pretoria

Copyright © 2008 by Christiaan Bakkes
English translation by Elsa Silke
Edited by Louise Steyn
First published in 2008 by Human & Rousseau,
a division of NB Publishers,
40 Heerengracht, Cape Town, 8001
Photographs in book and on cover: Chris Bakkes, Steven Dell,
MS Erasmus, André Gildenhuys, Simon Mayes, Emsie Verwey,
Cas Bakkes, Matilde de Jager
Cover design by Etienne van Duyker
Set in 11 on 13 pt Plantin by Alinea
Printed and bound by Paarl Print, Oosterland Street, Paarl, South Africa

ISBN-10   0-7981-4928-0
ISBN-13   978-0-7981-4928-0

Dedicated to the conservationists, game rangers,
community game guards, trackers, field guides,
safari leaders and wildlife scientists doing the
good work in Africa

Thank you to

Brent Pirow and John and Ingrid Ferguson
Alida Potgieter, for years of support
Suzette Kotzé-Myburgh and Elsa Silke, for their expertise
Emsie, for sharing my dream

Contents

The elephants of De Wagensdrif   9
Village baboon   13
Hunting season   19
The leopard   25
Training   38
Routine patrol   42
Deception   46
Moment of truth   51
Hailstorm   61
Croc in a pisvel   68
Guweni pool   79
Brothers   84
Culling   90
Hitching through Africa   96
February 26, 1994   102
Turning point   107
The battle for the mealie fields   109
The hunt   123
Die-hard   129
Amakange borehole   134
Bush law   137
The dog   142
Experiment   150
Gatvol   158
A dog without a master is a dead dog   169
Ecotone   172
Mountain zebra at Okondekafontein   176
Rainy season   178
Gemsbok near Ogamsfontein   186

Ozohavera   188
Magic safari   192
Confluence   201
The Etendeka mountains   204
Steppenwolf   209
Afrikaans must stop   213
Detour   218
The day of the cats   224
Veteran I   232
Veteran II   236
Piet Renoster   239
Rhino watcher   244
Christmas in the desert   249
No-man's-land   267
Tier   275
Reunion   282
Moments   285

Glossary   293

The elephants of De Wagensdrif

"Hear that, Boude?" My brother looked at me, wide-eyed. "There it is again. On the other side of the river. In the bushes. Can you hear?"

I was beginning to worry.

"What?" I asked.

"Sh! There it is again. Can't you hear it?"

"No. What is it? Tell me, man."

My brother cocked his head towards the opposite side of the river. He listened. I didn't like the tone of his voice. Fear gripped me. All I could hear was the murmur of water over pebbles. I saw the expression on his face: an awareness of something terrible.

"What is it, man?"

I was really anxious now; there was fear in his eyes.

"O, jirre, Boude. Elephants! Hurry! We have to get away from here!"

He jumped up, kicked sand over our cooking fire and stuffed the plastic mugs, waxpaper and half-empty bottle of cool drink into his canvas backpack. With a single bound he cleared the sandy bank and landed in the reed bush.

"Boude! Come on, man!"

My knees were weak with fear. I stumbled as I tried to get up from the sand. Panic overwhelmed me.

"Marius! Wait for me, man! Waaaiiit!"

His long legs reappeared on the sandy bank above. Then he was beside me. He grabbed me by the arm and dragged me up the slope. We fled headlong through the reeds, my feet barely touching the ground.

I was five years old, he was twelve.

As usual, we had been in the veld since the crack of dawn. My mom had wrapped buttered rolls and a piece of sausage for each in wax paper. She'd mixed some cool drink, poured it into a Coke bottle and put everything into Marius's backpack.

Since the beginning of the weekend I'd been looking forward to a day in the veld with my brother. Early this morning we followed the footpath through the gorge until we reached the river. We walked downstream along the river bank. It was a fresh morning and the sun sparkled on the water. While we were walking, Marius told me how the Voortrekkers had clashed here with the Matabeles. In my mind's eye I saw bearded men firing their sannas at warriors bursting unexpectedly and terrifyingly from the undergrowth, assegais at the ready. My brother's history lessons were always riveting stuff.

"The name of the farm is De Wagensdrif, because the first group of Voortrekkers pulled their ox-wagons through the drift here. Look, right here, where the river bank is not so steep. See how shallow the water is? And you can still see the tracks of the old wagon trail."

"Yes, I see. It's the best place to pull the wagons through."

My brother was very clever.

"The Voortrekkers hunted elephant here too," he mentioned in passing.

Beyond a dense reed bush lay a snow-white stretch of sand. He and I had discovered it during one of our previous expeditions. We were the only ones who knew about it. It had become a regular resting place.

We were sipping the lukewarm, watery cool drink (my mom always added too much water), and getting ready to roast our sausages on a stick in the flames, when my brother heard the elephants.

Now we were fleeing through the reed bush, heading for the ridges. My brother let go of my arm and drew ahead, bounding over the stones like a grey duiker, hair and shirt flapping in the wind.

"O got, jirre jissis! Today they're going to trample us, for sure!"

"Marius! Wait for me! I'm going to tell Ma!" I wailed from behind.

My brother slowed down and we reached the top of the ridge together. We jogged down the slope of a narrow gorge and up the other side. Under the boekenhout with the owl's nest my brother stopped. Winded. I caught my breath and wiped my eyes. My brother looked at me gravely.

"I think we're safe now."

Then he winked and a smile lit up his face. I realised I had been tricked once again.

I sniffed only once. "I'm going to tell Ma."

When we'd left the West Coast the year before and my father realised he would have to raise his children in the city, he'd used his savings to buy a farm nearby. It wasn't much of a farm. Fifty morgen of sandstone ridges and half a kilometre of the Elands River. None of it was suitable for cultivation or pasture, so my father was able to get it for next to nothing. It was sixty kilometres outside Pretoria and we spent every weekend there. Under flatcrown wild syringas we parked the caravan and pitched our tents. My little sister played under the trees most of the time, close to my mother. My eldest brother took the .22 and was off to shoot doves. My other brother and I went on journeys of discovery. Soon that farm was my entire life.

Of course there were no elephants. The last elephants had probably been exterminated to make room for farmland more than a hundred years before our arrival.

Because of my brother, the farm was to me a world peopled by Matabeles, Voortrekkers with flintlock muskets, lions and elephants. A world where anything was possible and every expedition was filled with the promise of adventure.

Since then our ways have parted. He no longer calls me Boude. He works in a large office block in Johannesburg nowadays, where he sits around a table with politicians and the rich and famous. Now and again I see his photograph in a newspaper or *De Kat* magazine. I stayed behind on the farm and from there my road took me away from the sandstone ridges in search of bigger adventures in greater wildernesses. In time my life became entwined with the fortune of elephants.

Village baboon

The baboons were milling around the concrete reservoir. A few were running round and round the high wall. As the bakkie approached, they scampered away one by one, barking as they ran into the hills. A few lingered, but their courage failed them when we stopped at the water point. Only one remained behind: a large female. She was standing on the wall, looking at something inside. Januarie and I got out of the bakkie. It was an icy winter morning in the Bushveld.

It was clear that the female found herself in a dilemma. She was reluctant to leave the dam wall. Whatever was on the inside was keeping her there. She bared her fangs at us and barked anxiously. It was only when we reached the high dam wall that she gave up. She jumped off the wall and seemed to be following her troop. But some distance away she sat down on a rock. She was watching us.

The other baboons were calling her from the ridges and the wooded ravines. She answered, but remained where she was. Watching us suspiciously.

The wall of the concrete reservoir was close on two metres high. Januarie and I clambered up. We sat on the edge and looked inside. The dam was half full. In the middle floated a small baboon. The little head was submerged; one hand was struggling feebly. Januarie jumped back down and walked into the veld in search of a stick.

The farm Kwarriehoek was a new addition to the Skuins-draai reserve. The previous owner had been bought out and we had just acquired the farm. Although it had been a cattle farm, Kwarriehoek boasted a healthy population of impala, kudu and warthog. There were also mountain reedbuck and klipspringers in the ridges. The addition of Kwarriehoek enlarged the reserve by two thousand hectares, of which about a thousand were mountain veld. The rest were plains with thorn bushveld. The reserve now had enough open plains to support giraffe. We planned the resettlement of giraffe as soon as Kwarriehoek had been added to the rest of the reserve by means of a gameproof fence.

Because it had been a cattle farm until recently, the existing water points still consisted of concrete reservoirs with drinking troughs. In due course we would construct sunken waterholes more suitable for game. Birds and baboons regularly fell into the high concrete dams, where they drowned and poisoned the water.

Januarie returned with a sturdy sickle bush stick. He handed it to me and scaled the dam wall again. I leaned over, hooked the small baboon and pulled it closer. Januarie hung over the edge and lifted her out by the scruff of her neck. She was soaking wet. We climbed down and laid her on the ground. The large female had now rejoined the troop. They were watching us curiously from the rocks.

The small baboon's stomach was distended from the water she had swallowed. Her fingers and toes were pale blue with cold. The eyelids were half closed and the brown eyes stared without registering anything. She could not have survived much longer in water that cold. But now she was showing signs of life and making feeble groaning sounds.

I took an old cloth from behind the seat of the bakkie and began to rub her dry. I massaged her belly until she threw up water. Her head rolled limply on her neck and her eyelids remained half closed. When she had thrown up all the water in her stomach, the groans became louder.

I decided that body heat might warm her up. I held her against my chest. Her open fingers found my woollen jersey and she wrapped her legs around my waist. She pressed herself tightly against my body, hungry for heat. Her little hands clutched more firmly at my jersey and within moments she was stuck to me like a leech.

I had to carry on with my rounds. The fencing crew was waiting. On the back of the bakkie were the last rolls of wire and the droppers they needed. I wanted to inspect their work. Afterwards I would take a drive through Kwarriehoek to see whether I could spot any game in the early morning. The baboon could stay with me until she was warm enough. Then I would return her to the veld.

Before we left, Januarie and I looked for a sturdy, gnarled stump. We lowered it into the water. If a baboon fell in again, at least he'd have a ladder to climb out. We resumed our patrol.

We drove through the veld – Januarie and I, with the baboon clinging to my chest. The day grew warm and sunny, but the baboon showed no signs of thawing. Her head was resting on my chest and she seemed to be sleeping, her arms and legs still clutching me in a firm embrace.

It was all very well while we were in the veld, but there was a problem: It was the end of the month. I had to go to town.

We got back to the old farmstead that served as ranger station, but the baboon was still holding on tightly. Januarie and the game rangers were getting ready for their excursion to town. I collected my monthly reports and requisition forms in the cramped little office and shoved them into my leather bag. The little baboon was uttering soft grunting sounds.

The town of Marble Hall lay thirty kilometres from the reserve. It was where I did my admin and planned my logistics. Januarie sat next to me in the cab; the other rangers were on the back. The baboon was still nestled against my chest.

I left the rangers in the centre of town to do their shopping. We had arranged to meet in the same place later. I drove to the co-op at the edge of town to stock up on barbed wire and posts.

The man at the co-op knew me well; I bought all my supplies from him. One day he had discovered a python in one of his storerooms. I had removed it for him and released it in the reserve. While his assistants were loading the bakkie, we talked about the baboon.

At the supermarket people weren't all that pleased to see a baboon clinging to my chest. I bought bread and milk and left in a hurry. The men in the liquor store found it hilarious. They tugged at her tail and touched her ears, but she showed no reaction. At the butcher's store the owner wanted to know if *that* was the fresh meat I had promised him.

Only the bank and the post office remained.

The plump girl at the bank raved about the cute little monkey on my chest. She asked if she was my little pet. How had I managed to get her so tame? As usual when I went into the bank on business, she wanted to know when I was going to invite her to the reserve. She was crazy about the outdoors, she informed me.

At the post office I mailed my monthly reports and the wildlife and bird lists to the head office in Pietersburg. Relieved that all my tasks had been completed, I walked out into the sunny street. Now all that was left was to fill up the bakkie.

Suddenly I felt a change come over the baboon. I looked down. Her little head was no longer resting against my chest. Her eyes were wide open. Startled, she took in the unfamiliar surroundings. Her head turned from side to side and her grip around my body relaxed. With my left hand I grabbed her by the scruff of her neck. She gave a terrified scream and I sprinted for the bakkie. She let go of my jersey and put up a desperate struggle. I tightened my grip on her neck. People stopped and stared at the strange spectacle.

In the wink of an eye the baboon had made a full recovery. Holding on to the screaming, squirming creature, I made a dash for the bakkie. When I threw open the door, she slipped out of my grip and dived into the cab. She tried to jump out on the other side but was stopped by the closed window. She fell back on the seat. I jumped in and slammed the door shut.

Like a thing possessed she threw herself repeatedly at the closed windows. I couldn't allow her to escape. There would be chaos if she escaped in the middle of town. It would be cruel to her as well. I had to return her to the veld, to her troop.

The rangers came running across the street with their shopping. They had witnessed what was happening. The townspeople stood motionless, staring at the spectacle. I motioned to the rangers to jump on. My fuel tank was almost empty; I had no choice but to fill up.

The poor little baboon was now panic-stricken. She darted to and fro in the cab like a whirlwind. Her fear, added to the large quantity of water she had swallowed, led to a predictable reaction. A streak of yellowish brown faeces squirted over the inside of the windscreen, the seat, my briefcase and my lap.

As the rangers jumped on the back, I switched on the bakkie and headed for the garage. The baboon was now spattering the roof, the rear window and my neck. At the filling station Januarie urged the petrol attendant to make haste. I handed him the key through a chink in the window. Januarie berated the attendant for staring instead of filling up. Slowly the man came into action.

Now the baboon had turned her attention to me. She wrapped her arms around my shoulder and bit me in the ear and neck. Though her fangs had not yet grown out fully, the bites were nonetheless painful.

Once more I grabbed her by the scruff of the neck and plucked her off me. I threw her onto the floor on the passenger side. She jumped back up and grabbed me by the hair, sinking her teeth into my scalp. I struggled to free myself. Her nails dug into my cheek. This time I threw her down more roughly, and for a while she crouched on the floor, dazed. It was getting hot inside the cab. Through the streaks of shit on the windows I could see that the rangers and petrol attendants looked both worried and amused.

It seemed like years before the tank was filled. Through

the chink in the window I paid and received the key. The baboon launched another atttack and I felt blood running down my neck. Then she crawled into the space behind the seat and cowered in the dark beside the jack and the wheel spanner.

Under the staring eyes of the townspeople we departed. There was no chance of opening a window. It was hot as hell in the cabin by now. The stench of baboon shit hung heavily in the air. Sickly sweet. The soiled windows obstructed my view.

It became a long drive back to the reserve. Fortunately the baboon remained behind the seat.

The sun was low on the western horizon when I reached the concrete reservoir at Kwarriehoek. All was silent in the ridges. I stopped beside the dam and threw open the door of the bakkie. Then I pushed the backrest forward and stepped back.

Cautiously the little baboon came out. She looked around for a while before she realised where she was. She jumped out. She glanced at the rangers and at me. Then she made off across the veld, heading for the ridges. On a rock, etched against the sky, a large baboon appeared. She gave a shrill cry.

The little one was swallowed by the undergrowth at the foot of the ridge. A while later she reappeared against a rock, halfway to the top. Again the female cried. I waited till they had been reunited and disappeared over the skyline together.

In the quiet of the evening I wondered who exactly had been the village baboon today.

For months the stench of baboon shit lingered in the bakkie.

Hunting season

In the last rays of the setting sun the sickle bush thicket was streaked with red. Through the telescope part of the kudu's shoulder was visible through a gap in the bushes. I was racked by uncertainty. I had the .243 Musgrave, a light rifle for a kudu. Riaan had taken the 30-0-6 Brno. By now the sun had sunk into the branches.

All I could see was a patch of grey hide with a thin white line twisting and diverging across it. I imagined the kudu watching me through the bushes with dark eyes. Ears pricked and nostrils flared. Should I or shouldn't I? A .243 bullet could easily be deflected by a branch. It was growing dark. I crouched there in two minds. Through the gap I studied the nearly invisible kudu hide for clues. All I could see through the telescope was grey hair intersected by a white line.

Beside me Hendrik Mahlangu stirred restlessly. The tension was building. The guys from Siyabuswa, the nearest village, wanted the meat the next morning. Perhaps Riaan would find something. What should I do? I didn't want to wound the animal in the fading light.

Hendrik Mahlangu and I had been in the veld all day. We had seen a lot of warthog and impala, but we had never got a chance. The animals here were wary of hunters. Half an hour earlier we had first noticed the kudu's white tail at a waterhole. We had taken his spoor.

Hendrik had had to point out the kudu to me. My eyes were still untrained; it had taken a few minutes before I recognised that which was visible of the kudu. Now it was my decision. My ears began to buzz. Slowly but surely destiny was taking over. The telescope approached the eye. The cross hair rested on the spot where the white line diverged. The butt bored into my shoulder. A final hint of indecision and then resignation. My forefinger pressed down on the trigger.

There was the dull thud of a bullet on flesh. The blotch that had been the kudu disappeared behind the thicket. Hendrik Mahlangu got a head start on me and was already making his way through the sickle bush. I followed but soon lost sight of him. I ran blindly in the direction in which I had fired the shot. Thorns scratched my arms and legs. The next moment I almost collided with Hendrik.

He stood there, smiling. At his feet lay the kudu. Judging by the froth in the blood the bullet had found the lung. It was a young bull. One and a half twists to the horns. Not nearly trophy size, but to me the most beautiful kudu I had ever seen. The year was 1987, my first year as a student ranger. It was my first kudu. The hunting season had opened.

At the time my fellow student Riaan van Zyl and I were in charge of a number of game farms for the South African Development Corporation. The farms varied in size; some were a respectable seven or ten thousand hectares, others were hardly more than game camps of one or two thousand hectares. Some boasted beautiful stony ridges and dry river beds. Others consisted of monotonous expanses of thorn bush, choked with sickle bush and umbrella thorn and suitable only for kudu, impala and warthog. The bigger farms had giraffe, and at Sandspruit there was even a small herd of white rhino. Riaan and I loved working there; it felt like Big Five country.

The farms were not far apart. Riaan was stationed at Tierpan and I at Kwaggavoetpad. Our work overlapped and the two of us regularly camped on the other farms.

The plan was to enlarge the farms systematically by buying adjoining land and developing them as game reserves. For the time being, however, they were no more than hunting farms for government officials. On weekends Riaan and I accompanied the hunters who had come to shoot blesbok and red hartebeest. In the evenings we had to socialise with them and try to keep them from demolishing the lapa or setting it alight.

After my first kudu I gained confidence. There were many opportunities for getting my eye in. Riaan and I were required to control the numbers of impala and kudu. We worked out quotas in accordance with game counts. On each farm a certain number of animals had to be culled.

At night we went out in the bakkie, taking our rifles and a shooting lamp. Hendrik Mahlangu was in charge of the lamp. One night I would drive while Riaan shot and the next night we would change places. The small herds of impala stood blinded and petrified in the beam of the lamp; with the .243 we'd pot them one by one with a single shot to the head. Some nights we shot impala ewes and lambs. On other nights we'd shoot kudu – cows and heifers. In time our marksmanship improved.

We undertook a daylight hunt for the impala rams and kudu bulls. At the crack of dawn we would set off on foot in opposite directions, each heading for a remote corner of the farm. Our goal was to see how many buck we could shoot before eleven o'clock. I shot my trophy kudu and a few sizable bulls.

Riaan and I were young and bloodthirsty. We competed. Sometimes we would return with five or six impala each. We sat in the veld, roasting the livers and kidneys on the coals. We were both slightly amazed that we were being paid to do this work.

Hunting opportunities came from other quarters. The government vet asked us to shoot warthog to run tests for swine fever. On each of the farms we shot a number of warthog. With a large hypodermic syringe we drew blood from the heart and froze it in a test tube. At the end of the month we took the samples to Marble Hall.

The Development Corporation also had a sheep and goat breeding project in the district. Black-backed jackal were a problem, and Riaan and I were summoned. The pelts of the jackal we shot were enough for a single bed kaross.

Word was sent that the officials at Siyabuswa wanted to decorate their new boardroom. Elandsfontein bordered on the Highveld. It was open country and we did not often hunt there. The zebra were tame. Riaan and I made a day of it. We moved stealthily among the boekenhouts and the termite hills. The walls of the new boardroom at Siyabuswa were hung with the skins of four zebra stallions.

At times there were wounded blesbok or hartebeest to be put out of their misery after a weekend hunt. By the end of the hunting season Riaan and I had become sharpshooters. I loved my job.

The director asked me to shoot one last blue wildebeest; he wanted the skin for the floor of his office. I drove across to Hartbeeshoek. Soon I found a herd of blue wildebeest. As I approached, they gazed at me, snorting. I sat on a low termite hill and cocked my rifle. This time I had the 30-0-6. A large bull stood somewhat behind the others, hidden by a heifer. That one would look good on the director's floor, I decided.

I waited for the herd to stomp and wheel a little and suddenly the bull was in front. He snorted defiantly in my direction, facing me. I took aim. I pointed the gun at his neck. An easy target, I thought. Too easy. I raised the barrel for a shot in the head. Halfway up, my hand closed too soon and I pressed the trigger.

The shot echoed emptily in my ears. I saw the bull shake his head and leap into the air. The herd made off in a cloud of dust. Before they disappeared into the thicket, I caught a last glimpse of the bull. Something hung from his mouth. I had shattered his jaw.

I searched in vain. I found bloodstains on the rocks. Drops of blood on grass blades. For the rest of the day I followed the spoor. Now and again the herd came into view through the trees in the distance. They would not allow me to approach again. Towards late afternoon their tracks mingled with the tracks of other wildebeest and I became confused.

Failure lay heavily on my mind. For a while I considered

keeping the whole episode to myself. Covering it up. Then my conscience got the better of me. I swallowed my pride. I radioed Riaan; he and Hendrik would have to come and help.

We were up before dawn. Hendrik Mahlangu got us back on the spoor. We found the herd. The bull was no longer with them. Towards afternoon we found the place where he had rested under a horn-pod tree. The grass was flattened; there were drops of blood and larger splashes of serum. But he had got up and carried on.

I thought of the wildebeest. It was a wound that would not heal. Apart from the pain of the injury, he was doomed to die of hunger and thirst. I hated myself. How hesitant I had been with that first kudu. How careful and discerning had been my behaviour during the entire hunting season. And now this. In a flash I had undone everything. And all for a bloody rug for the bloody director. No, I admonished myself, it wasn't the director's fault. I had wanted this commission, a final opportunity before the hunting season closed. It was my own bloodthirst and cocky behaviour that had caused this misery.

The blue wildebeest seemed to have disappeared off the face of the earth. For three days we criss-crossed the farm from one end to the other. I found it hard to believe that two thousand hectares could be so big. In the evenings around the fire Riaan tried to cheer me up. Hendrik Mahlangu seemed unconcerned.

All I could think of was the wildebeest slowly wasting away. Just a few days before he had been master of his herd; now he was crazed with hunger and thirst, dumb and uncomprehending. At night I dreamed of him. I dreamed I found him. With his disfigured mouth he asked me why. I dreamed of taking aim. The trigger was stiff and refused to budge. I pulled with all my might. Then the gun went off and spat out the bullet just a few metres in front of the barrel. The wildebeest disappeared in a cloud of dust.

Towards late afternoon on the fourth day Hendrik Mahlangu arrived at camp. Riaan and I had given up, but Hendrik had tracked him down.

We found him in a lekkerruikpeul thicket beside a stream. It looked shady and peaceful, a good place to die. He was lying in the grass. He watched as we approached, but did not get up. His skin was dull and grey. His hipbones and ribs were jutting out. His jaw hung slack, his tongue lolling from his mouth, parched and brown.

I cocked the rifle and approached. With a shot through the brain I ended his life.

The leopard

The leopard was young and inexperienced, but confident enough to keep trying. Unnoticed, he crept up to the bushes that grew against the kraal. He lay there late at night, waiting for a few restless calves to wander away from the safety of their mothers and the herd. One or two even moved in his direction at times, unaware of the danger on the other side of the stockade.

Every night the leopard misjudged the situation. Sometimes he charged too early and at other times he lingered after he had made his presence known. Pandemonium would erupt and the stampeding cattle would flatten the stockade and disappear, lowing, into the dark bushes.

This carried on for a month. Every third or fourth night the cattle broke out of the kraal. Finally the farmer decided to call in the help of the ranger.

I was the ranger at the neighbouring game reserve. Just the previous year I had still been a student. I was inexperienced, but eager to make my mark and always on the lookout for a challenge. This one I wanted to handle properly.

I asked the advice of my senior colleagues in Pietersburg, and they told tales of how they had outwitted leopard in their day. At the National Zoo's breeding centre at Potgietersrus I borrowed a trap.

I made arrangements with the farmer. I would camp on the farm and look for the leopard's lairs. I would set the trap in such a place, but no one except me would be allowed to approach the trap. The farmer told me he had shot a large male leopard on the farm three years before. This one was probably a youngster that had moved into the older one's territory.

"What are you going to do with the leopard once you've caught him?" the farmer inquired.

"I'm going to release him in our game reserve."

The farmer looked at me gravely. "You'd better make sure you get to the trap first if there's a leopard inside. If I get there first, I won't hesitate to shoot him."

I pitched my camp among the tamboti trees. For days I explored the farm. I studied the tall trees, thickets and ridges. In game and cattle paths I found leopard tracks, in gorges and crevices the grey-haired herdsman pointed out places where the leopard had slept or recently caught a baboon. I enjoyed the time away from the reserve and learned from the old man who had spent his life tending another man's cattle in the veld.

At last I decided to set the trap in a game path that led through a sickle bush thicket. The leopard made regular use of the path. I drove back to the reserve to fetch my helpers and their camping equipment. The trap was brought along.

Meticulously we set the trap. First, the wire mesh floor was covered with sand. The leopard should not sense that he was entering a strange environment.

Next, we set the trap door. A metal rod on the roof of the cage kept the door open. Attached to the rod was a steel cable that ran through spools at the back of the trap. A young warthog that I had shot the previous afternoon was tied securely to the steel cable. The device was simple. The leopard would enter the rectangular trap and head for the back, where the dead warthog lay. He would bite into it and tug. The cable would stretch tightly over the spools and draw back the metal rod. The heavy trap door would descend and an angry, frightened leopard would be caught in the trap. The trap door had to be finely balanced on the end of the rod, because leopards are agile and this one would need only half a chance to slip through the falling door.

We camouflaged the trap carefully with freshly chopped branches. The trap shouldn't look strange to the leopard. It had to resemble any other thicket in which a warthog had died. Finally the trap, the branches and the surroundings were rinsed with water to remove the scent of man. At last only the door protruding above the trap remained visible.

The Pedi rangers and I returned to our camp in the clump of tamboti a few kilometres away. The Pedis settled in under the trees and began to cook porridge in a pot over a small fire. Soon it was quite cosy at camp. Now we just had to wait.

I took my binoculars and walked into the veld.

The rain had been early that year and had fallen abundantly. The green grass stood ankle-deep. There were veld flowers everywhere: yellow mouse whiskers and violet foxgloves. Butterflies fluttered in the morning sun. I relished every moment in the veld.

My first task at the beginning of the year had been to eradicate an unsightly blue gum plantation bordering on the main road at the boundary of the reserve. The Pedis and I had got busy with long-handled axes and double-handed saws. It was backbreaking work, and initially my student's body protested. Sometimes blood mixed freely with sweat. Slowly my body came to terms with the discomfort, and I grasped the handle of the axe more firmly. The blade splintered the trunk in exactly the right place. The Pedis noticed that the white man learned quickly and was undaunted by hard work. In the blue gum forest friendships were formed which would lay the foundation for future working relationships. By the time the plantation began to shrink, my body was bronzed and hard.

My work wasn't limited to the reserve. On Friday nights I kept watch from a koppie, on the lookout for shooting lamps. It was a part of the Northern Transvaal where game was abundant. At night herds of kudu, impala and warthog emerged from the bushes to graze on the verges of the untarred roads. After a few stiff shots of brandy, the men came from the bars in the neighbouring towns, and with bakkies, shooting lamps and enough guns to fight the third Boer War they set their sights on the game by the roadside.

Many a night I pursued these offenders, and regularly they evaded me. One evening, after a hot pursuit, I succeeded in cornering a bakkie at a farm gate. In court, the illicit hunters subsequently forfeited their bakkie, shooting lamps and rifles. Outside the building threats and curses were flung at me, but the message quickly spread. The new game ranger was not someone to be trifled with.

In winter there were game capture and culling operations. Excess game like zebra and wildebeest were exported to game farms. The capture team camped in the reserve for weeks, and I helped to build bomas and holding pens. The game catchers were veterans of the bush, and their tales around the campfire in the evenings fired up the younger men's lust for adventure.

There was also the commercial utilisation of superfluous game in the reserve. I either hunted, or I accompanied hunters. Soon my eye was taking steady aim and my finger on the trigger did not falter. Warthog, impala and kudu fell before my rifle. This target practice was bound to come in handy when I reported for military training the next year.

It had been a good year, I thought while searching for the piet-my-vrou concealed in the dense leaf canopy on the rocky ridge. The mysterious bird's loud call heralded the arrival of a new season, but the bird itself remained hidden in the shadowy foliage.

To catch a leopard would be a nice finishing touch.

In the mounting heat of the afternoon I walked back to camp. The Pedis, in the meantime, had pitched a large military tent and were now listening to a portable radio broadcasting a soccer match in Northern Sotho. Januarie Mabogoane looked up when I walked into camp.

"It's going to rain tonight, Morena."

When the rain began to fall that night, we all sat inside the tent.

Early the next morning Januarie and I left the rest behind and drove through the wet veld to inspect the trap.

"I'm worried, Januarie. We set that trap very finely. It's probably been sprung by the wind and rain."

"We'll see, Morena."

I stopped the Land Cruiser some distance from the trap and peered through the bushes.

"The door is still open, Morena," Januarie said.

It took me a while to see the trap door in the midst of the sickle bush thicket.

"Let's go back to camp. Our work is finished for today."

I spent the rest of the day in the veld. Januarie and the Pedis stayed at camp. The next day the trap was still unsprung. I drove to the reserve for the day to check on what was happening there. When I drove back to the camp under the tamboti trees that night, it was raining hard. Tonight the wind will make the trap door fall, I thought.

The day broke cloudless and clear. Water glistened on grass and leaves in the morning sun.

"The door is shut, Morena."

Damn.

I got out of the Land Cruiser to reset the trap that had been sprung by the wind and rain of the previous night. Januarie got out too and followed me.

I was ten metres from the trap when I heard a low growl coming from the shadows. I stopped in my tracks. The growl changed into a furious roar as a leopard dived at me from the rear of the trap, fangs bared and yellow eyes flashing. I felt the blood in my veins run cold. Januarie turned and ran for the vehicle. I had been so confident that I had left the twelve-bore shotgun on the seat of the bakkie.

The steel mesh of the closed trap door stopped the leopard and he fell back on the floor of the cage. Immediately he threw himself against the door again. Panting and growling, he strained with all his might. He clawed at the steel grate. As I watched, a nail was ripped off completely. The leopard glared at me furiously with piercing yellow eyes. I stood petrified.

The next moment Januarie was by my side, pushing the shotgun into my hand. "Shoot him, Morena. Shoot him."

Slowly I came to my senses. The trap was sturdy. The leopard couldn't escape. I had caught a leopard. When I had least expected it, a leopard had been waiting for me in the trap.

"Shoot him, Morena. Shoot him," Januarie kept urging.

I shook my head. "No, Januarie. I'm not going to shoot him. We're going to load the trap onto the bakkie and release the leopard in the reserve."

For a few moments Januarie stared at me in disbelief.

"OK, Morena," he said hesitantly.

We sped off in the Land Cruiser to fetch the other Pedis and the necessary equipment. Januarie roused the Pedis and soon they were raring to go. "Inkwe! Inkwe!" it echoed through the camp, as the men scrambled for spades, posts and a large groundsheet.

By the time we got back to the trap, the leopard was frantic. I reversed the bakkie up against the cage. The Pedis jumped off and stood to one side, watching. Shotgun in hand, I began to remove the sickle bush branches from the cage. Januarie was over the worst of his shock and took his place at my side. After he had made certain that the trap was a sturdy structure, his newfound courage made him scornful towards the other Pedis, who were approaching with caution. "Come and help, you scared buggers!"

One by one they joined us.

The leopard threw himself against the sides of the trap, and the Pedis jumped back in fear. He grazed his nose against the steel mesh. Growling, he lay down in a corner – fearful, furious and desperate.

Soon the sickle bush branches had been removed. Four steel rings had been fixed to the top of the trap, two on either side. Two sturdy wooden posts were pushed through them to lift the trap onto the bakkie. Januarie, two of the Pedis and I lifted the trap out of the thicket. The leopard roared loudly in protest. The sickle bush left bloody scratches on our arms and legs and our faces were beaded with sweat.

"Bring it forward and lift it high, guys."

A Pedi stumbled and the trap door caught the tailgate of the bakkie. As we set the trap down, the door was pushed open. Pedis scattered in every direction. I saw the danger. In my effort to lift the trap I had left my shotgun propped against the wheel of the bakkie. The gap in the door was big enough for the leopard to slip through and wreak havoc amongst us. Fortunately the leopard was too busy throwing himself against my side of the trap. But in a matter of seconds he would notice the gap.

Using all my strength, I tried to lift the heavy trap. I feared a blood vessel in my brain might burst. Sweat was pouring down my forehead. The trap did not drop any lower, but the gap was still large enough for the leopard to escape. I knew I would be the animal's first victim.

A leopard usually jumps for your throat and sinks its claws into your neck or scalp; with its hind claws it will disembowel you. It's all over, I thought, struggling fiercely with the last of my strength to raise the trap. I managed to lift it a few centimetres and the door began to slide shut. Suddenly Januarie was on the other side. He grabbed the wooden post and strained. Together we dislodged the trap from the tailgate, and the door fell down.

Januarie and I rested the front of the trap on the tailgate and breathed deeply.

"That was close, fucking close."

I pointed the shotgun at the leopard while the Pedis lifted the trap onto the bakkie and covered it. Under the large tarpaulin it sounded as if the leopard had calmed down.

I had a favourite spot in the reserve. In the southeastern corner was a sandy tract surrounded by sandstone ridges. It was open savannah with large camel thorn, sandvaalbos and raasblaar. There were a few large pans that filled up during the rainy season. At the moment there was plenty of water.

In the dry season I kept one of the pans full by means of an underground pipeline I had laid from a nearby windmill.

Small herds of zebra and tsessebe were fond of this grassland and giraffe came to browse on the camel thorn. The surrounding ridges teemed with dassie, baboon and klipspringer. Good leopard food. I liked to camp there during patrols. That was where I was going to release the leopard. On a previous visit I had noticed another leopard's tracks. It didn't matter. The reserve had room for many leopards.

The sixty kilometre drive with the trapped leopard under the tarpaulin went without a hitch. At the old farmstead that served as our headquarters I left most of the Pedis. Only Januarie and two others came along. I drove to the stretch of sandveld I had in mind.

Under a wild plum with an overhanging branch we unloaded the trap. A rope was attached to the trap door and thrown over the branch. I covered the cage with the tarpaulin again and took the Pedis back to the compound. I would release the leopard on my own.

It was late afternoon when I returned to the release site. Most of the Pedis had been happy to stay behind, but Januarie had insisted on coming along. It was *our* tiger, after all.

Together we removed the tarpaulin. The leopard raged and roared, his tail sweeping from side to side on the floor of the cage. There was no skin left on his nose and his claws were bloody. For a few more moments I admired the beautiful creature. Then I took the end of the rope that was suspended from the branch and walked to the vehicle.

Januarie and I got into the cab of the bakkie. We shut the doors and rolled the windows halfway up. One of the old rangers had told me that a leopard released from a trap was a dangerous customer. "Don't just stand on top of the trap and open the door. He'll fuck you up for sure," the veteran had said.

From the safety of the bakkie I pulled on the rope. It slid across the branch and the trap door was hoisted up slowly. For a while the leopard remained on the floor of the trap, growling. Then he realised what was happening. Like lightning he shot through the mouth of the trap. I watched his spotted golden body disappear into the tall grass.

"Go well, leopard," I called after him. Satisfied, I got out of the bakkie. "It's been a good day's work, Januarie."

"Yes, Morena."

"Early tomorrow morning we'll fetch the trap and set it again. We'll see what we can catch next."

When the leopard regained his freedom, his first instinct was to get as far away from the trap and the men as possible. He was too full of fear and rage to feel the pain of his raw, injured pads, broken claws and skinned nose. He lowered his head and sped off across the grassy plain to the thickets at the foot of the ridge. The open grassland was unsafe by day.

Soon he was swallowed by the buffalo thorn and other shrubs growing among the rocks. Still he ran, but now he felt safer. His acute senses took in the unknown territory in which he found himself. He veered sharply and with a few bounds he disappeared into a bushy ravine. Concealed by horn-pod trees, wild plum and wild sage, he vanished over the first ridge, eager to put distance between himself and his terrible ordeal.

Deep among the koppies he slowed to a trot. Now he became aware of exhaustion and pain. An uncontrollable thirst overwhelmed him. It didn't take him long to find cool rainwater in a pool among the rocks. He squatted in the shade and sipped slowly. The water revived him, but his bloody nose and paws were beginning to throb painfully. Exhaustion triumphed over panic.

In a soft, grassy spot between two rocks he lay down in the shade of a shrub. Licking his paws and nose, he tried to remain alert in his strange surroundings, but the day had been too much for him. The sun went down over the sandstone ridges. Before it was entirely dark, the leopard lowered his head onto his paws and slept.

Sometime during the night he awoke. He took in his

surroundings, but he was disoriented; he had no idea where he was. He was sore and hungry and thirsty. Yet he knew something was amiss. Then he understood. Everywhere – on bushes, tree trunks and rocks – was the unmistakable scent. Not the hated scent of man that he would henceforth associate with captivity, but a different scent, a different danger. He was in the territory of another male leopard. The scent on the rock wall told him that the other leopard was strong. Old and wise. He himself was young and inexperienced. He had to get away from here. Get away or die.

He got up to drink some more water. His paws were cold from lying still and every step on the tender pads was painful. His entire body was stiff, and hunger gnawed at his insides. He had to get something to eat and then find his way back to his own range.

He began to explore the ridges. The smell of food was everywhere. He smelled dassie and baboon, but nowhere close. He rested often, though movement warmed him and relieved his pain.

Daybreak found him on the crest of a koppie. Beneath him lay the bushveld, luxuriant and wet with dew. A family of dassies crawled from a cleft in the rocks and huddled against a cliff to thaw in the first rays of the sun. The leopard watched them closely from the shadows and considered his options. Unnoticed, he stalked from rock to shrub until he reached the edge of the cliff. All his senses were focused on the hunt. He was a only few metres from the dassies, which were oblivious of the danger lurking in the grass beside the cliff face.

A single leap and he landed amongst them. They started up too late and he sank his teeth into the neck of a large one. The others scrambled for the safety of the clefts. The leopard's paws slipped on the brittle sandstone and with the wriggling dassie clenched in his jaw he tumbled over the precipice. Nimbly he landed on his feet in the wet grass and thorns a few metres below. His paws were bleeding again, but the hunt had been successful.

He rested on a rocky ledge for a while before he began to eat. He knew he had to get away, but the dassie lay comfortably in his belly and the intensifying heat was making him sleepy. His nose and paws throbbed dully. He found some shade in a crevice and fell into a deep sleep. He was young and strong. While he was sleeping, his body was regaining its strength.

The leopard woke, refreshed. His head cleared immediately. Instantly he was aware of the scent where the other leopard had marked out his territory against trees and rocks. It was possible that the other leopard was already stalking him. He rose cautiously and crept through the bushes. He wouldn't be a match for his older rival. He had to get away.

At a rocky pool in a small ravine he stopped. He scanned the surrounding area at length before squatting to drink. The cool water refreshed him even more.

A soundless shadow appeared above him. In vain he tried to leap to safety.

The other leopard was a large male. The force with which he pounced drove the air from the younger leopard's lungs. The momentum of the attack sent both leopards over the edge. The older leopard had driven his claws into the younger one's shoulder and sunk his teeth into the loose skin of his neck. Wrapped in a lethal embrace, they rolled down the ravine.

A rock at the foot of the koppie broke their fall and they flew apart. Panic-stricken, the young leopard scrambled to his feet and fled blindly. The older leopard caught up with him from behind and knocked his hind legs from underneath him. The young leopard bit the dust. Before he could get to his feet, the other leopard struck him a blinding blow to the side of the head. A second blow with the other paw sent him flying head over heels into a sickle bush. The bush shot him back onto his feet. He was just in time to see his roaring opponent take a flying leap at his throat. The young leopard raised himself on his hind legs and swung with his left paw like a boxer. The blow struck the older leopard squarely in the chest, stopped him in his tracks and threw him heavily onto his shoulder.

He was dazed. He had not expected such strength and speed from the intruder. He was taken aback but still hostile.

Making full use of his advantage, the younger leopard took to his heels. He wasn't supposed to be there. He didn't want to be there. He had his own territory. He knew instinctively that he was running in the right direction. The older leopard gave chase, but not as zealously as before. The blow to the chest had been painful. He was no longer young, after all. In any case, the younger leopard had made it perfectly clear that he was admitting defeat.

The old leopard gave up the pursuit and watched the intruder race through the bushes, back in the direction from which he had come.

Meanwhile the sun had set for a second time. The young leopard was exhausted and hurt and scared, but he was on his way home.

Through the night he trotted. He crawled under fences and crept past villages and farmsteads unseen. He stopped often to rest. Then he found himself on a long white road that ran parallel with his own route. He trotted along the road. The distance between himself and his destination was shrinking. He slowed to a walk. The unpleasant events of the past few days were forgotten. He stretched himself out on the white road to rest for a while. Exhaustion overwhelmed him and he sank into a deep sleep. When he opened his eyes, the rumbling noise and the blinding lights were on top of him.

I couldn't believe my luck. I found immense satisfaction in the capture of problem animals. The previous day I had returned to the spot where the leopard had been released with Januarie and the Pedis and collected the trap. Then we had gone back to the farm and carefully reset the trap in almost exactly the same place. Afterwards we had returned to the place among the tamboti trees where our tent was still pitched.

This morning, on approaching the trap, we noticed immediately that the door was shut. This time I took no chances. With my shotgun at the ready I crept closer. An unearthly wail greeted me from inside. Carefully I pulled aside a sickle bush branch. In the furthest corner, huddled against the putrefying warthog carcass, I found a brown hyena, moaning nervously and watching me with baleful eyes.

In a flash the Pedis were ready and the trap loaded onto the bakkie. Another animal was being translocated to the reserve. My bosses in Pietersburg are going to be pleased with me, I thought. The farmer can rest assured that his cattle won't be disturbed again any time soon.

It was a sunny morning as I drove to the game reserve along the straight white corrugated road. The thorn bushes at the roadside were decked out in new leaves. Ahead of me something lay stretched out in the middle of the road. It was only when I was nearly on top of it that I realised what it was.

Training

Brand was a moffie. Some guys just can't hide it. It was evident in his speech, in his bearing, in his mannerisms.

To be allowed to remain in our Defence Force unit, we had to swear to three things under oath. We had to swear that we accepted Jesus Christ as our Redeemer. We had to swear that we had never used any form of drugs. We had to swear that we were not homosexual. Many of us had our own reasons for wanting to remain in the unit. Many of us lied under oath. Brand did as well.

We were divided into platoons alphabetically. Badenhorst, Bezuidenhout, Blake and I became sworn comrades. We did everything together. Then there was Brand.

In spite of his refined ways, Brand was never a burden on the platoon. He had been physically fit even before he was called up. During physical training and fitness tests he kept up with the rest of the pack. During inspection his locker and bed were more neatly turned out than any of ours. His uniform was pressed to perfection. At the shooting range he was a better than average shot. During bush phase he seemed unperturbed by the hardships we had to endure.

During basic training there's little time to think about someone's appearance. Soon Brand was just another platoon buddy. It was during second phase that the trouble started. There was enough time now for guys to develop problems with each other.

Alpha company's barracks were two enormous old aeroplane hangars. Every shed housed three platoons. We, platoon number one, were positioned against one of the walls. Number two was in the centre and three against the opposite wall.

The guys in the other platoons began to take the mickey out of Brand. It was not just good-natured banter. Soon he had a cruel nickname. He accepted it stoically. Said nothing.

Marais in platoon number two was the ringleader. He tormented Brand mercilessly. Many guys in our own platoon did not feel comfortable around moffies either, but Brand was our comrade. We had to stand up for him.

"Aw, shut up, Marais, you fucking prick," Blake once snapped at Marais when things were getting out of hand. On another occasion Bezuidenhout threw a staaldak at Marais. It nearly ended in a fight.

Badenhorst was the big, quiet one in the platoon. He had huge hands. When he said: "Marais, stop it now," it was enough to make Marais beat a sneering retreat. But most of the time Brand was left to fight his own battles.

Brand passed through all the selection boards. He was selected for the leadership course along with the rest of us. He passed the academic component of the course with flying colours.

The last big test before we were made lieutenant was Vasbyt. It was a gruelling exercise, stretching over four days and including a long route march. Exhausting physical and psychological tests were completed. Candidate officers were treated as prisoners of war and interrogated. Ambushes were simulated. Rivers had to be crossed.

We started preparing months ahead. Some guys even trained after hours. Equipment was checked again and again.

"Vasbyt is all in the mind," the company commander had told us during a morning parade. "Two-thirds of you won't make it. For Vasbyt, your mind must be right. It has nothing to do with physical strength."

During the past weeks the tension had been mounting. Everyone knew Vasbyt was just around the corner. No one knew exactly when it would take place.

Shrill whistles tore through our sleep. "Get up!" the corporal roared. "Line up! You've got two minutes!"

Badenhorst, Blake, Bezuidenhout and I were ready. We'd

been expecting this. Other guys were scrambling frantically. The entire barracks was in a state of chaos.

The shock was too much for Marais. He fell back on the floor in an epileptic seizure. He hadn't been entirely honest either: He had kept his condition a secret. "Medic! Medic!" a corporal shouted.

Heavy boots tramped past Marais as the men rushed outside to line up. I saw him being stepped on. Two medics tried to enter the barracks against the flow. One collided with Blake. He was pushed aside with the flat part of the R-4: "Fuck off, dude."

It was the small hours of the night. The winter chill cut through our greatcoats.

Three days later. On a windswept plain in the Northern Cape a band of exhausted troops lay sprawled. Their brown uniforms were filthy and soaked with sweat. Their hands and fingers were chapped and rough. Their faces were streaked, as sweat mingled with the Black is Beautiful night camouflage paste.

I looked at my comrades. Of the once proud platoon of forty-four only eleven had made it up to this point. Other platoons had fared even worse. Several guys lay sleeping among the rocks. Others were sitting back to back. Their faces showed no emotion, just total exhaustion. Some were searching their rat packs for energy food.

During the past three days and nights we had been tested to the limit. I had come to realise how narrow the gap is between man and beast. Only our instinct to survive kept us going. When there was time to rest, we slept and ate. When it was time for the route march to continue, we got up. Unthinking, like oxen in a team, we swung our backpacks and rifles over our shoulders and moved along meekly, goaded by the whiplash tongues of the non-commissioned officers.

As soon as there was a change in the routine and we were confronted with a new obstacle, men began to crack. The moment they were required to think or use their initiative, they threw in the towel. The easiest part of Vasbyt was throwing in the towel.

Bezuidenhout had taken off his boots. The sole of each foot was one huge blood blister. Tears were streaking through his night camouflage. "I'm finished. I can't go on. Sorry, guys, this is where I get off."

Blake rebelled: "I don't know why I'm doing this shit. I'm a British citizen, for fuck's sake. A subject of the Queen. I'm with you, Bezuidenhout. Fuck this."

Badenhorst agreed: "My father has a mealie farm in the Free State. I have a diploma in agriculture. I don't need this."

Bezuidenhout began to put on his boots. His decision was final.

Brand had been listening to the conversation in silence. He was leaning against a rock some distance away. Now he clicked his tongue and rolled his eyes scornfully. "Well, I don't know about you guys. But I know *I'm* going to finish Vasbyt."

Badenhorst looked at me and then at Blake. Bezuidenhout paused in the middle of lacing up his boots. We glanced at each other furtively. For a few seconds no one said anything. Then Badenhorst spoke: "Oh well." He got up and heaved his backpack onto his shoulder. Bezuidenhout tied his boots. Blake helped him up. Brand came over to lend a hand.

Ten hours later we walked through Checkpoint Charlie. Samils and field ambulances stood waiting. From the mobile kitchens the aroma of bacon, powdered eggs and coffee wafted through the early morning air. Beside a tent under a thorn tree stood the company officers and our battalion commander. A military policeman pointed us in their direction.

Stumbling with exhaustion, we filed towards the tent. Brand's tenor voice took the lead. The rest of us joined in:

I wanna go to South Angola
I wanna kill a Cuban soldier.

We never saw Marais again.

41

Routine patrol

Sergeant Major Les White slid out from under the vehicle on a trolley. He got up. His brown overalls were covered with dust and his hands were dirty. "There you are, Lieutenant. Your vehicle is fixed. Try not to fuck it up again." His steely blue eyes gazed earnestly at Lieutenant Chris Bakkes.

"Thanks, Sergeant Major. I'll do my best."

The sergeant major had just replaced a blade spring and an exhaust pipe on Chris's Land Cruiser. Both the spring and the exhaust had broken during Chris's most recent patrol. Every time Chris returned to base, something was broken in his Land Cruiser. The sergeant major was losing patience. "A serviceman feels fuck-all for military equipment," he grumbled, shaking his head.

Lieutenants Bakkes and Mayes got into the military Toyota Land Cruiser and pulled out of the transport park. Sergeant Major Les White gazed after them. His muscular forearms were planted on his hips.

They drove to the barracks under the trees on the edge of the flood plain. Two sections of Bushman troops were lined up, clad in different variations of the South African Defence Force uniform. Some wore brown nutria pants matched with a brown T-shirt. Some wore a bush shirt and black PT shorts, others were clad in overalls. Their bush hats were perched on their heads at different angles. Everyone carried a R4 rifle, webbing, water bottles, ration packs and sleeping bags. They loaded the equipment on the bakkie and climbed on the back.

The Land Cruiser left the base late in the morning. It was a routine patrol. Chris and Simon would deploy the Bushmen in teams of two on the edge of the flood plains of the

Kwando River to set up observation posts. Lately there had been an increase in activity from the Eastern Caprivi. People were crossing the river, ostensibly in search of honey or to hunt in the Western Caprivi. The colonel didn't believe that they were wandering around innocently. He wanted no unauthorised movement in the proximity of the base. Chris and Simon's troops had to maintain a presence, challenge any persons they came across, order them back across the river and make sure that they complied. It wouldn't take long to deploy the troops, and Chris and Simon would be back at the base by sunset, in time for a cold beer in the mess. In two days' time they would withdraw the Bushmen.

The troops would dig themselves in on wooded hummocks with a good view of the flood plains. Chris and Simon kept the vehicle close to the bushes in a bid to be as unobtrusive as possible. Impala fled before them and on the flood plain they spotted reedbuck and lechwe. The Bushmen headed out across the plains on foot.

They stopped for lunch under a jackal berry at the horseshoe lake and Simon opened a rat pack. They made a fire, heated up tinned beans and Viennas, and boiled water for coffee in a fire bucket. A group of hippos lay in the water. Through his binoculars Chris watched a colony of carmine bee-eaters building a nest in a sand wall. They ate. There was still a large part of the day to kill, so they decided to take the long route back to base.

It was late afternoon as the Land Cruiser snaked along the bed of the Malombe omuramba. Chris and Simon spoke about girls, parties and their student days in civvy street. Beside the double-track road grew dense stands of kierieklapper and ghwarrie bush. An elephant crossed the road ahead of them. Chris stopped to give it right of way.

Suddenly the bush around them was crawling with elephants. They were surrounded by large cows, smaller cows and calves. The elephants had been enjoying an afternoon nap when the Land Cruiser blundered into their midst. Now they were restless at being disturbed.

At that precise moment one of their number decided she'd had enough. She shook her head, ears flapping. She trumpeted and commenced with a brief charge. The vehicle was trapped – another elephant was moving across the road. Chris revved the engine. This provoked the irate cow and with lowered head she launched into a charge.

Her forehead struck the edge of the roof on the driver's side an enormous blow. The bakkie tipped over and balanced on two wheels. Chris slid and fell on top of Simon. Their rifles lay in a jumble between them. The cow raised her head and with a stubby, broken tusk punched a hole in the door. The window, which had been rolled down inside the door, splintered into a thousand pieces. A quick glance around them confirmed their worst fears. The other cows had lined up protectively in front of their calves and were getting ready to charge. Chris looked at Simon lying underneath him.

Simon looked back.

"We'd better get away from here."

"I think so too."

At that moment the enraged cow stepped back for a second charge, and the vehicle fell back onto its wheels. Chris slammed the bakkie into first gear, dropped the clutch and stepped on the gas. The second attack glanced off the tail of the bakkie as Chris pulled away in a cloud of dust. The rest of the elephants were coming at full speed now. The Land Cruiser burst through a stand of ghwarrie bush to dodge the elephants in the road ahead. The entire herd was following the speeding bakkie and gaining on it.

Chris changed gears and the vehicle gathered speed. The elephants kept coming. He steered the bakkie back onto the road and sped away from the elephants, leaving them behind. They abandoned the charge and disappeared from sight in the rear-view mirror.

A kilometre down the road, Chris pulled over. He looked at Simon. Simon was wide-eyed and pale.

"Fuckit," was all he said.

Sergeant Major Les White stood with his arms planted on his hips, just as he'd done that morning. His cold eyes and silver-grey handlebar moustache gave him a formidable look. Chris drove into the transport park. The sergeant major glared at the gash in the door and the dented roof. Chris tried to get out to explain, but the door was stuck. He threw his shoulder against it once, twice. With the third attempt, the door flew open and Lieutenant Chris Bakkes tumbled onto the concrete floor of the transport park and landed at the feet of Sergeant Major White. Sheepishly he looked up. Apprehensive.

The sergeant major shook his head. He gazed at Chris steadily. Then he laughed.

Deception

Once you know the omurambas of the Western Caprivi, you can't get lost. That's what I always used to say. The Western Caprivi is a uniform strip of sandy bushveld. The omurambas are a series of vaguely defined drainage lines that run in a west-southwesterly direction from Angola, joining up with the Kwando flood plain. The river and the omurambas are the only geographical features in the Western Caprivi.

Shortly after dawn I stopped my vehicle at the mouth of the Kasimba and Kombere omuramba. My plan was to patrol upward along the Kasimba omuramba. Then to cut across the tree-covered dune and return by way of the Kombere omuramba. With me were four officers of the Finnish parachute battalion. A major, a captain and two lieutenants.

With my .308 Steir-Manlicher over my shoulder, I led them into the wilderness. It was my goal to get them higher up the omuramba as quickly as possible. Out of earshot.

It was one of those mornings that send your spirit soaring. Birds were everywhere. Bradfield's hornbills flapped lazily ahead of us. A racquet-tailed roller sat high in an apple-leaf. Arrow-marked babblers and red-billed wood hoopoes competed to see who could make the most noise. In the game paths red-billed and crested francolins scurried out of our way. A bateleur circled in the blue sky overhead.

At the first pans we came across six tsessebes. A duiker ram bounded away. At the second pan there were nine zebras. I wrote down the numbers carefully in my notebook. I showed the Finns the notes I had made on previous patrols: seventeen sable antelope on one particular day and thirty roan antelope on another. It had been a remarkable sight.

Some distance up the omuramba we found the buffaloes. It was a herd of three hundred. They liked that omuramba. It was not very hot yet and the buffaloes stood in the open veld on the floor of the omuramba. I herded the Finns to a slight rise at the base of a termite heap. They reached for their cameras. They looked around excitedly. They took photos. This was the Africa they had come to see.

I pricked up my ears. There was no distant rumbling. The men were late this morning. We would have to stay away longer. Making a detour, I led the Finns past the buffaloes and deeper into the bush.

As we walked, it became hotter. Towards eleven we came across a herd of forty elephants at a large water pan. The Finns looked impressed. We watched the elephants from a downwind position. They drank noisily and frolicked in the water. The Finns took turns to pose for the camera with the elephants in the background. Their uniforms were grey. Their pistols hung from their hips cowboy style. They wore the light blue UN beret.

The Finns are known as formidable soldiers. During the Second World War they crushed the Russian army time after time. At the end of the war, despite being undefeated, they were forced to relinquish part of their country to the Communists.

The group of Finnish officers had arrived at our rangers' post the night before. The rangers had given them a warm welcome; there had been a braai and a lot of beer was consumed. We already knew why they had come. It had been my suggestion to take them out on patrol. We'd agreed on it earlier.

While we were watching the elephants, a dull rumbling reached my ears. There they go, I thought. I watched the Finns surreptitiously. Their ears were unpractised. Their mood was relaxed. They heard nothing.

I had been in the Western Caprivi for nine months. For the past five months I had been a game ranger. My job was to count game and catch ivory poachers. On 1 April 1989 the United Nations had implemented Resolution 435. The Cuban forces had to retreat to the fifteenth degree of latitude. South Africa had to terminate all military aid to Unita. The South African Defence Force units were withdrawn. The war was over and the first steps toward Namibian independence had been taken. As trained game rangers, a few other conscripted lieutenants and I were seconded to Nature Conservation.

We left the water pan. Now I was leading them through the bush, away from the omuramba.

Eventually I decided it was time to return to camp. Somewhere on the crest of a wooded dune, with the sun directly above me, I took the wrong turn. The dim rumble had reached my ears again. It was somewhere northeast of us now, the distant sound of diesel engines.

I gave the Finns a quick glance. They were getting tired. They had heard nothing. Before I knew it, we were standing on the Angolan cut line. Far from where we had left the vehicle.

"I'm lost," I told the Finns. They looked at me in disbelief. It was the hottest time of day. They were soaked with perspiration.

"I took a wrong turn. We've been walking away from where we were meant to be going. We're in the wrong omuramba. We'll have to turn round."

Since June certain allegations had been surfacing. They were first made by the Cuban diplomats during the peace negotiations and later by international reporters in Namibia. Reports came through that the South African Defence Force was still involved with Unita. The Foreign Ministry had denied it in the press, calling it cheap propaganda.

UNTAG, the military auxiliary force of the UN with the mandate to monitor the transition period, was told to investigate. Since then there had been a great deal of interest in our rangers' station. First came the Royal Canadian Mounted Police; they were the military police of the peacekeeping forces. I took them out on a river cruise during a hippo census. Afterwards I took them for a drive in the veld. We found twelve giraffes in the Delta omuramba. Back at base, the chief ranger made his reports available to them. That evening the Mounties were treated to a braai and the next day we parted like old friends.

A group of Poles and Italian chopper pilots flew in unannounced. We received them warmly. I took them on a unique safari in the veld. Later a group of American reporters arrived. Same story. The chief ranger was convinced they were from the CIA.

I allowed the Finns to rest in the shade of a mangeti tree. They were unaccustomed to the African heat. Their water bottles were nearly empty. The bush had lost its enchantment.

The Finns stumbled on, dragging their feet. Their major was a jovial chap and encouraged his men. The captain was suspicious. He inquired how it was possible for a game ranger to get lost. Wasn't he supposed to know the terrain? The lieutenants glared at me. They were soaked with sweat and scorched by the sun.

I began to doubt their effectiveness as peacekeeping troops. What would they do if we suddenly came upon a Unita patrol? Early in April, shortly after Resolution 435 had been implemented, heavily armed PLAN cadres had crossed the Angolan border into Namibia. An incursion had been feared and Martti Ahtisaari, the UN representative and a Finn himself, had approached the South Africans for help, his tail between his legs. Permission was granted to call in Koevoet and 101 Battalion. A bloodbath had resulted.

It was an exhausted group of Finns that finally reached the vehicle at the mouth of the omurambas.

That evening around the lapa fire there were T-bone steaks and beer. The rangers wanted to celebrate. The Finns went to bed early.

After the Finns had left the next morning, I was summoned to the cramped office of the chief ranger. He leaned back behind his desk.

"We had a hell of a struggle with the vehicles yesterday, Bakkes. Two Unimogs got flat tyres and another one's diff packed up. We had to transfer part of the consignment. It's a good thing you were able to keep them busy for such a long time. We managed to cross the border in time."

He was quiet for a while. "Well done, Lieutenant," he said.

"Thanks, Colonel," I said.

Moment of truth

For months they had been eluding us. We always arrived at the scene too late, the trail already cold.

It became an obsession with Simon and me. When he saw signs of them in his sector, he radioed me. When I found their trail north of the white road, I radioed him. Then we deployed the Bushmen in a joint operation.

We had just picked up the trail. Kakweche, Yaya and Frans Dwandamo were crouched down, taking their time deliberating. Simon and I waited. It was winter and the veld was warm and quiet. We had walked a long way to get there. Black dust clung to the sweat on our legs. Wordlessly we stared at each other while the Bushmen spoke in muted tones.

A tsetse fly landed on Simon's neck. He ignored it. I saw the mouth parts of the fly sawing into Simon's neck. He waited. When the sting drew blood, he raised his hand. Slowly. It would be hard for the fly to withdraw now. Simon grabbed it between thumb and forefinger and plucked it off his neck. I heard the tsetse fly wriggle, crunch and pop as Simon crushed it between his fingers. He flicked it away like a cigarette butt. The winter foliage threw flickering shadows on the sandy forest floor.

Frans Dwandamo stood up. He shouldered his rifle and came walking towards us. His yellow face showed no emotion.

"Two weeks," he said.

Simon and I looked at each other. We both knew we were not going to give up on this trail.

Late that afternoon we came across the first carcass. First

there were the vultures. We noticed them circling overhead. Then we saw them perched in the trees over a wide area. Before we reached the carcass, we heard the beating of hundreds of wings as the birds flew up ahead of us, heavy and replete. The stench was overwhelming.

That would be the pattern during the following days. The Bushmen, masters of the art, would stay on the trail. The vultures would point out the killing fields. The carcasses were in an advanced stage of decomposition. At night we slept on the trail, our rifles in our arms. No fire. Cold food from the rat packs.

At dawn we were up. We continued through the heat of the day, in the silent veld. There was no sign of life. As if every living creature was hiding because it knew. The endless winter landscape was grey. Then: vultures up ahead.

Simon and I were filthy. The dirt was more apparent on us than on the Bushmen. The grey sand of the omurambas formed a black layer on our skins when the sweat dried off. Our PT shorts stuck to our groins.

It was the fourth day. Five carcasses lay behind us. The food in the rat packs was finished. There was still water in the pans of the omurambas, but higher up it would be drier. The Bushmen were growing tired. They have a faster metabolism and need energy food. The meat on the carcasses was too putrefied to eat. They began to lose the trail. Simon and I knew it was deliberate. We'd have to make a plan.

Though we weren't in radio contact with the base, we had an arrangement. Every morning at first light either Spekkies or Steve would drive along the white road. In case of emergency we would send a Bushman.

We decided to replace the Bushmen with a fresh section. Steve or Spekkies had to bring rat packs and water. Furthermore, they were to conceal the vehicle with the food and water at an RV beside the white road and wait there. The fresh section of Bushmen would walk back on their predecessors' tracks and meet Simon and me in the bush.

The changeover took a day. Simon and I set up a temporary base and waited. We lay in the sand under a raisin bush and conserved our energy. We lay at the spot where the Bushmen had lost the trail. Simon and I could no longer identify it.

The next group of Bushmen reached us late in the afternoon. They were Benson Kupinga, Bert Mirinda, Maranda Duwonga and Thomas Dwasha. Good guys. We showed them where the others had lost the trail. Within moments Benson Kupinga picked it up and we used the last daylight to make up for lost time.

We found the next carcass early the following day. Same story. The vultures, the stench and the mutilated skull.

In the afternoon, vultures far to the northwest. But the trail didn't lead there. Maranda Duwonga and I left Simon and the others on the trail and walked in the direction of the vultures.

He had managed to flee from his attackers' bullets. Loss of blood had caused him to collapse. It took several days before the carcass decomposed sufficiently for the vultures to pierce the hide. A few had made a start on the thinner skin of the flanks and anus. It was usually the lappet-faced vulture that broke through first. Then the white-backed vultures came in flocks. Most waited patiently in the trees.

He was bloated, like a balloon. His legs grotesquely in the air. Clouds of flies and bluebottles flew up at our arrival. He must have been a fine bull. His ivory was thick and yellow. At some earlier point both tusks had broken off. They had grown out into short, sturdy stumps.

We left him behind to rejoin the others. We would return later to remove his ivory. Maranda picked up Simon and the others' trail two omurambas below us. We rendezvoused at sunset. They had come across another two carcasses. The ivory of these elephants had been crudely removed from the sockets.

The next day we lost the trail. It simply disappeared. Still, the Bushmen were fresh. They scoured the area. Simon and I were slowing down. For the next two days we wandered through the bush in circles. The search was fruitless and there was no chance of picking up the trail again. We would have to regroup.

At an omuramba we found a group of pans with water in them. Simon and I set up a temporary base in a thicket and sent the Bushmen to the chalk road. We washed ourselves. It made us feel better. In the shade of a Zambezi teak we found a suitable place to lie. From there we had a view across the pan. We tried to sleep, but to no avail. We didn't speak much. We both knew we were involved in something bigger than ourselves. It gave us courage. All we could do was wait. This thing had to be done properly.

Two days later Frans Dwandamo, Kakweche and Yaya returned. They brought rat packs. We were rested and ready to continue. Where should we begin?

I don't remember how we decided on a course. We set out at first light. Towards afternoon we found a trail. A clear trail. Five people, Frans Dwandamo said. When the light began to fade, we stopped for the night.

We found the carcass the next afternoon. Our arrival was heralded by the heavy beating of vulture wings. But something was different. Simon and I didn't grasp it immediately. Then we saw that the Bushmen were once again engaged in deep, muted conversation and we realised something was amiss. Quietly we stepped aside and waited. The Bushmen studied the carcass and spoke in their ancient tongue.

Frans Dwandamo was the oldest and the yellowest. Here and there his crinkly head was peppered with grey. As a young man he'd been one of Colonel Cardoza's "fletchas". Later a member of Alpha group during Operation Savannah. He seemed baffled that we couldn't see it. His gaze didn't meet ours. He spoke tersely.

"The hunters are tired. They took meat. They cut open the back."

He waited while Simon and I examined the animal's back, which had been slashed open. The wounds were not the result of an attack by hyena or lion. They were gashes made by a crude knife or axe. Chunks of meat had been butchered from the carcass.

Frans Dwandamo continued: "That is why the vultures are here. The hunters have opened the meat for them."

He waited before delivering his verdict: "This elephant was shot yesterday. Shortly after we found the trail."

That night we slept on the trail for the last time. We knew, when we lay down as night fell, that the hunters had become the prey.

The sun had just risen over the treetops the next morning when we walked into their lair.

Since we found the last carcass we had been walking with our rifles in our arms. Cocked and ready – safety catch on "rapid fire". Simon and I scanned the bushes in front of us. Every now and then we looked at each other. Tension showed in our posture. We knew that at any moment something could happen. Simon's bright green eyes gleamed in his dirty face.

It could so easily have been different. In spite of our vigilance we could have walked into an ambush. But here we were standing in their hide-out. Strips of elephant meat hung from the lower branches of a Zambezi teak. Handmade axes and butcher's knives were stowed in the forks of the tree. Higher up there were blankets and bedding. There was a blackened pot. In the undergrowth around the base of the trunk five grass beds surrounded a small camp fire. The coals were still glowing. We found the place where their tracks led out of the camp. Not half an hour old. We withdrew and laid an ambush. We kept the game paths leading to the camp open.

From my position under a raisin bush I could see only Simon to my right. Opposite me, to the left, lay Yaya. Kakweche and Frans Dwandamo were facing Simon, hidden from view. It was going to be a long day, but we were ready for them.

When I originally arrived in the Western Caprivi, I had had no idea of the strange, dark world I would be plunged into. In many respects it would be my first encounter with the true Africa. The Africa of which I had read in Joseph Conrad's novel.

At first I couldn't believe my luck. The boat patrols on the mysterious river with its islands, tributaries and papyrus beds. The exhilirating encounters with hippos. My first glimpse of a sitatunga. The foot patrols with the Bushmen, who taught me about tracking and veldkos. My friendship with Simon Mayes.

It didn't take long, however, before I discovered that this pristine world was in truth a battlefield. As I became familiar with my surroundings, I kept coming across bones. Old skeletons of black rhino and newer ones of elephants. Simon and I were determined to make this problem our own. Get involved. Do something.

My thoughts wandered back to the past few days. The people we were pursuing. The devastation they had left in their wake. It was an epidemic. Africa's wilderness areas were being plundered of their big game. From what we had heard it was happening in Zimbabwe, Zambia and Mozambique. Not to mention Angola. And here. Here we were in the middle of it: Simon, the Bushmen and I. Warriors in the fray. We lay waiting. It was war. Somewhere in the bushes, not far away, the enemy was on the move. They would have to return, some time or another. And we were ready for them.

The plan we had decided on was to lie low until after dark. As soon as they got ready for the night, we would sneak up and overpower them. But silently I vowed: Fuck that. Today we're going to make them pay.

Slowly the sun moved across the sky. We lay motionlessly, rifles at the ready. Through the branches and the dry stumps I had a good view of the camp. I turned my head and looked at Simon. Bright eyes, teeth gleaming in a grin. I suspected he had the same plan. I lay so still that a violet-eared waxbill landed centimetres from my nose. It hopped from one twig to another. Its beady eyes studied me inquisitively. Then it hopped down onto the forest floor to peck at seeds. An unforgettable encounter.

The sun moved in behind the treetops in the west. The day cooled down. The francolins announced the end of the day and peace descended on the land. There was the beating of a francolin's wings as it flew up. Yaya attracted my attention and motioned in the direction of the camp. Like phantoms they came walking out of the shadows. Simon's eyes flashed as he looked at me.

Two threw themselves down on their grass beds. One propped a rifle against the tree. He climbed up and handed down the blankets to his comrade on the ground. Another one stood quite still for a while. He had his rifle in his hands. It was a heavy calibre, bolt action rifle. An elephant rifle. I identified him as my target. There was a ringing in my ears. My heart beat wildly and I raised my rifle.

That was when I realised that there were too many bushes and branches in the way to get a clear shot. Dry stumps obstructed my view.

I was still wondering what to do, when the man with the elephant rifle came walking in my direction. The sun disappeared into the branches of the thickets. I looked at Yaya. Then at Simon. Fuck! flashed his eyes. What now? asked my own.

My heart was hammering out of control. My throat was constricted. The man kept coming. His dark eyes bored into mine. His rifle sat comfortably in his hands. He looked confident and relaxed. Like someone who had been doing this job for a long time. He was coming to kill me. I lay petrified. I had my rifle ready, but I could not get a shot at him.

I looked at Simon again. He was trying to signal something. His gaze was urgent. I did not understand. All I realised was that the barrel of my rifle lay amid the branches of the raisin bush and I would have to stand up to get a shot at the man. By time it would be too late.

Suddenly I remembered the story about my great-grandfather. How he had died. In times of crisis you think of the
strangest things. My great-grandfather couldn't get a clear
shot either – the grass was too long. He served in the Heil-
bron commando under General Christiaan de Wet. It was
during the battle of Swartbooiskop, a resounding victory for
the Boers. Two hundred Khakis fell in that battle. Eight hundred were captured. My great-grandfather was shot in the
neck in front of the British positions. The grass had been too
long. He couldn't get a clear shot. He'd had to stand up. Was
it a family thing?

What was I going to do? Simon signalled frantically with
eyes, eyebrows and lips. Suddenly I understood. I was lying
behind their wood pile. The man was coming to fetch firewood. He didn't know I was there.

I stood up out of the bushes. The fold-in butt of my LM4
found my shoulder. The peep sight found the man's chest. I
saw the utter astonishment on his face, saw him raising his
rifle, his fingers finding the bolt.

Many things flash through your mind before you shoot a
man. That second before you pull the trigger. With him in the
peep sight of the LM4, his rifle pointed at you. You know you
have the advantage. Your brain is crystal clear. Your aim dead-
ly. How many elephants had this man shot? During this expedition alone – ten. What about the other, older carcasses that
lay scattered across the veld? This man was the enemy. He was
the opposite of everything I stood for. My finger curled more
firmly around the trigger. My hand closed.

Then – hesitation. To pull the trigger was to cross a line.
This wasn't shooting a buck. This man had a mother. How
many elephants are worth one man's life? I couldn't do it.

A shot tore through the branches overhead. It didn't come
from his rifle. It came from their camp. He turned and ran.
For another moment my sights were trained on his shoulder
blade. Then I pushed the barrel upward and fired a volley
over his head. I took off after him. Kakweche appeared beside me. He shot from the hip while running. I sent another

volley over the man's head and he dropped his rifle. I caught a brief glimpse of Simon, Yaya and Frans moving towards their hide-out. More shots were fired.

Night fell and Kakweche and I lost the man in the bushes. We turned and walked back. Kakweche retrieved the elephant rifle. Disappointment lay heavy inside me. Back at their camp Simon's face told the same story.

Every single one had escaped. They had left everything behind. Axes and knives. They'd run clean out of their shoes. Apart from the elephant rifle, a .458 Winchester Magnum, there were also a double-barrel twelve-bore shotgun and the full magazine of a semiautomatic G3.

Simon stopped next to me, out of breath. "Jesus Christ, man. We fucked this one up."

Simon and I, scrubbed clean, sat in the corrugated iron building that served as an office. We shifted uncomfortably in our chairs. The man who entered was not an imposing figure. He was small and his shoulders were bent. His wild red hair stood on end. A scar ran across his face and his nose had been broken sometime in the past. His game ranger's uniform was loose and ill-fitting.

His appearance might have been unimpressive, but his record was certainly not. Sandhurst Military Academy in England; Rhodesian SAS; Selous Scouts; Reconnaissance Commando. He had been badly wounded in the battle of Quito.

The man's small eyes flitted from Simon to me as he spoke. His voice was soft.

"The rangers at Katima got three of the five. The rifles that you seized made it easier to arrest them. Their leader was caught. They've been looking for him for a long time. He's an old poacher. The other two have fled to Zambia."

He picked up a foolscap page from his desk. He read in silence for a while. Then he continued: "The chief ranger's report says it was 'excellent work by inexperienced game rangers'."

He fell silent again, and thought for a moment before he continued. Here it comes, I thought.

"But as far as we are concerned, it is more important that, in the first place, it was a bloodless exercise. No one was hurt. No one died. That's good. It keeps us out of the spotlight. No police, no reporters. No questions and investigations. And in the second place: It gives us credibility. After this breakthrough – *your* breakthrough – no one will question our presence here. There will be no further speculation about who or what we are. We are game rangers in the employ of Nature Conservation."

A slight smile appeared on the colonel's face. Then he spoke again: "Lieutenant Mayes, Lieutenant Bakkes. Thank you, you have rendered excellent service."

Hailstorm

The hailstorm caught Dan and me a kilometre from camp. It was a tradition for us to explore the bush and granite ridges on the afternoon after a safari. I enjoyed being in the veld without clients, and he needed to escape from the kitchen.

The granite mountains of the Lowveld are beautiful. The most beautiful among them lie between the confluence of the Nsikazi and the Crocodile Rivers. The tallest monolith is Mpakeni. Our camp lay in its shade. On the opposite side, north of Nsikazi, were Khandizwe and Matjulu, the highest points in the Kruger Park, but smaller than Mpakeni. To the northwest you could see Pretoriuskop, Numbi and, on a clear day, Legogote in the distance.

In the well-watered gorges of Mpakeni grew Pride of De Kaap and matumi. On the ridges above, Lowveld chestnuts formed a dense canopy of leaves. Cape teak and wild pear grew against the slopes.

"Dan, are you ready to go?"

"In a minute, Blue. I'm just stripping off me whites and putting on me khakis." He crammed a battered straw hat on his head.

On the floor of the valley lay the spoor of bush pig. Every so often a bushbuck would burst from the thickets ahead of us. The mysterious bush loerie flitted through the foliage overhead. Butterflies and beetles filled the air around us. To Dan and me it was a mystical place.

After we had explored for a while, we would sit down on an overhanging rock or beside a rock pool, and talk. Dan Peoples was a traveller from New Zealand, who had been on a trip round the world for many years. He had left his country after completing an apprenticeship as a butcher. He had worked in restaurants and on boats all over the world, gaining valuable experience in the catering business. I had just returned from Namibia, after completing my military service. Dan's tales about Australia, Italy and Turkey were fascinating to someone whose only international experience was a stint of border duty.

Dan had met his girlfriend on a Greek island. They had worked in the same restaurant. She was from South Africa, from White River in the Lowveld. Because of the country's politics, Dan had had no desire to visit South Africa. Tired of being on the move, he had been planning to return to New Zealand. His girlfriend, also on her way home, had convinced him to visit South Africa. "Just come and see," she had pleaded. That had been three years before. He had never left.

The clouds were dark and threatening overhead when we came out of the gorges and into the open. We took the double-track road back to camp. The first hailstones were small, yet they whacked us painfully on the shoulders. We thought it a joke and broke into a jog. The next moment a hailstone the size of a golf ball struck Dan, sending his straw hat flying. His eyes glazed over as he grabbed his head with both hands. Soon whopping great hailstones were pelting down on us. It was no longer a joke. I grabbed Dan's hat and handed it to him. "Come, Dan. We have to run."

We made a dash for it. Around us branches and leaves were being stripped from the trees. Hailstones pounded our heads and shoulders. Though my bush hat was made of stronger fabric than Dan's straw hat, it was far from adequate protection. I was dealt several blinding blows to the head. The stones striking my shoulders and back sent a burning pain through my body. I realised we were in trouble.

Dan was faster than I. He urged me on as he outpaced me. By this time the storm was so violent that bouncing hailstones were pelting us from below. One struck me a painful blow on the kneecap. The earth turned white with hail.

We considered finding shelter, but there were no overhanging rocks in sight. Around us the devastation became apparent through sheets of sleet. My lungs were burning, but I realised if we stopped now, we could be dead. With a burst of speed, I caught up with Dan.

"Come, Blue," he urged.

Ahead of us the camp came into view, though it was still a long way off. Too long. It seemed like an eternity. We were being chastised mercilessly from the skies above. Blood stained the back of Dan's shirt. I felt sure I was also bleeding. From time to time hailstones the size of golf balls made way for ones the size of tennis balls. I felt my legs grow heavy; I had never been a sprinter. An enormous hailstone narrowly missed Dan's head. It would have struck him down for certain.

The lean-to where we parked the Land Rovers was up ahead. We made a beeline for it. A huge hailstone struck me between the shoulder blades and drove the air out of my lungs. I fell to my knees, but kept moving. I reached the corrugated iron lean-to on all fours and fell down next to a vehicle.

The noise was earsplitting. I looked at Dan. He was doubled up and panting. His straw hat was in shreds and his brow had been split open. Slowly I got my breath back. In the fading light I watched as dents appeared all over the roof of the lean-to. Dan's breathing had also subsided. We looked at each other long and earnestly.

"Fuckit, Blue," was all he said.

After a while we inspected our bodies for damage. Red bruises and lashes, an abrasion here and there. Dan's brow didn't look good. A few lumps on the head. But it could have been much worse. Our heads and bodies aching, we went to bed.

The next day broke clear and sunny. When I got up, I was stiff and sore. Some of my bruises had now acquired a bluish green tinge. I walked out on the veranda of my hut and looked out over the valley. An astonishing sight met my eyes. Destruction lay across the bush in a broad swathe. It was as if a huge combine harvester had travelled in a straight line across the mountains and valleys. Bare branches formed a stark contrast with the surrounding foliage that had escaped the devastation of the storm.

Dan and I both reached the breakfast table late. Only Chris Greathead was there. A few of the other men were out in the veld, taking stock of the damage. Greathead was feeding fruit salad to two tame black-collared barbets. "I hear you were nearly killed," he remarked.

I was also keen to survey the aftermath of the hailstorm, but my body protested. The coffee was refreshing. Dan was reluctant to go to the kitchen. He, Greathead and I lingered round the table, talking about rugby.

The receptionist, Angie, came over to us.

"Blue, you must go. Inch and Marco have found an injured zebra. They don't have a rifle with them."

The name Blue had started with Dan, and everyone in camp had taken it up. It was the Kiwis' peculiar nickname for a redhead.

I placed the .375 in the gun rack on the dashboard of Greathead's Land Rover. In bright sunlight we drove out of the pock-marked lean-to and down the mountain.

We found Inch and Marco in the valley below, standing beside their Land Rover. They were gazing through their binoculars at something on the slope. "We didn't want to go any closer. He ran away when we arrived. It's his left eye," Marco said.

Through my own binoculars I saw the zebra walking up the slope, his head hanging. His hindquarters were facing us and we couldn't see what the problem was.

I took the rifle. Greathead and I walked through the treeline on the valley floor and began to climb the slope. I had met Greathead three years before in circumstances very different from the way I had met Dan. We had been platoon buddies during basic training at Diskobolos and afterwards we had both been selected for the officers' training course. He had gone to the Mozambican border as second lieutenant and I had been sent to the Angolan border. Quite by chance we had both found employment at the reserve after our national service. It had been the start of a long relationship.

The wind blew in our favour as we approached the zebra. He was walking slowly. I still couldn't see his injury. We tried to get abreast of him unnoticed. It was easier said than done. If we disturbed him, he would disappear over the ridge. We followed at a distance and hoped he would afford us an opportunity.

Suddenly the zebra halted, as if he had become aware that something was following him. He turned sideways and for the first time his head came into view. I raised the binoculars.

Where an eye had once been, a bloody cavity was gaping in his skull. His cheek was covered with caked blood that had grown hard and dark. Through the lenses of my binoculars I stared for a while, astonished by the damage a hailstone could do. Then the zebra turned and carried on walking up the mountainside.

Greathead and I realised we had a better chance of getting close to him if we stayed on his blind side. Slowly we caught up with him. His disfigured face was clearly visible now. The raw wound glistened red in the morning light.

Slowly I slipped off the safety catch. I cocked the rifle. The zebra stopped again. A .375 is a heavy calibre. Its bullet rapidly loses momentum. I would have liked to get even closer, but the zebra had heard me. He could make off at any minute. It was my last chance. I took aim. Poor creature, it flashed through my mind as I pressed down on the trigger.

The bullet broke his neck. He tumbled headlong down the slope, flipping over a few times before coming to a halt in a lifeless heap.

Back at the vehicles, I told Inch and Marco to fetch a team of helpers to skin the zebra. Greathead and I continued on our tour of inspection in the Land Cruiser.

We were entering the area that had been worst affected by

the storm. A scene of total devastation greeted us. Every leaf had been stripped from the branches and the trees stood bare and grey against the blue sky. The road was carpeted with shredded leaves. The grasslands on the mountainside looked as if they had been mowed down with sickles. Every stream bed we crossed had been eroded. Slowly we drove on.

We began to come across dead animals. Half buried in a carpet of leaves, or entangled in branches. First a Cape hare in the road. A large-spotted genet with its skull crushed. A young vervet monkey. A crested francolin lay almost completely camouflaged by leaves. Like forgotten kites, a few hornbills, a grey loerie and a purple-crested loerie hung suspended from the leafless branches. White-backed vultures, a bateleur and a few tawny eagles circled overhead. Jackal buzzards sat in the trees, on the lookout for small injured animals.

Greathead saw the klipspringer first, on a granite ridge among stinging nettles and wild sage. We raised our binoculars. A klipspringer has a unique coat. Its dense fur is rough and every hair is coarse and hollow, almost like a small porcupine quill. This dense covering forms an excellent cushion against sharp rocks and lends protection in case its agility leaves it in the lurch and it happens to fall.

Large tufts of hair dangled from the klipspringer's coat. Where the hailstones had struck, the skin was exposed. We looked into hollow eye sockets. The eyeball jelly formed streaks down the cheeks. Greathead lifted the rifle from the rack. The klipspringer heard us. It stumbled away blindly. First it blundered into a lavender fever berry. Then it seemed to find its direction and disappeared over the ridge.

"I'm going to fetch him," I told Greathead. I pulled my hunting knife from its sheath and began to climb the ridge. On the other side I saw the klipspringer standing on top of a rock. The ridge was strewn with granite boulders and my progress was slow. It was a little ram with pointed horns. He heard me coming and lifted his grotesque head to pinpoint my direction.

I jumped forward to close the gap. He was blind, after all; I should be able to catch him without any difficulty. He bounded away and landed on a ledge higher up. He stood there, perfectly balanced, ears pricked to catch any movement. Out of reach. I clambered over the rocks and tried to make up ground.

A klipspringer has short legs that end in small, rubbery hooves. This adaptation makes him ideally suited to mountainous areas, as those small hooves enable him to adhere with surprising effectiveness to any rocky surface. Now the blind klipspringer was leading me across the rocks in a macabre hunt. With faultless precision he jumped from rock to rock.

His luck ran out when he collided with the limb of a round-leaved teak and was flung aside. Skilfully he regained his balance and continued to flee, desperate to put distance between us. I stumbled on, clambering across rocks, knife in hand. Rough surfaces grazing my elbows and knees. Nettles striking me in the face. Sweat pouring from me.

Then the klipspringer jumped into a bush and became entangled. I tried my best to reach him. I was panting for breath. He fought, freed himself and took another leap. Panic and confusion got the upper hand, and he crashed into the rock face. Jumping sideways, he wedged himself into a crevice.

My hand closed around his neck. I pulled him out. He kicked frantically. I held him close to stop him from kicking me. A desperate bleat, shrill and protracted, rose from inside him. The sound spoke of his failure to understand what had happened to him. What was happening to him. It gave voice to his agonising fear. I felt it rip through my soul.

Holding his small, disfigured head, I bent it backward. The throat was exposed. My hunting knife cut deeply, through the gullet and artery. Blood spurted over my hands, my legs, my knees. It splashed over the rocks. His body grew limp in my lap.

Croc in a pisvel

"Wait! Stop the bakkie."

"What? Why?"

"Crocodile."

"No! Don't talk shit, man."

"Crocodile. I'm telling you. Stop the bakkie."

"What would a croc be doing here?"

"Jeez, man. Just stop the fucking bakkie and I'll show you. I'm not fucking blind, am I?"

Sceptically, Daniel slowed down and pulled off the road. Chris jumped out and jogged to the water's edge. Steve, who had been sitting between Chris and Daniel, got out too and followed Chris.

"It was probably a leguaan," he said. Chris's look said it all. His eyes were searching the surface of the water and the reeds on the opposite side. Daniel looked resigned as he got out as well and walked towards them.

Chris was crouching on the dam wall. He motioned for his friends to be quiet. For a long time they stared at the water. Steve saw it first. Chris and Daniel were watching the reeds, when something broke through the surface in the middle of the dam. To the unpractised eye it looked like a rough piece of bark. Steve touched Chris on the shoulder.

"Chris. There it is."

"Ja, wragtag," Daniel had spotted it too.

"Well, there you have it," Chris declared, gratified. As if he needed confirmation, Daniel went to the bakkie and fetched his binoculars. One look, and all remaining doubts were dispelled.

"What's he doing here, I wonder?"

The three friends were standing on the wall of an earth dam beside the main road. Beyond the dam the dusty plain was dotted with a haphazard collection of tin shanties and clay huts as far as the eye could see. Rubbish was scattered everywhere and plastic bags were fluttering from the thorn trees.

Chris turned to Steve and Daniel.

"Guys. Tonight we're going to catch him."

Chris, Steve and Daniel worked on game ranches in the KwaNdebele homeland for the Department of Agriculture. They had been on their way to the office in Kwamhlanga when they had spotted the crocodile. Now they were making enquiries. The crocodile had been there for some time. The children threw stones at it and the police had tried to shoot it. Where it had come from, no one could say. Perhaps it had come overland from the Elands River, sixty kilometres away. The people had been resenting its presence for a long time.

Much later Chris and his friends would find out that a baby croc had been kept in a fishpond at a nearby police base. Apparently it had been the riot squad's mascot until it had grown too big for the pond. It was unclear whether it had escaped itself or whether the policemen had released it in the dam.

The three men handed in their monthly reports and log sheets and announced that they were going to hunt a crocodile that evening. They drove back to the game ranch to plan their operation.

In the shed on the ranch there was an old fibreglass boat, covered with dust and debris. There were no oars, so two makeshift oars were hammered together out of leftover plywood and planks. Daniel asked for three volunteers among the Pedi rangers and, as usual, John Peba, Josef Mokoa and Petrus Sepogwane declared themselves willing.

They discussed their strategy and made a list of the equipment they would need. A powerful shooting lamp was taken out of a steel locker. Steve and John Peba fashioned a hoop out of galvanised wire and fixed it to the end of a broomstick. A noose of nylon rope was attached to it with masking tape. The plan was to get the hoop over the crocodile's head and then to pull on the rope so that the noose would tighten around the creature's neck. Josef and Petrus went into the veld to chop sturdy forked sticks from a kierieklapper. At the hunting camp they stripped an old mattress cover – known since their army days as a pisvel – off a bed and cut a bicycle tube into strips. They took along an old panga and a roll of mutton cloth. They also took a large coil of rope.

They loaded the equipment and tied the boat onto the back of the bakkie. They all donned long-sleeved overalls. It was late afternoon when they left the ranch.

The sun was just setting as they reached their destination. Chris and the three Pedis walked around the dam. They spotted the crocodile among the reeds. Daniel and Steve removed the bakkie's battery, while Chris and the others untied the boat, launched it and anchored it. The battery was placed in the prow and the flex of the lamp was connected to the terminals. Two men would row and one would hold the lamp. The rest would stand by with the hoop and the forked sticks to capture the crocodile. During the delegation of each person's duties, Petrus Sepogwane stood to one side.

"What's the matter, Petrus?"

"I can't swim, Morena."

By eight o'clock it was dark. John Peba and Josef Mokoa rowed awkwardly, and the boat wobbled over the water. Steve swept the light across the surface. Chris held the broomstick with the wire hoop and Daniel wielded a forked stick.

The light picked out the crocodile in the middle of the dam. Motionless, it hung in the water. The sharp light cleaved through the brown water and for the first time the men had a good view of the crocodile. It wasn't a big one. Not yet two metres long. Its armoured hide was olive green and yellow and its belly white. It seemed in excellent condition, and a dead platanna hung from the side of its mouth. Its eyes glowed red in the beam of the lamp.

Splashing and rocking, the boat approached the crocodile. Chris was reminded of the title of a children's story: *The Simpletons Hunt Crocodiles.* The crocodile lay still, blinded by the light that Steve kept trained on it. It felt like an eternity before the boat came abreast of the beast. No one said a word. Steve shone the light unwaveringly on the crocodile. It might not be big, but those teeth sticking out at the side of its jaws looked dangerous enough to inflict serious damage.

The boat was now almost right beside the crocodile. Still the creature hung motionless in the water. Chris brought the hoop with the noose into position. Slowly he began to immerse the hoop in front of the crocodile's snout. Carefully he brought it closer. The hoop was now level with the crocodile's mouth. In the boat everyone watched with close attention. The shadow of the hoop passed across the crocodile's speckled yellow eye. With a thrust of its tail and a kick of its webbed hind legs the crocodile dived down. In a flash he had disappeared into the brown depths of the dam. On the boat the men looked at one another. They would simply have to try again.

Four hours later they were still on the dam. By this time the boat was half filled with water. The men were cold and wet and feelings were running high. After the first attempt, the croc had permitted the boat to come reasonably close a few times, only to give them the slip and hide underwater for several minutes before emerging on the opposite side of the dam.

From the tin shanties on the plain a few people had seen the light moving on the water and had come to investigate. Petrus Sepogwane provided a running commentary for the benefit of the onlookers. The boat had probably crisscrossed the dam at least fifty times. What had begun as an exciting adventure had now deteriorated into a repetitive farce, and the men on the boat were slowly losing interest.

It was then that the crocodile changed its strategy. The unabated pursuit and the blinding light must have unnerved it in the end. Now it sought shelter among the reeds on the dam wall. In places the reed bed was so dense that the boat couldn't penetrate it at all. Now and then the shooting lamp would pick up the crocodile's red eye, only to lose it seconds later in the reeds. The boat cruised back and forth at the edge of the reed bed. The men were at their wits' end and becoming impatient. The water was shallow and now and again the keel scraped on the muddy bottom.

Steve's lamp picked up the crocodile's eye again and on Daniel's command John and Josef rowed the boat closer. The crocodile now seemed to be hiding in an inlet in the bank. The boat was a few metres away when the croc dived again and disappeared from sight. Chris was discouraged, but Steve saw their chance. Because of the shape of the inlet, there was only one way the croc could escape and that was by passing underneath the boat.

Steve shone the light into the water, illuminating the bottom of the dam. Things happened fast. Among the algae, reeds and debris Chris saw the armoured scales on the crocodile's back as it vanished under the keel.

"Great stuff, Steve!" Now he had to be quick. He flung away the broomstick and grabbed the forked stick out of Daniel's hand.

He plunged the stick into the water where he had last seen the crocodile. The water exploded in a churning brown mass as the struggling, squirming croc was pinned to the bottom. The forked stick shuddered and shook in Chris's hands and he had to muster all his strength. Two metres of brute force was fighting to escape down below and soon the water around the boat had changed into foaming chocolate soup.

As his shoulders and arms pushed down on the stick, the boat began to move under Chris's feet, gliding into deeper water. John and Josef struggled in vain to hold the boat steady with their oars. Soon the water under the keel became too deep. The balance shifted and Chris tumbled into the brown water on top of the crocodile.

His grip on the struggling creature did not relax. He

simply couldn't afford it. Sinking into the muddy bottom up to his knees, he kept his grip on the forked stick. The crocodile was still out of sight, but around Chris the water was boiling and churning. "Bring the boat closer and come help me, guys!" he shouted.

Petrus Sepogwane appeared at Chris's side and stood knee-deep in the water with a rope in his hand.

"I don't know which end is his head and which his tail. If I put my hand into the water now, it could be bitten off. You'll have to help. Steve! Keep that light on the water."

Daniel got out of the boat and waded towards them, the roll of cloth in his hand.

"Wrap it around your hand and feel where the tail is," he suggested.

It wasn't the brightest idea, but no one seemed to have a better plan. Chris put out his hand and Daniel began to wrap the bandage around it. With his other hand he kept pushing down on the forked stick. Petrus also grabbed hold of the stick. For a fleeting moment Chris feared that he might have impaled the crocodile.

John, Josef and Steve took the boat ashore.

With his bandaged hand Chris found the crocodile's tail and lifted it out of the water. Daniel, who had taken the rope from Petrus, looped it around the tail a few times and tied it securely. He, John and Josef held on to the rope.

"OK, Chris, you can let go," he said.

Chris and Petrus relaxed their grip on the forked stick and Daniel dragged the still struggling crocodile through the reeds and out onto the dam wall. Steve kept the light on the crocodile and Petrus handed Chris the bicycle tubing. With its jaw wide open the crocodile swung its head from side to side, but it was blinded by the light and with a single movement Chris slipped a length of tube around its mouth, tightened it and tied it securely. Petrus grabbed the croc around its body and Daniel tied its hind legs. John held on to the tail and Josef ran to the bakkie to fetch the pisvel. Steve was still lighting up the scene with the shooting lamp.

Soon the crocodile was inside the pisvel, the battery back in the bakkie and the boat loaded onto the back. They set off for Elands River to release their catch. John, Josef and Petrus were in the back, underneath the boat. Daniel was driving and Chris and Steve sat beside him, balancing a crocodile in a pisvel across their laps. On the dam wall they left behind a group of astonished spectators.

At regular intervals Daniel had to apply the brakes in order to avoid cattle and donkeys in the road.

"Let's sleep over at Boet's house. We can release the crocodile in the morning," Chris suggested.

"Yes, I want to get out of these wet clothes," Daniel agreed.

Steve looked at his watch. "Boet will shit himself if we arrive at his place at this hour with a crocodile in a pisvel. It's half past one in the morning."

"It's high time we terrorised him again. Let's go."

"Yes, let's go. Fuck Boet anyway. He's been sleeping peacefully while we've had to catch a crocodile."

Boet was manager of a game farm on the banks of the Elands River. He was Chris, Daniel and Steve's more serious colleague. On Saturdays, while the other three were listening to rugby on the radio, having a braai and drinking beer, Boet would spend the day in the veld with his binoculars and his bird book. Chris and the others knew that Boet valued his privacy and therefore they made a point of arriving at his place at the most inopportune times.

In the cab the conversation revolved around the croc capture operation. Each person gave his version of the story. They replayed the events and laughed heartily. They agreed that the operation had been a great success. Once again the game rangers had prevailed in the interest of nature. The crocodile would have been shot some or other time, or it would have grown large enough to take a child. But now it had been captured and they were relocating it to the Elands River, where crocodiles were still spotted regularly. They would release it there to enjoy a peaceful existence. They were guardians of nature and saviours of man and beast alike.

Across their laps lay the crocodile in its pisvel.

After prolonged hooting, the watchman at the gate came out of his hut sleepily and unlocked the gate of Boet's game farm. The double-track road to Boet's house wound through thorn trees. Hares and genets fled before the bakkie's head-lights.

Boet was half asleep and seemed on the verge of tears when he opened the back door, candle in hand. Chris, Steve and Daniel burst into the house exuberantly. Under his arm Steve carried the crocodile in the pisvel. He put it down on a counter in the kitchen and walked over to the gas fridge, where he retrieved three beers and a block of cheese. He handed two of the beers to Chris and Daniel, cut off a big chunk of cheese with his pocketknife and stuffed it into his mouth. Boet looked desperate.

"Oh sorry, Boet. Do you want a beer as well?"

"Boet. We're looking for a place to sleep. We want to get out of our wet clothes and we have something that's going to sleep in your bath," Chris said.

"What?" Boet asked.

Chris winked and took the pisvel from the kitchen counter. "Come and see."

Chris, Daniel and Steve led the way to the bathroom. Boet followed dejectedly with the candle. Chris shook out the pisvel over the empty bath. The crocodile fell out, still tied up securely. It squirmed a few times before realising it was helpless. Then it lay still.

Boet stood open-mouthed.

"You can't leave that thing in my bath," he said, almost beseechingly, staring at the crocodile.

"Well, Boet, if you have a better place for it, please feel free to take it out."

Boet gave up and went back to his bedroom, grumbling. He slammed the door behind him.

Daniel lit another candle and the three friends finished

their beers in the lounge. They were still grinning at Boet's reaction. Then they took off their wet overalls and each grabbed a sofa or available bed. Petrus and the rest of the Pedis had left for the compound as soon as they had arrived.

A crested francolin announced the start of a new day. The three crocodile hunters began to stir. Daniel got up and made coffee in the kitchen. Chris stepped out into the yard in the half-light to take a leak. The morning star was still visible in the grey sky. It was going to be a beautiful day. He remained outside for a while and felt the bushveld awakening around him.

When he returned, the coffee was ready. Daniel had appropriated a box of Ouma rusks in Boet's pantry and he and Steve were dunking them in strong, steaming coffee. Boet woke up and joined them in the lounge. He seemed to have had a good night's sleep and even showed some interest in the crocodile adventure. Chris, Steve and Daniel filled him in enthusiastically. Everyone roared with laughter at the previous night's escapade and Boet particularly enjoyed the account of Chris tumbling into the water. The sun rose over the tops of the thorn trees and shone through the lounge window.

"Boys, let's go and release that crocodile in the river," Chris announced. Everyone got up and went to the bathroom. Chris was talking to Steve and glancing over his shoulder as he bent over the side of the bath to pick up the crocodile by the scruff of its neck.

"Watch out, Chris!" Steve shouted and grabbed him by the shoulder.

Using its tail, the crocodile half lifted itself out of the bath. Quick as a flash its mouth moved in the direction of Chris's outstretched hands and when its jaws snapped shut, it sounded like a rifle shot. The tubing that had been tied around its hind legs and mouth lay in heaps inside the bath. Chris and Steve tumbled backward and sent poor Boet flying so that he cracked his head against the wall. The three ended up in a heap on the bathroom floor. Daniel landed on his back in the passage. The crocodile fell back into the bath and struggled fiercely, but its feet couldn't get a grip on the smooth enamel sides.

Chris and the others sat up, wide-eyed. Boet was rubbing the back of his head.

Chris inspected the damage. The crocodile had narrowly missed him. "Bliksem!" was all he said.

Inside the bath the crocodile was going mad. Daniel fetched the forked stick from the bakkie.

The bakkie wound its way through the bushveld along a rutted track that led to the river bank. A herd of impala watched them from a clump of sickle bush. A warthog burst out of the tall grass beside the road and fled ahead of them, its tail held high. The bakkie stopped on the flood plain at the river's edge. Boet pointed at a sand bar.

"I saw a huge one there last week."

Chris lifted the crocodile out of the bakkie, once more tied up securely and wrapped in its pisvel after a furious struggle in the bathroom. Carefully he shook it out on the sandy bank. Petrus held its head and Steve its tail. Chris untied the tubing round its hind legs and jaws.

The men stepped back, cautiously and respectfully. For a while the crocodile lay still. Then it raised itself on its short legs and walked to the water's edge. It slipped in and disappeared. After a while its head reappeared in the middle of the Elands River. It was making its way downstream.

The Elands River flows in a northeasterly direction and later joins up with the Olifants River. Further east, the Olifants River runs over the edge of the plateau and into the Lowveld. In the Kruger National Park it flows through a deep basalt canyon, creating rapids and potholes. Here large shoals of freshwater fish gather, migrating upstream during the breeding season. It is a good hunting ground for crocodiles.

Before the Olifants River reaches the basalt canyon, another tributary flows into it. The Timbavati is a seasonal river. For the best part of the year it is a meandering dry stream bed. After the November rains it is filled with floodwater and flows strongly for two weeks. Fish, crocodiles and hippos migrate upstream from the Olifants River to occupy its pools. At the start of the dry season the pools dry up. The fish die and most of the hippos and crocs move back. Some occupy earth dams along the banks of the Timbavati and stay a little longer.

Chris and the crocodile would meet again.

Guweni pool

"Why do you say the rain is over for this year, Filliosse?"

"Look how low the lesser masked weavers are building their nests over the water. This year the Guweni is going to run dry."

And so the drought of 1992 began. The severest drought in the history of the Kruger Park.

The Sweni is a tributary of the Nuanedzi River. The Sweni itself has several tributaries, that flow from the south-west across the broad turf plains like the fingers on a hand. They are the Nungwini, the Murandzuloku, the Magonkolweni and the Guweni. All four these tributaries meet at a fault in the rhyolites in the foothills of the Lebombo mountains and flow into the Sweni together.

The Guweni is the largest of these streams. In one place it forms deep pools, where I liked to stop when we took tourists on wilderness trails. On the banks grow sausage trees, weeping boer-bean and fever trees. There are also dense stands of magic ghwarrie and red spike-thorn through which game paths meander to the water's edge.

Here you have to tread carefully. Lions love these pools. They have a way of surprising you in the undergrowth.

At one magnificent pool weaver nests dangle from the yellow switches of the fever trees. A large variety of waterfowl can be seen on the clayey banks: African openbills, woolly-necked storks and white-backed night herons.

The pool is large enough for a small herd of hippo, numbering perhaps five or six. The muddy water is also home to several crocodiles: two big fellows of three metres and several smaller ones.

Our tourist camp was situated on the southern bank of the Sweni River. On the opposite side we kept a muddy pan filled with water from the overflow of our borehole. As the veld began to dry out, the game would gather around the pools and boreholes.

In the heat of the day, when it was too hot to walk in the veld, we would sit under the thatched roof of the lapa. Endless rows of game filed past to drink: impala, zebra, blue wildebeest, warthog, kudu, giraffe. A few old buffalo bulls. Sometimes you saw more game at camp than during an entire day spent walking in the veld.

Late afternoon is a good time to take a drive and explore the vicinity of the Guweni pool on foot. It's a desolate backveld region. The animals are wary of venturing into the ghwarrie thickets, for it's the ideal place for an ambush.

If you approach the pool in the late afternoon, when the pale yellow fever trees contrast sharply with the dark evergreen of the weeping boer-beans, and you don't see any game on the plains, you can be certain: there are lions around.

Filliosse and I would then slip our rifles from our shoulders and cock them. He would stay with the hikers while I would weave through the ghwarrie bushes. The tension and anticipation always thrilled me. Once I'd made sure it was safe, I would return and beckon to Filliosse: the hikers could approach.

On the banks we would watch the hippos, crocs and waterfowl for a while. Then we would search for fresh lion tracks, for the region was known for its large prides of lion.

Often we'd find the lions on the plains, where they lay sleeping among knob-thorn bushes. We would watch them for several minutes. Some lay stretched out on their flanks, fast asleep, with only a tail twitching now and again. Others lay on their backs, belly up.

Filliosse and I would stand motionlessly for a long time. We would allow the tension to build. Then one of us would cough.

Surprised, the lions would look up. The males always fled

first, without thinking twice. More heads would pop up, previously hidden by the tall yellow grass. Some dangerously close. Cubs of various sizes would scatter in every direction.

The females would always take a defensive stance. They'd utter a few menacing growls. Ears flattened, bodies close to the ground, crouching, ready to pounce. Their tails would crack on the ground like whips. Sometimes one or two would launch a stiff-legged charge in our direction and kick up a cloud of red dust before breaking away and joining the cubs. The smell of lion and dust in the late afternoon sun will stay with me for ever.

Filliosse and I would have our rifles at the ready and urge the hikers to stay calm. After all the lions had fled, Filliosse would produce a deep belly laugh. We found it great sport; the hikers found it incredibly exciting. The largest pride of lions that we ever encountered there numbered forty-three.

When the pool began to dry up during the drought of 1992, the hippos were first to leave. They didn't all leave together. First a cow and a calf, followed later by another cow and calf. At last the bull was left behind on his own. By that time the pool was very shallow, no more than a muddy pond. It was dangerous. Once the bull charged halfway up the bank in pursuit of me, but fortunately it was too steep and he returned to the mud. Hippos that refuse to leave their pools during a drought sometimes hide in the bushes on the river bank by day. They feel vulnerable. The sun dries out their hides and they become fractious. Jack Greeff once had no choice but to shoot a hippo bull coming at him from the thickets, because a hippo doesn't usually back off during a charge. I was lucky.

When we arrived at the pool in the late afternoon, we would find only the hippo bull and the crocodiles there. The plains were hot, dusty and deserted, with a dry southeaster blowing. The zebra and wildebeest had already left in search of perennial water. At last the hippo also left and only the crocodiles remained. On the bottom of the pool deep cracks appeared in the mud.

During that time Filliosse and I often found crocs hiding in the bushes very far from the water. Many of the crocodiles trekked overland in search of perennial water, but most of the crocs in the Guweni pool stayed behind. They hollowed out the clay banks and went into hibernation.

In the following weeks, as the countryside dried out, the crocodiles became thinner. The two big ones had dug themselves in deeply. We searched for their dark caves for a long time before we spotted them. One of them seemed to have been involved in a fight, perhaps with his comrade. One afternoon we found him halfway out of his tunnel. The tip of his tail was missing.

The tunnels of the smaller crocodiles were not as deep. They soon became emaciated. They looked like skeletons covered with crocodile skin. Their metabolism had slowed down. The only proof that they were still alive was their shining yellow eyes.

Then the leopard discovered the young crocodiles. One afternoon on our way to the pool we found his tracks in the game path. At the pool he had dragged three crocodiles from their tunnels, hung them in a fever tree and eaten them halfway. Every day there was another piece of crocodile biltong in the trees. It was a macabre sight to see the half eaten crocodiles dangling from the yellow branches. To me it epitomised the drought.

One day we came across the leopard. He lay fast asleep in dense shade in the stream bed. We watched him from the opposite bank. He was unaware of us. Minutes passed. After a while his eyes opened. For seconds he stared at us. The next moment he disappeared into the undergrowth. Gone.

The Guweni pool was now just a dusty hollow. The last moisture had disappeared from the bottom. The days were searing hot. Far in the west, behind the mountains, it looked as if clouds were accumulating. But the rainy season was still in the distant future.

The two large crocodiles, Stub-tail and his friend, were the only ones left in the Guweni pool. Sometimes they lay outside the mouths of their caves. Their skins were sunken over their bones. They looked dead. Filliosse touched one with the barrel of his rifle. Like a spring trap, the animal spun round and almost knocked the rifle out of Filliosse's hand with his jaws. The hikers jumped back. My old Shangaan friend laughed so that his eyes were mere slits in his face.

As the weeks dragged by, the days became more oppressive. October remained dry, November too. The wilderness trails were no longer a pleasure. Clouds built up in the west and looked promising, but then the southeaster would come up and drive them back.

Filliosse and I stood by the Guweni pool, the place we once knew as a leafy oasis.

"There's going to be good rain this year," Filliosse said. "Not just yet. Almost. But not now. The weavers have only just started building their nests."

My heart went out to the two crocodiles. Doggedly they clung to life with the last of their strength. A crocodile can survive on dry land for months on the fat reserves in its tail.

One day there was a change in the weather pattern. It was as if a tug-of-war was taking place between the coastal winds and the winds from the mountains. Clouds scudded and whipped across the land. The dry, hot air seemed to be sucking in moisture from the sea. Nature held its breath for rain.

We found Stub-tail on the cracked bottom of the Guweni pool. The leopard had not even bothered to hang him in a tree, but had begun to eat him right there. In the end Stub-tail had had too little tail to get him to the rainy season. His mate was left behind on his own.

That night the heavens opened. The Guweni River came down in flood and filled all the pools.

Brothers

It was night. We heard the two male lions approaching along the dry river bed. At first the roars were distant. Then closer. Now they were close to us, just beyond the reeds in the river bed. We even heard the soft rattle in their throats. I knew these two lions well. They ruled over this river bed.

It was late November. The rain had not yet fallen. Oom Bennie Erasmus, Filliosse Mula and I were camping on the banks of the Shisakarangondzo. We were busy with anthrax control.

When the lions had passed, Oom Bennie spoke in Afrikaans: "Ek hoop nie die epidemie vorder so dat die leeus aangetas word nie" – I hope the epidemic doesn't spread to infect the lions.

"Hmm," Filliosse concurred in his guttural baritone. He threw another red bushwillow log on the fire. Filliosse never spoke Afrikaans. But when a bush veteran spoke, he understood.

"A lion with anthrax is a terrible sight," Oom Bennie continued. "His head swells until it is so big that he can't close his mouth. There is nothing you can do, except shoot him on the spot."

The epidemic was now in its second week. Only kudu and buffalo had died so far. Filliosse, Oom Bennie and I made up one of the monitoring teams. For the past ten days we had been walking in the veld, searching for carcasses. We had taken blood and tissue samples. Then we had burned the carcasses. It was hard, hot work. But sometimes there was a surprise.

Yesterday morning, vultures in the trees had alerted us to

the carcass of an impala. The impala ewe had not been dead for long. When I knelt beside her, a caracal had jumped out of a raisin bush next to me. It was rare for a caracal to catch an impala.

Oom Bennie told me about anthrax.

"It breaks out at the end of the dry season, when the condition of the animals and the veld is poor. The spores of the *anthracis bacillus* are found in the mud of the waterholes. There are small cuts on the lips of the animals because the grass and leaves they feed on are dry. When they drink water, the anthrax spores enter their bloodstream through the cuts in their mouths. As soon as the rains fall, the anthrax threat disappears."

"Why are we monitoring it?"

"In the Kruger Park we don't conserve only wildlife, we also conserve the ecology. Anthrax is part of the ecology. We don't want to eradicate it, but we must control it. And we have to prevent it from spreading to the stock farms. Vultures are the main culprits. They feed on the carcasses, then fly to the farms and bath in the drinking troughs. That's why we burn the carcasses. Lion and hyena also spread it. If the rains are late, all the animals become infected in the end. Elephants too."

Oom Bennie was an interesting man with a lot of stories to tell. He used to live in Mozambique. He stared into the fire, pulled deeply at his cigarette and took a sip of whiskey.

"I had a large farm next to the Gorongosa game reserve. I farmed with cattle. Lions were a big problem. Later it became more profitable to hunt; the Portuguese sugar farmers paid a lot of money to hunt lion. When they saw the large numbers of buffalo, they offered me a contract to shoot buffalo – meat for the labourers on the sugar farms. I shot hundreds of buffalo. Made a lot of money. Sometimes I even shot unlawfully in Gorongosa. Now *there* you found a lot of buffalo."

The lions were roaring in the distance now. It was quiet on the banks of the Shisakarangondzo. Filliosse threw another log on the fire and went to bed. He lay down in his bedroll against the wheel of the bakkie. Oom Bennie was reminiscing about the distant past.

"One of my neighbours was an eccentric old German. We suspected he was a Nazi who had been in the SS and had come to hide in the bush. He kept to himself and was always suspicious. My other neighbour was a mestizo with beautiful dark-skinned daughters." He stared into his tin mug and smiled. "Yes, they were pretty. It was a lonely place."

When the war broke out in Mozambique, Oom Bennie left. He became one of Doctor Bolton's veterinary technicians in the Kruger Park.

The next morning we came across two lions on a buffalo carcass.

"They mustn't come and eat here," Oom Bennie said. It was just the two of us; Filliosse had stayed behind to change a tyre.

The lions got up from the carcass menacingly. They were in their prime. One had a blond mane, the other one's mane was almost black.

Oom Bennie and I approached them. We waved our revolvers and spoke to them in loud voices. Dark-mane made a stiff-legged charge and growled angrily. Then he broke away and he and his companion trotted away. They watched us from the shade of a mopane.

I kept my revolver trained on them, while Oom Bennie took the blood and tissue samples from the carcass. They were two fine lions. Male lions learn quickly that a coalition is more effective than a monarchy. Together they fight other males who threaten their leadership. They ascend the throne together. I knew – I had put the old male out of his misery. While one had attacked him from the front, the other one had come from the side and snapped his spine. When I found the old male, he was a pathetic, crazed figure. With his forepaws, he dragged along his paralysed hindquarters. He had been their father.

Together the two young lions patrolled the Shisakarangondzo. They watched each other's backs. They took turns to mount the lionesses along the river bank. The young cubs belonged to either of the two. Unity is strength.

When Oom Bennie had finished, we began to build the funeral pyre. Filliosse had rejoined us in the meantime. We dragged heavy mopane stumps nearer. With difficulty we rolled the buffalo over and got as much firewood underneath him as possible. Then we covered him with wood. The lions had left. Filliosse fetched the jerry can from the bakkie. We soaked the pyre with diesel and set it alight.

A buffalo carcass takes a long time to burn. We would have to return later in the day to put more wood on the fire. We drove to Orpen and delivered the blood and tissue samples. Doctor Bolton would analyse them in his field laboratory. The other teams had also come in. They reported dead kudu and buffalo everywhere. All our carcasses tested positive – all except the impala ewe.

The next few days were stifling hot. We burned a lot of kudu and buffalo carcasses. Filliosse and I climbed Masala koppie. In the surrounding bush we counted twelve columns of smoke. Everywhere anthrax teams were burning carcasses. The veld was parched and grey.

Anthrax control became hard work. Buffalo are water-loving creatures and the sick ones came to the water to die. We regularly had to pull carcasses out of the waterhole with the bakkie and a tow cable. The water became contaminated. The heat increased. Far in the west, over Mariepskop, clouds began to gather.

One afternoon Filliosse, Oom Bennie and I came across the lions again on the opposite bank of the Shisakarangondzo. They were half hidden in the undergrowth. Oom Bennie realised immediately that something was wrong. "I hope it's not what I think it is."

The three of us looked through our binoculars. I scanned the bushes. I could see only the blond lion. His eyes seemed swollen shut. Blood ran from his nose and mouth – a symptom of anthrax.

"We'll have to go closer," said Oom Bennie. He took his .375 Winchester Magnum from behind the bakkie's seat and checked it. I did the same with my .458 Brno. Filliosse took the R-1 and cocked it. Oom Bennie looked at us gravely.

"If these lions see us, they will run away. We'll have to outwit them. We have *one* chance. When I shoot, you must shoot."

We crept through the reeds downwind. Then through the dry river bed of the Shisakarangondzo. I was aware of the familiar hollow feeling at the pit of my stomach. Oom Bennie led the way. I was close behind him; Filliosse brought up the rear. We held our rifles at the ready.

We followed a game trail up the opposite bank. There were fresh lion tracks. Oom Bennie knelt to point out drops of blood in the sand. The lions were somewhere ahead of us in the riverine bush. I felt sweat pouring down my back. Oom Bennie's eyes scanned the undergrowth. We moved forward quietly. The cicadas screeched.

Filliosse saw them first. He made a soft hissing noise through his teeth and I looked round quickly. His eyes gleamed in his ebony face. He pointed: ahead, to the right. Oom Bennie had already seen them. The butt of his rifle came up to his shoulder. The lions were still out of sight in the undergrowth. The blond one sat up. He had not seen us yet. I looked at his swollen face, his bloody nose. Dark-mane was lying flat in the grass. It looked as if he was sleeping.

Oom Bennie leaned back. His eyes never left the lions. Filliosse and I leaned forward to hear what he was whispering.

"We have to make certain. Aim at the blond lion. I'm going to wait for the other one to raise his head. Shoot as soon as I have shot. Not before."

The blond lion showed his profile. I slipped the safety catch off and pointed my rifle at a spot diagonally below his ear. Oom Bennie aimed at the other lion. We waited. Seconds became minutes. Sweat stung my eyes. The lion swam in front of the sights. The tension was building. I kept my focus.

Then I heard Oom Bennie whisper beside me: "Goeie bliksem!"

Dark-mane had raised his head.

Af first I didn't register what I was looking at. Then it became clear: Half of Dark-mane's face was missing. His cheek had been ripped off. The wound looked raw and painful. The grotesque face stared in our direction. He didn't see us. Then the head sank down again.

Oom Bennie and Filliosse lowered their rifles. I did the same. Silently we fell back.

At the bakkie Oom Bennie lit two cigarettes. He gave one to Filliosse. They drew deeply.

"Yes," Oom Bennie said through clouds of smoke, "they're OK." For a while he was lost in thought. "Sometimes brothers also disagree."

Culling

It was my second year as wilderness trails ranger in the Kruger Park. Elephant culling season had come round again. The chief of wilderness trails required of each ranger to shoot at least two elephant bulls. In-service training. He wanted to keep us on our toes. The year before I had to shoot four elephants. The first two didn't go smoothly.

The breeding herds were usually culled from a helicopter. This was to ensure that the operation was as successful as possible, for not a single elephant could be allowed to escape. It was the task of the young trail rangers to shoot lone bulls from the ground. A charge was simulated, so that the men might gain experience.

The helicopter taking to the air was the signal for the operation to begin. The vehicle procession came under way. Everywhere people jumped into bakkies or onto the backs of bakkies and flat-bed trucks. In a cloud of dust they headed for the area where the operation would take place.

The helicopter soared overhead. Then, out of nowhere, hundreds of vultures descended from the thermals high above, floating in the wake of the helicopter. In columns they followed the procession of vehicles. They were mostly the white-backed variety, but there were also lappet-faced vultures with their red turkey heads, hooded vultures and white-headed vultures. There was even a Cape vulture or two.

Patiently they soared, close behind the helicopter. In rows or single file. Some swept up and over the procession, others circled lazily overhead, rejoining the rest after a while. They knew, as we did and the elephants too, exactly what was going to happen today. Like monstrous angels of doom they followed the helicopter.

At the prearranged place the procession came to a halt. The helicopter had spotted the elephants there during a reconnaissance flight earlier in the day. Now we waited. Systematically the helicopter began to herd the elephants in the direction of the trucks. The vultures perched in the dead trees around us. In the east the chopper thrashed and churned above the treetops. Somewhere below, outside our field of vision, were the elephants. Man and vulture waited for the machine to do its job.

Then came the signal – a ranger received a message on the radio. He nodded at the men beside him. They motioned for everyone to get going, into the veld, where the chopper hung motionlessly in the air. The trucks tore a broad strip through the bush, uprooting young trees in their way.

The procession reached a place where a herd of thirty elephant lay in a motionless pile. Their soft brown eyes were open and aware. Rangers got out of their bakkies. They pressed the barrels of their rifles into the hollow where an elephant's skull and cervical vertebrae meet and delivered the fatal shot. Only those younger than five years were spared.

To make the culling operation as effective and clinical as possible, and to prevent elephants from being wounded or escaping, they were first darted from the helicopter with an overdose of scoline. Scoline is a powerful muscle relaxant that paralyses the animals. In effect they lie, helplessly suffocating under their own body weight, until the rangers arrive to put them down.

To maintain the balance of nature, it was initially decided to destroy entire herds indiscriminately. Until a smart young scientist pointed out that valuable genetic material was being destroyed. That was why it was decided to spare the lives of calves younger than five years. They too were darted from the helicopter with a narcotic drug. But they weighed less and didn't suffocate when their diaphragms pressed on their lungs, as the older ones did. Later they would be exported to second-rate game reserves like Pilanesberg and Madikwe. There they would grow to adulthood and become "problem animals", trampling tourists who left the safety of their motorcars.

While cranes were unloading the heavy steel crates from the flat-bed trucks, technicians and scientists took the measurements of each elephant, dead or alive. Height from the shoulder, length from head to tail, circumference of foot (fore and hind). Everything was noted down carefully and preserved for posterity. Veterinarians took blood and tissue samples. Put them into test tubes and plastic bottles, each with a label. Young students, mostly girls, rushed about, keeping the sleeping youngsters cool with buckets of water.

In the meantime, the team of slaughterers had begun to remove the entrails. Rangers kept a close eye on the surrounding bush, rifles at the ready. It had happened before that a vengeful elephant had stopped by to pay them a visit.

The crates were positioned in front of the sleeping youngsters. The wilderness rangers and the Shangaans took up their positions. The girls poured water over the elephants one last time. The vet had the antidote ready. The syringes and needles were lined up in his medicine chest. A cameraman jostled for position. The vet set his watch. He pushed in the needles.

A minute and a half later the young elephants woke and smelled the blood and guts of their dead mothers, brothers and sisters. They smelled diesel, man and steel. They struggled to their feet, only to be bundled into a dark crate by a group of shouting, stinking men. A heavy door slid into place noisily.

The wilderness rangers had great fun. Elephant shit and mud all over the place. The dirtier the better.

The cranes lifted the loaded crates onto the trucks. The disembowelled carcasses were hoisted onto the flat-bed trucks and covered with heavy green tarpaulins. The tourists would be spared the sight. The late afternoon sun fell in shafts through trees and dust clouds. The vultures waited patiently while the men finished their business.

Rumours about the day's results spread among the wilderness rangers, sending a wave of excitement through the men. Information filtered back. Piet: two elephants two shots; Bryan: one elephant three shots, one elephant five shots; Max: froze up again. He was out. It had been his last chance.

I grew quiet and withdrew from the noise. It would be my turn the next day. It was going to be a long night.

Wayne and I would be shooting the next morning. Wayne went first. I sat beside the pilot to provide ballast for the helicopter. The figures of Wayne, Mick and Louw dwindled under the knob-thorns as we lifted off. We followed the course of a dry river bed; the pilot had seen two elephants around there earlier. Now they were gone. The pilot kept the helicopter low over the riverine bush.

In the distance, near the upper reaches of the stream, their backs became visible in a red spike-thorn thicket. We headed in their direction. Huddling close together, the elephants tried to hide among the spike-thorns. The pilot manoeuvred the helicopter in an effort to drive them into the open. We came in low overhead, so low that I could see every furrow and wrinkle on their grey hides. They kept their heads averted from the helicopter, concealed among the leaves, refusing to give up the meagre protection of the bushes. They knew exactly what was going on.

"Come on, you bastards. Get the fuck out of there," the pilot muttered beside me.

Desperately the elephants clung to their futile shelter. The helicopter made a wide turn. Came in low again. The first elephant's courage failed him. He broke away from his mate and burst out of the red spike-thorns. Like a giant wasp the helicopter descended on him, driving him across the plain. To where Wayne, Mick and Louw were waiting, a long way downriver.

The elephant tore across the veld. I tried to imagine his

overwhelming fear. A huge, powerful beast, diminished and humiliated. Helpless against the power of technology. Degraded. Loathing rose inside me.

Across the open plain the elephant fled to meet his certain death. He knew it. Urine and faeces spurted from his body in an uninterrupted stream. He was tiring but he still had far to go. Desperately he tried to swerve, but the helicopter kept him in line. Running was his only hope.

As he fled, he pushed his trunk down his throat and sucked up his own stomach fluid, squirting it over his head.

From the air I recognised the knob-thorn under which the men were waiting. Wayne and the others came into view. Not far now. Just let it be over.

The elephant made straight for the knob-thorn. Three tiny figures stepped out of the shadows. They looked deceptively defenseless.

I watched as the barrel of a rifle was raised. I watched as the elephant collapsed. The helicopter broke away. A dim popping sound reached my ears.

The scene repeated itself with Wayne's second elephant bull. It was clear: To an elephant the sound of a helicopter was the sound of death. The elephant plunged to the ground, head first. One tusk ploughed into the earth and sent up a cloud of red dust. Then he got up. He charged at Wayne. Mick and Louw raised their rifles too and the elephant reeled. After he had collapsed, I heard the belated pop-pop-pop of the rifle shots over the noise of the engines.

Now it was my turn. Wayne took my place in the passenger's seat. Carrying my .458 and wearing my ammunition belt, I took up my position with Mick and Louw.

The helicopter brought my first elephant bull. He came charging along with flapping ears. Fleeing before the helicopter, unaware of the men on the ground.

I stepped out of the shadows, cocked the rifle and sighted on the first wrinkle below his eye. I allowed him to approach. Then I pressed the trigger.

He stopped in his tracks as if he had charged into an

invisible wall. Then his forelegs collapsed and he tumbled forward. His tusks stuck into the ground. The hindquarters and legs were still erect, but they were wavering. I reloaded and ran closer. The rest of the body sagged to the ground. I pushed the barrel into the hollow at the back of his head and pulled the trigger. A small fountain of blood pumped from the bullet wound. I pushed my finger into the dead eye, unloaded and stepped back.

Now the helicopter was bringing my second elephant. He came from the side, slightly off course. I wanted to get it over with. He saw me as I stepped out from under the knob-thorn. I raised my rifle. It was the signal for the chopper to break away. The elephant saw his chance. When the helicopter lifted, he veered and fled, away from the helicopter and me.

I ran after after him. I heard myself shout. The pilot noticed that the elephant was getting away and brought the helicopter in low. Then he saw me close behind the elephant and hung back.

I ran, holding the rifle high in front of me. From the corner of my eye I saw Mick and Louw. They were shouting and waving. They were trying their best to keep up, but they were middle-aged and overweight. The elephant and I were leaving them behind. The helicopter was no longer following. For moments the elephant and I ran together. Then he began to draw away from me. I slackened my pace and saw him gaining ground.

I stopped. He was growing smaller. "Go well!" I shouted after his retreating form. I watched as he was swallowed by the bushes.

Mick and Louw caught up with me. They were out of breath. They looked flustered and bewildered. They eyed me quizzically, but said nothing. In silence we turned round and walked back to the bakkie.

Hitching through Africa

It was half an hour before sunset when the two came walking into the Kruger Park. I watched them from my stoep. What's this? I wondered. Both wore faded jeans and boots. Both had hefty packs on their backs. There was resignation in their attitude. They aroused my interest.

The man and the woman walked into the rest camp and headed straight for the small building that served as reception area and shop. I saw Hein Grobler coming out onto the stoep and waiting for them, hands on hips. I set down my beer next to my chair. This could get interesting. I swung my feet off the railing, got up and wandered across to reception.

From a distance I could hear there was an argument.

"It's out of the question," Hein was saying.

"But it's what the book says," the woman retorted, tourist guide in hand. The man looked baffled. Hein noticed me. He looked relieved; reinforcements had arrived.

"Chris, now I've heard everything. These two want to hitch to Satara."

It was late on a Friday afternoon in June at the Orpen gate, the southern central entrance to the Park. Sixty kilometres ahead lay Satara, one of the larger rest camps. An hour before sunset tourists were no longer allowed to travel from Orpen to Satara.

"Look," Hein explained, "even if I could allow you to hitchhike, it's too late now. No one is permitted to travel to Satara at this hour. Besides, it's weekend. All the camping spots and bungalows are occupied. I'm sorry."

"But see here what the book says," the woman insisted desperately.

Hein took the book; it was a British tourist guide. I read over his shoulder: *Hitchhikers are welcome in the Kruger Park.* It was early in the 1990s. South Africa was undergoing a period of transition. Increasing numbers of foreigners were visiting our shores. Dozens of tourist guides were being published, but a lot of the information was inaccurate.

I lost interest. It was my first free weekend in a month; I had completed a wilderness trail on the Sweni the day before. Before that I had stood in for a colleague at the Olifants River. I was looking forward to a quiet weekend at home. The ranger at Kingfisher Spruit had invited Hein and me for a braai that evening. I didn't feel like dealing with misinformed tourists.

I turned to leave, but then I saw the distressed look in Hein's eyes. The two hitchhikers were now sitting dejectedly beside their backpacks. They had lit cigarettes.

Orpen lies where three game reserves meet: the Timbavati, the Manyeleti and the Kruger. We were surrounded by bush. What were we going to do with these people? Night was falling. To send them back to the highway was unthinkable. There were no cars at night and the place was teeming with lion and hyena.

I sighed. Oh well. "Come and pitch your tent at my place."

They jumped at the invitation. Grabbing their backpacks, they followed me.

I showed them the kitchen and the bathroom; they were welcome to use them. I pointed out a spot on the lawn where they could pitch their small tent. For some reason I didn't offer them my spare room. South Africa was isolated from the rest of the world in those days. The Park was isolated from the rest of South Africa. I was mistrustful.

"I'll take you back to Hoedspruit tomorrow morning. You can rent a vehicle there. Or get a lift with a tourist."

While they were pitching their tent, I showered. I met Hein at his house. We got into my bakkie and drove to Kingfisher. On our way we discussed the two travellers. We knew tourists. They drove in from the city to visit the Park. The adventurous ones came on a wilderness trail with me.

To us tourists were a necessary inconvenience that made it possible for us to make a living in the Park. But these two were different. They showed the kind of enterprise that commanded respect. Hein and I looked at each other. They had stirred something inside us. Where were they heading? Where did they come from? They lived from day to day. Uncertain about the future, yet carefree. There were always new places to see. New adventures to experience.

As we were driving back from the braai, I decided. I wanted to find out more about these people. Besides, I was in a position to make a difference to their lives. The last shred of doubt disappeared when I walked into my bathroom. An aroma of soap and perfume lingered in the air and it smelled good. When was the last time I'd enjoyed the company of a girl?

The man I will always remember as Burt from Australia. Long curly hair protruding from under his woollen cap. The woman I would remember even better. She was Joanna Milward of Surrey, England, otherwise known as Jo. She was dark-skinned, with long black hair.

I walked out of the house to their tent. They were fast asleep. I spoke to them; they answered hesitantly.

"Be ready. Tomorrow morning at five we're going for a drive through the Park."

Before dawn we were up. We gulped down coffee and rusks in the kitchen. They were excited.

"Let's go," I said. "We have to be on the road before the tourists. We'll drive until we find elephants. Then I'll take you back to Hoedspruit."

They seemed more than satisfied with the arrangement.

At first light we found two lions at the roadside. We stayed with them until long after sunrise. It was a male and a female, mating. It was the first time Burt and Jo had ever seen lions out of captivity. "It's not every day you come across lions mating," I explained.

Jo was sitting between Burt and me and leaned across me to take photos. I smelled her perfume again.

The plains were dotted with blue wildebeest and zebra. Impala gleamed golden in the morning sun. Jo found it beautiful.

They told me about their travels. They had started in Cape Town. For two weeks they stopped there; it's a wonderful city. Then they followed the Garden Route. Had a great time with the hippies at Knysna. Next came the Wild Coast. They considered it the real Africa; the coast was idyllic and the Xhosa culture fascinating. In the Free State they spent some time on a farm with a farming family. Everyone had been so good to them so far. They'd had a completely different idea of South Africa when they arrived.

We came across more lions – a pride of three lionesses and six cubs in the road. They were basking on the tarred surface in the winter sun. It was going to be a fine day.

From here Burt and Jo wanted to go to Zimbabwe. Then up into Africa. They wanted to try and reach the Red Sea. No, they weren't a couple. They had met in Cape Town in a backpackers' lodge and decided to travel together.

When we drove into Satara, we still hadn't seen any sign of elephants. "Let's have a meat pie," I suggested. While we were eating, I decided we might as well make a day of it.

I bought a crate of beer. The lady behind the counter asked about my dishevelled friends.

We continued on our journey. At the Nuanetsi River a large herd of buffalo grazed on both sides of the road. We stopped for a long time to watch a group of giraffes. The beer tasted good. We laughed and talked. It grew hot and the game began to look for shelter in the shade. It was quiet on the plains at the foot of the Lebombo mountains.

Burt asked about the history of South Africa. I spoke about the Boer War. Yes, he knew about Breaker Morant; he'd seen the movie. In Australia Morant was a hero.

Morant's unit, the Bushveld Carbineers, operated not too far from here, I said. He was imprisoned at Pietersburg. To the Boers he was just another war criminal.

Slowly I turned the bakkie west. We took a detour back to

Orpen. I enjoyed the feeling of a girl's body against mine in the bakkie. The number of animals we saw increased as the day progressed, but we had still not seen elephants. Jo sat dreamily in the middle, beer and cigarette in hand. It was good to know she was enjoying the outing.

Burt began to hum "Waltzing Matilda". I urged him to sing. Then I sang my favourite ballad: "The Band Played Waltzing Matilda". He was surprised that I knew it and joined in. Now we were all singing. Jo sang popular Beatles songs. Next came Creedence and The Eagles. Burt began to recite poetry. He captivated us with Banjo Paterson's "Clancy of the Overflow" and "The Man from Snowy River". We were having a good time in the bakkie.

There was still no sign of elephants. I had a plan, but for that we would have to leave the tourist route. I turned into a firebreak. We drove past a large No Entry sign.

"That sign doesn't apply to us. I'm the game ranger around here," I said smugly.

Next to me Jo was squirming with excitement. Their visit to the Park had surpassed all expectations.

We drove far into the veld. At Red Gorten waterhole we found elephants, just as I had expected. There was a throng of bulls and breeding herds. We stayed there for a long time. Jo took a lot of photos. The calves frolicked in the water.

After half an hour I said: "There you are, now we can go back."

It was late afternoon when we drove into Orpen. Jo and Burt were thrilled. Hein was waiting for us on the stoep, his hands on his hips. He shook his head and smiled, winking at me.

We stopped in front of the house. "Listen, guys, it's too late to drive to Hoedspruit now. You'll have to stay over. Move into the spare room. Pack up your tent," I said.

Jo and Burt looked visibly relieved.

Hein locked up and came over. He brought a packet of meat and a crate of beer. We made a fire. We laughed and chatted. Recited poetry and sang.

100

Hein went home; he had to open up early the next morning. Burt went to bed. Jo took a shower. I went to the sitting room to listen to music. Jo joined me after a while. She looked fresh and beautiful. She smelled good. She sat down on the sofa beside me. We listened to music. I played her my favourite songs. She paged through my books. We talked till late. At half past one I excused myself and went to bed. I don't know whether she had wanted me to stay.

The next morning I drove them to Hoedspruit. I left them on the far side of town on the road to Phalaborwa. We said goodbye fondly. They thanked me again and again.

I turned and drove back. In my rear-view mirror they grew smaller. Inside me there was a yearning. Part of me wanted to join them on their travels. They were heading blithely into the unknown, in search of fresh adventure. What an experience it had to be. Yes, the Park wasn't everything, after all. Perhaps some day.

In the months that followed I received an occasional postcard from Jo. The first one came from Zimbabwe. Later there was one from Uganda. They'd seen gorillas. There was a card from Ethiopia. The last one came from the Red Sea. Then, after a long silence, a thick letter from England. She described their trip in detail. Their adventures. The windfalls and setbacks. The wonder of it all. Every moment of it worthwhile. Now she was working in the office of an insurance broker in Surrey. She missed the sunshine and the freedom enormously.

I wrote back, but I never heard from her again.

February 26, 1994

The romance of the wilderness trails was beginning to wane. I still enjoyed walking in the bush, but I was getting tired of answering the same old questions and regaling tourists with the same old stories. Of playing host to overworked city dwellers in search of amusement and excitement. I was no longer interested in other people's stories and wisecracks around the camp fire. In the evenings I retired to my tent early, and by day I walked farther and spoke less. Was it time for something different? Settling down, getting married? The thought scared me.

Orpen, my present home, was considerably quieter than Skukuza. But even here friends and drinking buddies came looking for me. Like that Saturday morning in late summer when Brent, John and John's wife, Ingrid, showed up.

I had just completed two walking tours in a row at the Sweni River and directly afterwards stood in for a colleague in the Napi wilderness area. I'd had to deal with the whims of demanding tourists. Afterwards I'd had to rush across two-thirds of the Kruger Park to attend a boring meeting at Letaba. I felt in need of a quiet, peaceful weekend alone at home.

The minute they walked through the front door, Brent tore the wrapping from a sixpack and started handing out beers. I opened one, went over to the hi-fi and soon "Tommy Gun" by The Clash was thundering through the Orpen rest camp. Quiet weekend, my arse.

"Come along. We're going on a game drive and afterwards we'll have a late breakfast at my camp in Timbavati."

"Brent, my entire life is one long game drive. One gets fed up with watching game, you know."

102

"We'll make it a short one. We'll spend the rest of the day at my camp. There's enough cold beer."

I allowed myself to be convinced. As I walked out, I grabbed my revolver from the table. On the hi-fi The Clash was hammering out "I fought the law".

I got into the cab with John, a forester from Swaziland, and Brent and Ingrid climbed on the back of the bakkie. We left Orpen in a cloud of dust, heading into the Timbavati.

I called out to Ingrid at the back: "You and Brent look out for game. John and I will be too busy talking kak!"

John laughed and we clinked our beer cans.

A leguaan scurried across the road. John slammed on the brakes, I jumped out and gave chase. I grabbed the leguaan just before it reached the safety of a log. My hand closed around its thick neck. Laughing, I walked back to where the others were waiting beside the bakkie. I held the creature at arm's length. Ingrid stepped up to touch it.

"Wait," I warned, "it hasn't crapped yet."

Scarcely had Ingrid withdrawn her hand when a jet of brown and white shit spurted from the leguaan, barely missing her. The men found it hilarious.

"Now you can touch him, Ingrid."

After a thorough examination the poor leguaan was released and scrambled into the bushes. John spun the wheels and we pulled away in a cloud of dust.

There are two earth dams in that part of the Timbavati. Drinking places for game. Each dam has a resident crocodile. When the water gets low in one, the crocodile sets off overland to move in with his friend in the next dam.

The bakkie stopped at the edge of the fuller dam. On the opposite bank lay a crocodile of more than three metres. I jumped out and jogged to the water's edge.

"I'm just going to cool down," I called out to Brent.

"Chris! Don't!" Brent shouted. "Both the crocs are here."

"No, man, I see only one."

"Chris!" I heard Brent shout as I dived.

It was a tradition that had started in the Caprivi. On a hot day on patrol along the Kwando River I would dive in quickly and wade back out immediately. I had often done it in croc-infested waters. Once or twice even in the Zambezi. And I had always wondered whether the day would ever come.

I turned round and began to wade back. My eyes fell on my three friends' petrified faces. The next moment a pair of yellow eyes broke through the surface. With enormous force the crocodile locked its jaws around my right shoulder. Immediately it swung its heavy tail and folded me in half. My head disappeared underwater. The crocodile shook me like a dog.

Brent had been right.

The first thing I realised was that my feet were still touching the muddy bottom. The crocodile was struggling to knock me off my feet and very nearly succeeded. I had to remain on my feet, I decided. I also had to breathe. The crocodile was drowning me.

I struggled upward against the strength of the creature and felt the muscles of my shoulder being stripped from the bone. There was no pain whatsoever. My head broke through the surface and I took a gulp of fresh air. Around me the brown waters were churning, as the crocodile thrashed with its tail. For a moment I looked into its eyes. Then I looked at my friends on the bank. They were running around, searching for sticks and stones to beat off the crocodile. I had to speak to them.

I turned my head to look at the opposite side. The second crocodile had slipped into the water and was heading straight for its friend and me. I knew it wasn't on its way to lend me a hand. The crocodile that was latched on to my shoulder was getting the better of me and for the second time my head disappeared underwater.

I lifted my feet out of the mud and took my first step in the direction of the bank. The crocodile renewed its efforts to drag me off my feet. I took another step towards the shallows. I had to make contact with my friends. Again I stretched my neck above the surface and felt flesh and sinew being ripped from my shoulder blade.

My eyes found those of John. "My revolver is in the bakkie. See what you can do."

He nodded and made a dash for the bakkie. I looked round. The other crocodile was very close now and I knew I wasn't going to beat it too. I took another step closer to dry land and the crocodile bent me double again.

Slowly, too slowly, I dragged the crocodile into shallower water. Its iron grip on my shoulder did not relax. It shook me from side to side, but I remained on my feet. It was easier now to keep my head above water. John was standing knee-deep in the water. Around me heavy bullets hit the water. Suddenly I knew I was going to survive.

Then the second crocodile was there. I was waist-deep in the water. Bullets were flying around me.

The first crocodile realised it wasn't going to drag me off my feet. It let go of my shoulder and swam away. With my mutilated arm I reached out and grabbed John's wrist.

"Look out!" Brent shouted from behind John.

I turned and threw my left arm up in defence.

The second crocodile lifted itself out of the water from three metres away. Its powerful tail propelled it forward. Its jaws closed around my forearm. It sounded like another gunshot as the crocodile, with a twist of its body, bit clean through my forearm, splintering my upper arm. For a moment I stared at its heavy body as it fell back into the water, my hand protruding from the side of its jaw.

I fell backwards into the water and stumbled out on dry land.

"It's tickets," I said. Blood spurted everywhere.

"We'll get you to a doctor," Brent said.

He pulled off his T-shirt, tore it in half and began to bandage my shoulder. John put me on the back of the bakkie and used his shirt to stop the bleeding. Ingrid climbed on too. Brent jumped in behind the wheel and raced through the veld like a maniac, back to Orpen. John held my head in his lap.

105

At Orpen Ingrid stormed past me into the house and grabbed blankets from my bed. She handed them to John, who tore them in strips and applied more bandages. I heard the camp manager's wife say: "Oh, merciful Lord. I'll radio for the ambulance."

I saw John throwing up over the edge of the bakkie. I felt the sun beating down on me. The wide legs of my PT shorts were pulled up almost to my waist. I drew John's attention. "John, please pull down the legs of my shorts. My balls are being roasted."

I heard John laugh.

"Chris, you're going to make it."

Turning point

It was a year and a half after I had met Jo Milward from England in the Kruger Park. I lay on a white beach somewhere on the shores of Lake Malawi. I was tanned and lean. My hair was long and bleached by the sun. I was over the worst diarrhoea and felt stronger every day. For four months I'd been hitching through Africa. I looked at the scars on my body and took another sip of beer. I searched for a postcard and a pen in my backpack.

I looked out across the lake. A group of boys were driving a herd of speckled cattle along the shore to the water. Opposite me a few men were sitting beside their dugout canoes, preparing their nets for the evening's fishing. Next to me three girls were sunning themselves. We had met a few days before.

I began to write:

Jo
Like you, I'm travelling through Africa on foot. Crocodiles have bitten off my arm and I lost my job in the Kruger Park. I don't know where I'm headed.
Love,
Chris

A month later I reached Mwanza on the banks of Lake Victoria in Tanzania. I bought a ticket on a minibus that would take me through the Serengeti and back to Arusha. There I'd contact my brother and arrange for more funds. Plan the rest of my trip.

Four days later I arrived at Arusha. I booked in at the

YMCA and left my backpack there. I walked out into the street and bought a few postcards at a stall. It was overcast. I went into a coffee shop, ordered coffee and samoosas and sat down to write to relatives and friends.

As I looked up, Allistair McKinnon, whom I'd met on the road a while ago, walked through the door. It was a warm reunion. Allistair had joined up with a group of Australians and they had been on a trip to the island of Zanzibar. They had just arrived in Arusha and were looking for lodgings.

I accompanied them to the hostel where I was staying. That evening Allistair, the Australians and I did the rounds of the bars in Arusha.

The next day I started walking back to the snake park which I used as a temporary base while travelling through Tanzania. There I'd befriended Wade Bale, the manager of the Meserani Snake Park. His parents ran the bar and the camp site. Allistair and his friends stayed behind to organise a safari. He promised to call on me at the snake park.

I took the road across the Masai plains. An open green Land Rover approached from the direction of the snake park. It was Lynn Bale. Seated next to her was Wade's girlfriend, Melinda. They saw me and stopped. I jogged over to the vehicle.

Lynne and Melinda were excited.

"Chris. We have an urgent message for you. You have to stop by the Arusha police station immediately."

"Why? Am I in trouble?"

"No, man. Your parents phoned. There's a man in Namibia who wants to offer you a job. Get in. Sergeant Joseph at the police station has all the details."

The battle for the mealie fields

The Aap River meanders across the Beesvlakte. The name Beesvlakte could not have been more descriptive. It is a wide plain where large herds of Herero cattle trample the earth to dust. In the late afternoon, clouds of dust hang in the air as the cattle return to the boreholes at the settlements of Omuramba, Kowares and De Wet.

The Aap River flows from the mountains in the north. It is a small, dry stream bed with numerous tributaries joining up with it from the ridges. Its banks carve their way through rugged calcareous crust and hardpan. On the small flood plain the banks are overgrown with thorny scrub that is almost impenetrable. The bush is interspersed with flatcrown umbrella thorn and stately camel thorn.

At Omuramba the Aap River continues where the Beesvlakte ends at the mountain range in the east. Umbrella thorns cover the lower slopes of the rocky hills. It is here, under these flatcrown umbrella thorns, that the Omuramba borehole can be found. The windmill has not worked for years. It stands forlorn beside the concrete reservoir, and buffalo weavers have built their nests in it. A Lister engine pumps the water from the borehole.

The soil is good here. When the rains come at the end of February, heralding a brief wet season, the people of Omuramba cultivate small patches of mealies and watermelon. Traditionally these people are not crop farmers. They are proud cattle farmers who eke out a living in a harsh land. In bygone days, when droughts or wars had destroyed their herds, they survived by hunting.

In the late nineteenth century another group of people

trekked through this forsaken region. Before moving on again, they taught the local inhabitants to plant mealies.

It is also at this borehole that the elephants visit the drinking trough at night. Here they don't have to venture out on the open Beesvlakte. They come from the ridges unseen and force their way through the umbrella thorn barricade. They remain in the shade all day, browsing undisturbed along the river bank on juicy shoots and camel thorn pods. At dusk they gather on the outskirts of Omuramba.

There they wait. Listening to the clacking noise of the Lister engine, the lowing of cattle, the calls and whistles of the herdsmen, the barking dogs.

At close of day the engine will die. The herdsmen will return to their dwellings on the open plain and take their dogs with them. The elephants will wait a little longer. Night will descend and take over. When only a sporadic lowing can still be heard at the waterholes and the scops owls are calling from the trees, the elephants will leave the cover of the bushes and gather around the borehole.

It was late February 1996 when I first arrived at the Beesvlakte. I had just begun my training programme with the community game guards and had been given the task of tracking down the community rangers scattered across the length and breadth of the Kaoko. I depended heavily on a Shell road map and a young Himba assistant.

I approached the Beesvlakte from the south, having driven through the Kowareb Schlucht and turned north at Ombaadjie, at the junction of the Aap River and the Ombonde.

The powdery, dusty plain with its deeply rutted tracks and stunted mopanes did not impress me. There are more scenic places in Kaokoland.

In the north, towards Opuwo, black clouds were gathering. Lightning flickered across the sky.

"We won't be sleeping dry tonight," Kuva, my assistant, declared morosely. He had just joined me and we were still strangers to each other.

At Kowares the first large raindrops struck the bakkie's

windscreen. The rain came down for about ten minutes and then the heavy shower diminished to a drizzle. The powdery dust had changed into sludge and the tail end of the bakkie began to skid dangerously around the bends. Being new to the area, I slowed down. I would overturn the bakkie at least once before I got the hang of those treacherous surfaces.

Towards late afternoon the mud-spattered bakkie stopped at the village of Omuramba. I got out. It was still raining. I noticed that the groundsheet was flapping in the wind; part of my bedroll was soaked. I cursed softly. Damp camping wasn't my idea of fun.

Presumptuously, I waited for someone to emerge from a hut to welcome me and inquire what I wanted. Nothing happened. From the doorways of the square lattice and dung dwellings black faces stared at me expressionlessly. Small, smoky fires were smouldering outside.

The rain was beginning to soak through my shirt and I climbed back into the bakkie indignantly. I had a lot to learn. This was Kaokoland. Every white newcomer was regarded with suspicion. There would be no hero's welcome. The newcomer would be put to the test first. After all, white people never stayed long.

With a slight smile, Kuva said: "Let's set up camp before it gets too dark." He had also seen that my bedroll was wet.

Over the northern hills the clouds were still low and heavy. Under a stand of mopanes we found slightly higher ground and spread our groundsheet. With diesel from our jerry can, I managed to get a fire going. I parked the bakkie close to the fire and draped my wet blankets over the railings.

Through the mopanes something on the plain caught my eye. It was almost dark and I had no idea what I was looking at. Kuva came to stand next to me and the two of us watched in amazement.

Across the plain a line extending as far as the eye could see was creeping closer. Ghostly white, almost like a silver veld fire. Then we heard the rushing. A mass of water engulfed the bases of trees. It filled the ruts in the road and darted like a tongue ahead of the creeping wave. It swelled and moved and roared. Before our eyes a blanket was being drawn over the Beesvlakte. A blanket of water.

The flood reached our camp. We just had time to toss the groundsheet on the back of the bakkie. The water washed over our feet and ankles, but did not rise any higher. It passed underneath the bakkie. It wasn't a strong flood.

I had never experienced anything like it. In the Lowveld I had seen the dry stream beds fill with fiercely rushing water. In the Caprivi I had seen the water on the flood plains rise gradually, until only the tips of the grasses were visible. This creeping sheet of water across the denuded plains was different. Kaokoland was different.

About an hour after dark the water had subsided. Only puddles and muddy silt remained. We didn't try to light the fire again. Kuva curled up on the bakkie seat and I spread my bedroll, now even wetter than before, on top of the trunks and the groundsheet on the back of the bakkie. A restless, uncomfortable night followed.

The first mug of warm, sweet tea brewed on the diesel fire the next morning thawed the body. From the direction of Omuramba two men were approaching. They were clad in khaki overalls, canvas boots and bush hats.

They introduced themselves as Filemon Hungwa and Kambanga and crouched beside the fire. They knew I was looking for them. They were glad I had come. They'd been waiting for a long time. They were the game rangers.

Filemon Hungwa and Kambanga accompanied us back to Omuramba. There they introduced me to Councillor Tjavira, a taciturn old man dressed in dark blue trousers and jacket and a broad-rimmed felt hat and carrying a carved mopane kierie. A Herero version of a boere oom.

Towards afternoon the clouds dispersed and the sun came out. In the days that followed Filemon Hungwa and Kambanga showed me the Omuramba area. We found substantial herds of springbok and ostrich sharing the plains with the cattle. I was still suffering from the Kruger Park syndrome and found it difficult to reconcile cattle with game. The denuded plains confirmed my view that cattle upset the balance of the African ecology.

The rangers took me to the ridges and gorges on either side of the Beesvlakte. I found it exciting. Tall leadwoods and mopanes grew along the stream beds. We found kudu and baboon. They showed me the hidden fountains and we even came across a herd of mountain zebra.

Filemon Hungwa impressed me. He was enthusiastic and eager to tell me about the wildlife in the area.

"There are many elephants here. Now that it is raining, they walk around, but this is their place. They live here."

In the next three years Filemon Hungwa would prove himself one of the best game rangers I had ever met.

A month and a half later I returned to Omuramba on the Beesvlakte. In the meantime my quest had taken me to the Epupa Falls on the Kunene, the Marienfluss and Hartmann's Valley. In search of Himba rangers.

I came from the north, from the direction of Opuwo, past Ombombo. The Beesvlakte had undergone a transformation. Seasonal grasses grew knee-high as far as the eye could see. The cattle were in prime condition and everywhere herds of springbok leaped across the veld. It lifted my spirits, and I looked forward to seeing Filemon Hungwa and Kambanga again.

At Omuramba Councillor Tjavira looked grave. He introduced me to Headman Japua, who had come from Okaruviza. There were serious matters to discuss. An important meeting was planned for the next morning under the camel thorn tree. They had just been waiting for me to come.

I was surprised. What could be so serious? And what did it have to do with me?

It was a fresh morning under the camel thorn tree near the Omuramba borehole.

Since early morning people had been arriving. Councillor Tjavira looked dapper in his blue suit and tie, his hat and his kierie. Headman Japua sat on a folding chair, dressed in a black suit. Around them sat councillors and elders, all in their Sunday best. The two game rangers were in uniform. The younger men wore jeans and T-shirts. Some distance away a group of Herero women were sitting on the ground, decked out in their colourful Victorian dresses and horn-shaped headpieces.

"If the women are present, it's important business," remarked Kuva, who had in the meantime become an invaluable source of enlightenment.

The meeting was opened with a prayer. Councillor Tjavira got up. His face was grim when he began to speak. He gave me an accusing look. His young secretary acted as interpreter.

"Our people have been living here for years. We were here first. Others came later. Some came, stayed for a while and moved away. This is a hard land. But we survive here.

"Now a newcomer has come here to teach us to look after our game. Since we first came here – our forefathers – we have been looking after our game. You can see this just by walking across the Omuramba Beesvlakte. The wild animals graze among our cattle. We know about game conservation.

"Today I want to know from this newcomer in our midst: Are you here just for the game? Are you here for the game, or are you here to learn how people and wild animals can live together? Wild animals which sometimes threaten these people's food supplies?

"What are you going to do to earn your keep here? We don't need you. We have been managing well without outsiders. What are you going to do that will make a difference to our lives?"

He fixed his gaze on me intently. Seated on a canvas chair beside him, Headman Japua regarded me earnestly. Eyebrows raised, like a headmaster waiting for an explanation from a naughty child. I began to feel uncomfortable. Some of the young men looked at me and sneered. Others pulled down the corners of their mouths scornfully.

Councillor Tjavira remained quiet for a moment. I felt small and vulnerable. Unwelcome. I was still unfamiliar with the Hereros.

Councillor Tjavira continued. This time he tried a different angle. "There are women here in Omuramba whose husbands have died. They are poor, because they don't own any cattle. We have to look after them. But how can we? How can we if our resources are being destroyed? What are you going to do to prevent our women and children from starving?"

Councillor Tjavira's arm swept in the direction of the acacia thickets beyond the forlorn windmill, and for the first time I noticed the mealie fields in the clearing.

Filemon Hungwa touched my shoulder and I woke immediately. He, Kuva and Kambanga were already out of their bedrolls. "They're here," said Filemon Hungwa.

I sat up in my bedroll. The whites of Kambanga's eyes were clearly visible in the moonlight. It was after midnight and the surrounding veld was dead quiet. We sat together, listening. Seconds dragged by. Silence reigned. I pricked up my ears and opened my mouth. The Himbas were crouching on their haunches.

Then we heard it: the rustle of a mealie stalk. Followed by the sound of young mealie leaves brushing lightly against a large, slow body. Then all was quiet again. We sat motionlessly, waiting for the next sound. It took a long time, but it cracked sharply through the night air as a mealie stalk was snapped off. Again the rustle of leaves. Followed by the crunch of a mealie plant being mashed into pulp by gigantic molars. The familiar sweet scent filled my nostrils. I felt my heart beat faster.

The men stepped back when I got out of my bedroll. I took my .303 and looked out across across the mealies, surrounded by a stockade of thorny branches. I must have been sleeping soundly. The others had woken up when the animal had ploughed through the fence. In the moonlight I made out the back of a single elephant in the middle of the mealie field. A bull for certain.

As quietly as possible I cocked the rifle and raised it to my shoulder. I swung the barrel in the direction of the bull. I set my sights over his head. I waited a moment longer and then pulled the trigger. The barrel spewed fire and the explosion ripped through the quiet night.

A brief trumpet. The sound of mealie stalks and thorn branches being smashed. Then silence.

I turned round. Beside me was Filemon Hungwa. Kuva and Kambanga were hiding behind the bakkie.

"Come, guys," I said. None of them knew how to drive. I gave the rifle to Kuva. He got in on the passenger's side. I handed the shooting lamp to Filemon Hungwa and Kambanga, who had climbed on the back. I moved in behind the wheel and pulled away.

We drove around the mealie field and found the place where the fleeing elephant had burst through the surrounding fence. We wound through the mealie fields and thorny thickets and inspected the thorn stockades in the glow of the lamp light, but we found no further signs of elephant activity. We drove back to our camp under the umbrella thorns.

I instructed Kuva to get the fire going and boil water while I crawled back into my bedroll. Our battle for the mealie fields had just begun.

For the next ten days we camped beside a different mealie field every night. Fortunately the fields were small and close together. Every two or three hours we went on patrol in search of elephants. Usually the drone of the bakkie or the beam of the shooting lamp was enough to make them melt into the dark thickets, but now and again I was forced to fire a shot over their heads.

We identified four elephants. One large old bull with stubby, broken tusks. His stumps protruded from their sockets in short, splintered fragments. His ears were tattered and you could see he was a crabby old fighter.

The other three were his askaris and apprentices. They were all in their mid-twenties and early thirties. It was he, the old man, who was teaching these elephants to raid the mealie fields.

The elephants got wise and started to come later every night. After the first week they would only come at two or three in the morning. Kuva, the game rangers and I were getting more exhausted by the day. It was hard to stay awake at night.

One night the elephants stripped the field furthest from

where we had been lying. We had slept soundly and hadn't noticed a thing. They destroyed about half the crop.

A subtle change was taking place in the attitude of the community. During the day Filemon Hungwa and Kambanga would speak with great bravado of their elephant adventures the previous night. The people would listen wide-eyed and laugh heartily at Kambanga's bragging. Everyone knew that he was actually very afraid of elephants. Even Councillor Tjavira would show a trace of a smile.

One afternoon, while we were taking a nap under the thorn trees, a group of young men approached. Among them I recognised a number of those who had regarded me with such apparent scorn at the meeting. Now their attitude was completely different. In faultless Afrikaans they inquired what they could do to help save the mealie fields.

"Guys, I have to go back to Sesfontein for a day or two. My food supplies are finished. I want to get a good night's sleep. Take all the empty cans and bottles and rope and wire that lie scattered around your houses. Tie them onto the fences. Perhaps the noise will scare the elephants away. It will definitely help to wake us when the elephants come into the fields."

Back at Sesfontein I spent the night at the police station. Sergeant Gert van der Linde, the station commander, made a legendary curried venison potjie. From the first day I had liked this genial giant. He was the only other white Afrikaner in this vast region. He was completely at home among the Damaras, Hereros and Himbas of Sesfontein. He had been there for nearly twenty years and had been accepted as one of the community.

He maintained law and order with a light touch. He dealt with cases that appeared before him with judgments like: "Petrus Narieb, if you start stabbing people again after you've been drinking, I'll eat your balls for breakfast. Do you understand?"

"Yes, Sergeant. Sorry, Sergeant."

Besides admiring Gert van der Linde for his kindness and hospitality, I saw in him the last link to my home: the Afrikaner friends and family that I had left behind in my exile.

After a hearty meal, a few cold beers, a Boere conversation and some solid sleep, I felt ready for Omuramba again the next morning.

I stopped the bakkie in front of Efraim's cuca shop. When I entered, the bush telegraph had preceded me. Efraim welcomed me warmly. "I hear you're busy with the elephants on the Beesvlak."

His daughters had baked fresh doughnuts and filled them with red jam. He lifted the lid off the enamel bowl on the counter. A fragrant cloud of steam escaped and made my mouth water. I wolfed down a few on the spot. I bought mealie-meal, tinned meat, canned fruit, tea, sugar and powdered milk. Outside, Kuva loaded the supplies on the bakkie and we drove off in the direction of Kowareb.

We arrived at Omuramba in the afternoon, after a long, dusty trip. The fences around the mealie fields were covered in tins and bottles. That night we waited in vain.

At dawn the elephants arrived. We were ready for them. We tried to drive them from the thickets, so that we could chase them across the open plains. In vain. They disappeared into the bush and stayed there. No vehicle could follow.

I took the .303 and crept closer, staying downwind. From behind a fallen tree, I took aim and fired three shots over the elephants' heads. There was a distinct sluggishness in the way they made off, deeper into the bush. I realised they knew I was bluffing.

For the rest of the day Filemon Hungwa and I explored the ridges east of the Beesvlakte. Towards dusk we emerged on a cliff above the plain. Directly below us meandered the dry bed of the Aap River. The vast plain with its waving grasslands lay before us. Herds of cattle were making their way to the borehole. To the north we could just make out the windmill among the trees. Here and there we saw herds of springbok and ostrich.

Below us a breeding herd of elephant emerged from the wooded banks of the Aap River one by one. Finally there were thirty-seven elephants on the open plain. There were adult cows and young bulls. There were calves of every age.

Unconcerned, they set off across the plain. Not towards the water point, but heading for a mysterious destination somewhere in the nebulous ridges on the far side of the Beesvlakte. They ambled past the cattle and the springbok.

I gazed after them until they grew small in the twilight. Somewhere in the ridges I heard a baboon bark and I knew I was in Africa.

The next afternoon a white police bakkie arrived at our camp.

"Not much is happening at Sesfontein. We've come to help," said Sergeant Gert van der Linde as he and Constable Kenahama got out.

Gert had brought mutton ribs and beer. Soon Kuva had a big fire going and the night became a celebration.

With the arrival of Gert van der Linde, the battle for the mealie fields got a new lease on life. Early the next morning we came across the elephant bulls as they emerged from the bushes. Gert and I were ready for them. We cut them off from cover in our bakkies and herded them towards the plain.

Now they were feeling vulnerable. They raced across the plain, arses tucked in and ears flapping. Like cowboys, Gert and I drove them along in our four-wheel driven horses. It was a sunny morning and I felt my spirits soar. Adrenalin coursed through my veins. I whooped and looked at Gert in his bakkie some distance from me. He laughed and raised his thumb in the air. We were brothers.

We stayed on the elephants' tails. They made no attempt to stand and face us. Whenever we suspected they might break formation and choose another route, either Gert or I swerved and cut them off, herding them together again. At last they were so bewildered that they simply kept running.

For six or seven kilometres Gert and I chased them across the unbroken plain. Then the terrain became rocky. We were forced to slow down. The elephants drew ahead. They reached a donga at the foot of the ridges and Gert and I called off the chase.

The four elephants disappeared into the ridges. The next

two nights they did not return. Fortunately Gert had brought enough beer.

Gert, Filemon Hungwa and I were talking to Councillor Tjavira. By now I was used to his brusque manner. I suspected that he was beginning to accept me, though he still wanted to make it clear that the Beesvlakte was his domain.

"When the first Boers arrived here, my grandfather was a young man. He told me a lot about them. They came here with their wagons and oxen and horses. They were tired and asked if they could rest. They stayed for a long time and built houses at Otjitundua and Kaoko Otavi. Some outspanned their wagons beside the fountains. The Boers' cattle grazed among our own cattle.

"The Boers could shoot well and did a lot of hunting. After a while we grew afraid that they were going to destroy all the game. Later the Boers packed their wagons and trekked across the Kunene. To Angola.

"It was the Boers who showed us how to plant mealies. Before they came, we didn't plant anything. We were cattle farmers. When they left, we kept on planting. We plant only when it rains."

Councillor Tjavira was quiet for a while. His gaze was fixed on the ground as if a thought had suddenly occurred to him. He mulled over it for a while. Then he looked up at Gert and me. "The Boers taught us to plant mealies. Now it's the Boers that are looking after our mealies."

It was the closest he ever came to acknowledging our efforts.

The day before the elephants returned, three bakkies arrived, two from the north and one from the south. The two from the north came from Opuwo. It was Vossie Kaipurwa and a few other game rangers, armed with .303s and G-3s. They had come to lend a hand. The bakkie from the south belonged to the anti-poaching unit at Sesfontein. They had heard what was happening at Omuramba. They wanted to help too.

Now there were enough men and vehicles to protect the mealie fields properly. The mealies were swelling and ripening. They were very enticing to the elephants.

By this time I had summed up the situation. Usually the elephants avoided people. They browsed on the thorny shrubs. They came to drink when everyone was asleep. If they had a proper water point further down the Aap River, they wouldn't need to come to Omuramba.

A running battle ensued in the thickets between the four elephants and our augmented forces. Since Gert and I had chased them across the plains, they had never shown themselves in the open again. Now they tried to reach the mealie fields through the dense undergrowth. But wherever they tried, there was someone to cut them off.

Firing shots over them was no longer effective. It just made the old bull mad. He had begun to charge at people. Vossie Kaipurwa was very nearly trampled one morning. Just in time he managed to find cover behind a fallen tree. Then it was Toyvo John Toyvo, leader of the anti-poaching unit, who just managed to escape the old bull's rage.

"If his tusks had been longer, he would have got me, that's no lie!"

It became an exciting game of firing volleys and slipping away. Exciting, but dangerous. We all longed for harvest time to arrive.

In the heat of the day we reclined against our bedrolls under the trees and talked. As the days went by, I got to know the men well. Vossie Kaipurwa was a Herero from Ombombo. For many years he had served under the legendary Chris Eyre, veteran game ranger of the Kaoko.

Bakker Manuel, Vossie's colleague, claimed to be a direct descendant of the nineteenth-century hunter Henry Hartley. "Oubaas Hartley stayed over in my great-grandmother's kraal for a few days."

The scene reminded me of a modern-day Baines painting. The flatcrown thorn trees and the campfire. Instead of ox wagons, there were bakkies now.

There were Toyvo John Toyvo, a Themba of Omuhonga, and Alvo Kangara, a Himba, both of the anti-poaching unit. Both ex-PLAN soldiers. Officers trained in East Germany and Tanzania. They were neat, disciplined, efficient. There was Gert van der Linde, who had spent time with Koevoet. Filemon Hungwa, Kambanga and Kuva. Men who had grown up in the veld, herding cattle.

Here we were all sitting together. Eating porridge from the same pot and drinking tea from the same mug. I experienced no animosity from the PLAN men. Only respect for Gert and myself, who had been on the opposite side. No mistrust. There was work to be done. There was no time for things that belonged to the past. Why couldn't it have been like that from the start?

Toyvo and Alvo agreed. "It doesn't matter which side you were on," Toyvo explained. "We all served. We were all prepared to fight. We're all warriors. That's what's important. Not whose side you were on. War is a young man's work."

I had already made up my mind to approach my superiors with a proposal. A pipeline should be laid from the borehole, five kilometres away. Leading deep into the bushes to supply the elephants with a proper water point. Then they wouldn't have to come to Omuramba.

Councillor Tjavira came walking through the mealies with his hat and kierie. "The mealies are ripe now. We start harvesting tomorrow."

The next day camp was struck and the bakkies loaded. Toyvo came and stood beside me. "There's one thing I don't understand. Why did you volunteer to protect the mealie fields? It's not your job."

"I'm just looking after my own interests. We're the ones who taught you to plant mealies, after all."

In June 1998 Namibia, Botswana and Zimbabwe succeeded in getting the total embargo on the export of ivory lifted. Limited trade in unpoached ivory was once more permitted with Japan. Suddenly money became available.

With these funds a pipeline was laid. A waterhole was constructed in the bushes beside the Aap River, south of Omuramba. The elephants drink there now.

The hunt

Every two years a big hunt takes place in Damaraland and Kaokoland. Nature Conservation determines quotas and issues permits to the various headmen. Then Damara, Himba and Herero dust off their ancient rifles and go forth into the wilderness in search of the large herds. I was asked to lend a hand where necessary.

West of the Grootberg, among the flat-topped basalt hills in a rock-strewn mopane landscape, live the Riemvasmakers. It was late afternoon when I arrived at Palmpos from Sesfontein in my bakkie. The hunting team was already there. Markus Roman would drive my bakkie. Abram Mapanga, Oom Jantjie Rein and Oom Joël Hoëb were to do the shooting. Oom Joël's .303 dated from 1909, Abram's from 1916. Jantjie Rein's .308 was the only one with a telescope. I took my rifle from behind the seat. A .303 Lee Enfield model P14, with a peep sight. I broke new cartridges from their packaging and divided them among the hunters. A few of the younger men jumped on the back of the bakkie. They were going to help load the buck. The cooking and slaughtering teams stayed behind at Palmpos. There was an atmosphere of anticipation as the bakkie drove away.

We bounced over a rocky double-track road. Around us lay the winter veld: yellow, red and brown. A few springbok were watching us from a distance. We left them for the time being to try for something bigger.

An opportunity soon presented itself. A large herd of gemsbok stood some distance away on the opposite bank of a spruit. Jantjie Rein and I left the bakkie and discussed our strategy in muted voices before crouching and moving closer.

We crept from milk bush to mopane. For the moment the gemsbok were out of sight. The breeze was blowing in our favour. We approached the banks of the spruit, where the mopanes grew denser and taller. Through the leaves and branches we could make out grey patches where the wary gemsbok stood. We reached the river's edge.

In the dry bed below us stood five gemsbok of which we had been unaware. They stared at us, petrified. Jantjie and I shot simultaneously, too hasty in our excitement. Our bullets flew high over their heads and struck the bank.

Two of the gemsbok took it as a sign that they should flee. They dashed up the opposite bank and joined the others that were now well on their way to the ridges. Uncertain and hesitant, the remaining three gemsbok stood frozen in the stream bed, staring at us.

In a flash I had reloaded. They could be off at any moment. This time I had to make sure. The bead in the peep sight found the neck hollow of a large cow with long horns. I pressed down on the trigger. Her legs gave way and she collapsed. The other gemsbok leaped away and disappeared. That was easy, I thought and lowered my rifle. My enthusiasm dampened when I approached. The gemsbok had just drawn her last breath. I noticed her swollen udder. Milk was dripping from the teats. Somewhere in the bush a small calf would be waiting in vain for the return of its mother tonight.

It was no problem for the Riemvasmakers. Meat was meat, food was food and the hunt had begun. Life in Damaraland was hard. The bakkie arrived and the gemsbok was loaded. Back at the hunting camp at Palmpos, the slaughtering took place in the twilight. Vitallus Florrie set off in his Series 3 Land Rover to take the first of the harvest to the families on their farms.

That night the cooking team roasted the dripping udder on the coals. I didn't join in the feast.

The next morning we were in the veld early. We opened fire at a small herd of springbok. They all trotted away unharmed. All except one with a lame foreleg where it had been struck by a bullet. We sat waiting for him to become stiff and sore before we ventured closer.

When we approached, he made for the ridges on three legs, and we followed at the double. I was foolishly wearing sandals, as I had the day before. Now they were slowing me down over the rocky terrain. I tripped and caught my foot on a stone. To keep my balance I brought my foot forward quickly. It made contact with a larger rock and my big toe burst like a ripe plum. Hot, sticky blood poured over my toes and glued the sole of my foot to my sandal. I slowed down.

Jantjie and Abram passed me and the springbok disappeared over a saddle in the ridges. On the rocky plain far below us Markus was making slow progress in the bakkie.

I reached the top and walked across the plateau. My toe was very painful now and my stride had been broken. I began to climb down the other side of the koppie. The slope was not as steep. In the valley below Jantjie and Abram were bending over the springbok. His remaining three legs had finally given way. Abram stood up and raised his arms above his head. The rock in his hands crushed the springbok's skull with a single blow.

It was afternoon when we returned. My toe was throbbing dully. On the back of the bakkie lay three springbok. I hadn't shot any of them. Back at camp, mugs of tea were served. The men rested for a while and drew on their pipes. I pulled my boots on over my bloody toes before we left on a late afternoon hunt.

On the third day we hunted in a new area and saw a herd of seven zebra on the mountainside. The hunters tumbled off the bakkie hastily and hurried along, rifles at the ready. I followed. We ran to the foot of the hill and took up our positions. The zebra were mere specks on the slope above us. It sounded as if a battle had erupted around me as the men began to shoot. In the hail of bullets the zebras milled about confusedly. I disliked this hunting method, but I joined in the shooting nonetheless.

The zebras set off up the hill. One stayed behind, turned,

and ran in the opposite direction. I could see he was injured. Another one, that was trying to keep up with the herd, had a dangling foreleg. Abram took the initiative. He looked at me. "You follow the one that's on his own. We'll follow the herd."

The zebra that had broken away was disappearing around the hillside. I broke into a run, but lost sight of him. I followed his spoor along a game path and noticed large drops of blood on the stones. The zebra was keeping to the foot of the hill. It was a landscape of rolling hills and when I jogged over a rise, I saw the zebra disappearing over the next hill. He was still trotting.

Two hills further along, I saw him again. He was walking now and I was catching up. His head was starting to hang. He looked back and saw me. He resumed his trot and disappeared from sight. I followed the spoor. By the time he had crossed the next hill, he had weakened considerably. He was walking with difficulty. Under cover of some milk bushes, I approached undetected. Then I walked out into the bright sunlight.

I took aim and cleared my throat. The zebra stopped and looked back. My bullet shattered a cervical vertebra. It was a young stallion and he had been wounded in the stomach earlier. I turned his white belly in the direction of the plain so that the men in the bakkie would see him clearly.

It was a new day. Fresh gemsbok spoor lay on the floor of the valley. Abram and I were tracking on foot. The broken countryside and mopane thickets limited our sight. The steep sides of the valley towered above us. Our eyes searched for the buck among the trees. Apart from the cow we had shot on the first afternoon, the gemsbok had been evading us. We were moving along stealthily when my boot crunched on some loose stones. A black rhino bull lumbered to his feet in a thicket fifty metres ahead of us. We froze in our tracks. The massive head swayed searchingly, the ears listening in all directions. His nostrils were testing the wind.

We stood petrified. We were upwind and he would not pick up our scent, but he would react to the smallest movement and charge without warning. Minutes passed while the rhino stared in our direction, horns held high. Not a muscle moved in my body. Likewise, Abram was motionless beside me. Minutes turned into an eternity. Sweat poured into my eyes and the soles of my feet were burning. Then the rhino decided that it had been a false alarm and lay down. He lowered his great head in the dappled shade of the mopanes.

Not for a moment did Abram and I consider relaxing. Step by step we moved in the direction of the steep slope. It looked impossibly far. We never took our eyes off the rhino.

Another eternity later Abram and I were sitting safely on a rocky ledge, looking down on the sleeping rhinoceros. Now we could relax and admire him. How vulnerable he was. If we had been rhino poachers, he would not have stood a chance. I delighted in the thought, however, that I had the freedom of this rugged wilderness. The only place in Africa – in the world – where black rhino survive and breed outside a proclaimed conservation area. Truly the last of the old Africa. Without disturbing his rest any further, Abram and I sneaked away to join up with the bakkie at the mouth of the valley.

My eye picked up the spiralled horns in the shade of the trees on the opposite bank of the spruit. Crouching, I found shelter behind a bush. The kudu bull had nearly succeeded in making himself completely invisible. I crawled from one bush to the next until I reached the bank. The kudu stood motionless, its head concealed in leaves. I knew he was watching my every move. It was a matter of seconds before he would abandon the bushes and flee, but I was not yet in position and advanced a few more metres. I took aim, my elbow resting on my knee.

The bullet entered the kudu's shoulder and he leaped into the air before making off along the stream bed. Damned sharp-point ammunition, I cursed, and chased after him. I tried to reload, but the bullets had jammed in the magazine.

I crouched to try and set them straight. I slid a second cartridge into the barrel. There were specks of blood on the rocks.

In the shade of the trees that grew on the bank, the kudu appeared in front of us. My second shot found its mark behind the shoulder again, and the kudu collapsed.

That evening we sat around the fire at the Palmpos hunting camp. Justin Beukes and Lukas Prins of the cooking team were grilling roosterkoek on the hot coals. Kudu, springbok and zebra meat was simmering in pots on the fire. Each man had a steaming mug of tea in his hand. Quietly we discussed the successes and failures of the hunting expedition so far. Hunting trips of earlier years were called to mind. The warm glow of the fire became the glow of camaraderie, of brotherhood.

These are my people, I realised. The scene was timeless. It could have happened a hundred years, even two hundred years before. A white drifter and a group of dark-skinned pioneers, sitting around a hunting fire somewhere in the unspoilt northwest of Southern Africa. The next day I would be leaving to hunt elsewhere.

Dozens more gemsbok and springbok would fall before my rifle before the end of the hunting season. I would meet another rhinoceros on the way, and a few elephants too. The hunt with the people of Riemvasmaak had been my baptism of fire. After that it would become easier.

It had been my first hunt since losing my arm three years before.

Die-hard

The first herd of zebras had been captured the day before. Zebras are not subject to quarantine. They don't carry the same diseases as game with cloven hooves. After they have been captured they can therefore be transported to their new quarters immediately. The trucks had left for the Waterberg, however, with a consignment of impala and tsessebe of which the quarantine period had expired. They would only be back the following night.

The capture team didn't have time to waste. Koos Prinsloo, team leader, had decided to proceed with the capture and hold the zebras in the quarantine camps for the time being. The day's operation would therefore involve capturing zebras again.

Pilot Ben Kilpatrick had flown over the bush country of the Western Caprivi that morning and detected a herd beside a pan in the Manywa omuramba. In the Caprivi the soil is acidic. Apart from elephant and buffalo, no substantial herds of other game are found here. The Muhango Park had asked for twenty zebras. The herd we had captured the day before had numbered nine. The only truck available to the capture team was an ancient Mercedes. Not fast or reliable enough to transport game over large distances, but still suitable to move animals from the capture boma to the quarantine camps.

The boma was erected in the proximity of the pan. It is preferable to catch game in the late afternoon, when it is cooler. The boma, therefore, had to be constructed in the heat of the day. It was hard work. Kashupi, Daan Titos, Shorty and Sagous planted the posts. Hannes, Kaunda, Simon and Chris strung up the cables. Craig busied himself with pliers and galvanised wire. Samuel and the other Ovambos cleared the bush. Koos Prinsloo supervised with a hawk-eye. Everything had to be exactly right and woe betide the man who shirked his duties. Cables cut into the palms of hands and knuckles left their skin on posts. Splinters got stuck in fingers and sweat stung the eyes. But eventually the canvas sides were raised and the curtains strung up. Catching game is hard work, but the men were young, strong and cheerful.

The wide mouth of the funnel-shaped capture boma was carefully concealed among bushes and trees. The zebras should be unaware of the danger for as long as possible. The helicopter lifted off a second time. Next to Ben Kilpatrick sat the capture unit's veterinary surgeon, Doctor Alex Kemp.

At the boma the men concealed themselves near the mouth of the funnel. Soon they heard the helicopter approach. They couldn't see a thing through the trees, but they knew the zebras would be in full flight somewhere between the boma and the noise of the helicopter. They tried to be as unobtrusive as possible among the bushes. The helicopter could be heard southeast of the boma now and it seemed to be coming closer. At the mouth of the boma the anticipation increased.

Then the helicopter came into view low over the treetops. It manoeuvred from side to side, dived down on one side, rose up again, then flew to the other side, cutting off the herd there. From their hiding places the men heard the rumbling of hooves. The herd thundered past and into the mouth of the boma. Overhead the helicopter came in low. An alarm sounded. It was Ben's signal. Kashupi and Kaunda burst out of their ghwarrie bush, curtain in hand. The wire rings sang across the taut cable. The curtain was closed and the zebras were inside. Behind them a line of men moved in: Ovambos, Afrikaners, Englishmen and Hereros, each brandishing a sturdy bushwillow switch. The helicopter looked for a spot to land. Now the fun began.

The sides of the boma were made of woven plastic. Any wild animal could break through with ease, but because they couldn't see through the plastic, they thought it was a solid barrier. The funnel narrowed gradually and the final crush led

to a loading platform. At the end of the platform was the old
Mercedes truck with its high metal sides, and belting and hay
on the floor. That was where the zebras were supposed to go.

There were twelve. They ran deeper into the boma and
began to mill about in front of the crush. They kicked and
stamped and snorted. In the cloud of dust surrounding them,
they were silhouetted against the setting sun. Daan Titos drew
a second curtain behind the zebras and the men, dividing the
boma in two. Now they found themselves in a smaller com-
partment. Dust and the smell of dry leaves hung in the air.

The zebras stopped in front of the crush. A large stallion
brought up the rear and glared menacingly at the approaching line of men. A young mare barked nervously. The stallion
took the initiative. He cantered in line with the men, who were
brandishing their switches and whistling. He picked up speed
and made sure that his herd was following. Unexpectedly he
swung in the direction of the beaters and made for the gap
between Craig and Sagous. With widespread arms and waving
switches they tried to stop him, but the stallion was determined. Sidestepping a painful flick on the neck, he shouldered
Craig aside, and the herd burst through the line.

Now they were huddled against the curtain in the corner.
The stallion was angry and bewildered. He saw no escape.
The men regrouped and advanced towards the curtain. Koos
Prinsloo issued commands. Doctor Kemp joined the men in
the boma. Again the herd was driven towards the crush. The
stallion kept himself between the herd and their pursuers. The
men whistled and shouted, the herd milled about and the stallion began to canter. This time it was Hannes who had to step
lively to escape his hooves. The herd evaded the men again.
They galloped along the length of the curtain.

Now the men intended to trap them against the side of
the boma. Where the curtain ended against the boma's side,
the zebras swung left and trotted down the length of the
boma. The lower end of the line of men moved in behind the
herd in order to cut them off. The zebra were in single file
now, keeping close to the boma's side and heading for the

entrance of the crush. "Hang back, men. Hang back," Koos Prinsloo ordered. The animal in front, another fully-grown stallion, reached the crush and appeared to be hesitating.

"Now, men! Charge!" Koos Prinsloo ordered and an unearthly roar erupted from the throats of the men in the line. With switches raised high they fell upon the zebras like a Matabele impi. It was too much for the animals. The leading stallion slipped into the crush and the rest followed. Bringing up the rear was the big stallion. The men charged in behind them and Shorty drew the last curtain at the mouth of the crush.

There was chaos in the narrow gangway. The zebras trampled and milled about, barking. Wherever the men could reach, they beat the zebras across their rumps. A few men clambered up the sides and let them have it from above. A solid screen of dust hung around the crush. The zebras wheeled closer and closer to the ramp. The stallion in front saw a gap at the end. He galloped down the crush and onto the ramp. The others followed. Then he was on the truck. With the earsplitting sound of hooves on metal, the other zebras followed. All except the big stallion.

He was in his prime. It was clear that he'd been working hard to safeguard his herd and retain his position. On his haunches he wore the scar of a lion's claws.

When he reached the ramp, he baulked and kicked back with both hind legs. The dangerous hooves narrowly missed a few heads. Then he rose on his hind legs and in a single movement he turned round in the narrow crush. He was determined to get out. His pursuers saw his resolve and hesitated. He took his chance and charged. Men scrambled up the sides of the crush. Chris was too slow and was flung aside, receiving a painful bite on the shoulder. Samuel landed under the hooves and had to protect his head with both arms. Later Doctor Kemp would have to administer painkillers for a cracked rib. The curtain between the crush and the boma was not completely closed. The stallion threw himself at it. The curtain was ripped off the cables and trampled in the dust. The stallion stood in the centre of the boma. Around him the dust was settling and the late afternoon sun filtering through the autumn leaves shrouded him in gold. He stood his ground, snorting. Defiant. Hooves trampling the earth. You have taken my herd. You're not getting me.

At sunset the men were still struggling fruitlessly to get the zebra into the crush. They were exhausted and out of breath. Sweat trickled through the dust that had settled on their skins. The zebra evaded them time and again.

It was then that Doctor Kemp loaded the dart gun.

The Palmer dart gun used by the doctor shoots a dart with a capsule containing an immobilising drug accurately over fifty metres. The hollow needle penetrates the rump muscle and the impact forces the tranquilliser out of the capsule, through the needle and into the animal.

The men were waiting now. Soon the zebra's head was hanging. The men tried again. The zebra struggled to remain conscious. He snorted and glared at the approaching line of men. Then he jumped round and trotted away. The men closed in and the zebra realised he would have to make a break for it. He launched another charge.

The spring hare burrow was hidden in the grass. The tranquilliser had clouded the stallion's perceptions. He was exhausted and trapped. Two metres from the line and at full gallop his foreleg disappeared into the ground. With a sound like the crack of a whip his leg snapped under the full weight of his body. The earth shook as the zebra fell headlong.

Dazed, he got up and stumbled away on three legs. Helplessly he stared at the men from a distance. They stood around indecisively, looking guilty, like boys who had taken a game too far.

Silence had fallen over the twilit veld. Out of the silence respect was born. And the knowledge that the work was done.

Chris broke away from the line and crawled under the canvas. Moments later he returned with his R4. The sound of the bolt sliding home rang out sharply in the night air. Even sharper was the blast from the barrel.

Amakange borehole

When I woke up, the moon was low in the western sky. It was almost a half-moon, with a slight potbelly. In its dim light the mopane leaves flickered grey in the night breeze. The coals of the campfire were still glowing dimly. Beside me against the rear wheel of the bakkie Kuva was also awake. He raised himself up on his elbow and stared into the night. Next to the Land Rover on the other side of the coals Horace McAllistair cleared his throat softly. Just to let me know that he and Tjimbumba were also awake. Kuva lay back in his bedroll. We lay waiting in the quiet winter's night in the mopane bushes on the border between Kaokoland and Ovamboland.

The elephant came walking out of the night. Like a black ship in a sea of grey mopane. His path took him straight past our camp. He was on his way to the water trough at the borehole about thirty metres beyond our camp.

The night breeze gave away our presence. It bore the smell of woodsmoke, diesel and man. He stopped. A bull in his prime. His impressive ivory glimmered white in his dark head. He turned from his path and headed into the bushes, making a detour around us. He was alert but calm. Behind a taller stand of mopanes he came to a halt. The moon threw its dim light on the contours of his back, which was just visible above the mopanes. He stood motionless. Although I could not see it, I knew his trunk would be testing the air. In our bedrolls we didn't move a muscle. He stood like that for what felt like a long time, but was really no more than a few minutes. Then, still hidden from view, he walked on to the borehole. He came out into the open and walked around the water trough. Again he stood for a while. Just to make certain. Then he plunged his trunk into the trough and began to drink.

From the same direction came three more elephant bulls, walking in single file. Where he had left the trail, they left it too, took a detour and made their way through the tall mopanes and the bushes to the borehole.

We watched them as they drank in the moonlight. Aware of our presence, but unperturbed. They stayed for a long time. I dozed off and woke later from the sound of water being sucked up their trunks and squirted down their throats.

Horace sat up. He felt around for his tobacco and began to fill his pipe. He struck a match. For a moment it lit up our camp. The elephants stopped drinking and raised their heads. Horace drew on his pipe, the tobacco glowed and puffs of smoke rose into the air. The match went out. As quietly as they had come, the elephants left the trough and disappeared into the night.

At daybreak Kuva got up, stoked the fire and placed a mug of tea beside Horace, Tjimbumba and me. We sat around the fire. The winter sun was feeble and the morning was fresh. Horace filled his pipe while he spoke. With his long grey beard, faded khaki trousers and veldskoens without socks, he looked like a weather-beaten old Dorsland trekker.

"Subsonic communication among elephants is still a puzzle, but last night we saw another clear example of it. The leader followed his usual path to the water. When he picked up our scent, he left the path and stood at a safe distance in the bushes. He signalled to his comrades: Hang back, fellows. There are people at the water. They stood waiting in the thickets for the leader to assess the situation. He stood listening and smelling for a long time. When he was satisfied that we were asleep, he signalled back: 'OK, boys. It's quiet in the camp. They seem to be sleeping. I'm going in to drink. Come in carefully around the back. Just follow my tracks.' Then he went to drink. His mates picked up his scent without any difficulty. They walked on his tracks and came to drink. They only realised we were awake when I lit my pipe. In all my years in Kaokoland an elephant has never bothered me while I lay sleeping. They come close sometimes. A few times they even came very close, reaching with their trunks to smell me. Almost touched me on occasion, but never bothered me. Just walked away into the night after they had reassured themselves."

Horace put away his pipe. He stared into the fire. After I'd had my second cup of tea, we rolled up our bedding and loaded our camping equipment onto the bakkie. We started the diesel engines and left Amakange borehole to continue with our patrol.

Bush law

Uaromine was a young Himba man. Strong, lean and handsome, like most of his kind. He lived north of the Kunene River. He was a loner. Young men of his age went around in groups. When they had seen to their fathers' cattle and goats for the day, they swaggered through the veld from one onganda to the next, flirting with the red-smeared girls with the firm breasts and the alluring thighs.

Himbas are nomads by nature, but to Uaromine drifting was an obsession. He would appear from the bushes at an onganda out of nowhere and join the family for a drink of curdled milk. If it was late, he would stay the night, only to get up in the early hours and disappear. At daybreak, when the goats were taken out to the veld, the goatherds would discover that a kid was missing.

Finally his path took him south, to Opuwo. There he stole a radio and traded it to a hawker for cheap wine. He lay around the dusty cuca shops of Opuwo for a few days, got into a fight, stole a kid and disappeared into the bushes. Time and again he returned to Opuwo. Once the police locked him up for theft and on another occasion for assault. He gained the reputation of being an antisocial troublemaker. Then he decided it was time to get rich quickly.

Tako had been a corporal in the South West African territorial forces during the border war. If you saw him now, you'd hardly believe it, for his appearance was typical of the traditional Himba male in the prime of his life. His long hair was tied in a tight ondumbu, the distinguishing feature of a married man. He was naked from the waist up and round his neck hung his thick ombongoru of shell and ostrich eggshell beads, held together firmly with sinew and mopane resin. His loincloth was made of cotton and consisted of two parts. In front hung the short otjitati, neatly pleated, and behind hung the long ombuku that ended at mid-calf. It was suspended from an oxhide thong that encircled his waist three times. Fastened round his waist was a long handmade skinning knife in an oxhide sheath. From the oxhide thong hung his ombinga, or snuff case. In his hand was a short assegai with a long, flat blade that glinted in the morning sun. The shaft ended in a sharp metal spike concealed in a flowing oxtail. Somewhere in a trunk in his hut he kept a folded brown uniform, his webbing and a photograph of himself, posing with his R1 rifle.

Tako had found the tracks of a herd of cattle. The cattle were being driven north by one person. The herd was less than an hour ahead of him. He set out in pursuit and lengthened the strides of his long legs.

Late the previous afternoon the shocking news had spread from onganda to onganda: A herd of cattle that had been grazing unattended in the veld had disappeared. A gang of young men, armed with pangas, assegais and kieries, went after them. As usual, the bush telegraph had preceded them to Tako's onganda, and he had left his hut and found the tracks before the young men arrived.

Half a day's walk from the Kunene River Tako spotted a small fire through the mopane bushes. A young man was roasting a goat's rib on the coals. Around him stood a herd of cattle. Tako had heard the cattle lowing from a distance. He had sneaked up soundlessly.

When the young man looked up, Tako's assegai was already pressed to his throat. Defiance flashed in his eyes and he made a grab for his kierie, but the point of the assegai pressed into the skin just below his adam's apple and a droplet of blood appeared. Uaromine sat back resignedly. His glowering gaze held Tako's. His arms dangled at his sides. From the bushes behind them came the excited shouts of the young men, hot on the trail.

The young men reached Uaromine and Tako. From the crowns of their heads hung long, curved, plaited ponytails. The rest of the scalp was shaved and shiny with sweat. They were all for settling the matter on the spot, but Tako reasoned with them.

"We're going to take him to Headman Tjihange's onganda. You have to guard him. I'll ride to Epupa on a donkey and fetch the police."

The young men all spoke at the same time and waved their pangas menacingly.

Tako spoke earnestly. "You have to guard him. If you hurt him, the police will come and arrest you."

The young men pushed Uaromine roughly to Headman Tjihange's onganda. Tako had to intervene often and caution and cajole.

At Tjihange's onganda Tako again admonished the young men. "Listen to me. Wait for the police to come."

He mounted his donkey and rode to the police post at Epupa Falls.

Headman Tjihange came out of his hut and stood under a tree beside the sacred fire. Wordlessly he looked at the young men.

Uaromine's defiant gaze darted from one young man to the next, and the corners of his mouth turned down scornfully. They stood around him in a circle.

A young man stepped forward and raised his panga. In a single movement the panga sliced through Uaromine's throat and broke his neck. Writhing, he fell at their feet, blood spurting in every direction and spraying over the bystanders. Now all the young men joined in and hacked Uaromine to pieces. They danced around the body.

"Ongeama, huuu! Ongeama, huuu! The lion who caught our cattle is dead. Killed by the bravest of the brave."

On his donkey Tako heard the shouts and continued on his way to summon the police.

Eleven young men were taken to Opuwo by the police and thrown into the cells. They appeared in court.

The prosecutor and the magistrate opposed bail, shocked by the brutality of the incident. A young anthropologist from the University of Cologne, who had been doing research for her dissertation among the Himbas for two years, spoke for the defence. A Himba's existence revolves around his cattle. According to Himba law, cattle theft is punishable by death. Eleven young men from one community comprised a large part of the work force. Who would tend the cattle in their absence? The Ovambo magistrate, whose task was to implement the Western legal system, refused bail.

I sat at the back of the courtroom, listening. I had come to Opuwo for supplies and had heard about the incident from the girl from Cologne, who was a friend of mine.

The Himbas are an embarrassment to most of black Namibia. They refuse to relinquish their traditions and embrace the watered-down Western civilisation that the other Namibian tribes have accepted. They remind the Ovambos of the fact that they themselves sentenced cattle thieves to death not too long ago. Namibia is a developing country. Instead of being proud of their country's precolonial past, the average black Namibian is ashamed of it. And the Himbas are a painful reminder of that past.

To add insult to injury, the Himbas fought on the South African side during the war. This is something the Ovambos will never forget. And more importantly: All that stood between the Swapo government and a hydroelectric power scheme in the Kunene River at the time was the headstrong Himbas, who considered access to their ancestral graves on its banks as their birthright.

The eleven young Himbas were taken back to the cells. Accustomed to pristine surroundings, they had no resistance to the appalling conditions in jail and soon more than half of them were suffering from tuberculosis.

Months later the case came before the court again. The Himbas were illiterate, and the Western legal system was meaningless to them. The statements they had made were not binding to their conscience. Suddenly no one remembered who had swung the panga. It had not been any of them. They thought the fellow might be living in Angola now. Tako had told them to leave Uaromine alone. That was what they had done.

The prosecutor leafed through their statements and pointed out declarations that had been made under oath. They shrugged. We can't write. Perhaps you should ask the constable who took down that statement. Perhaps he's the one who killed Uaromine with a panga. Old people from Tjihange's onganda who had been eyewitnesses now no longer remembered, or suffered from poor eyesight. The hearing lapsed into chaos and the case was dismissed. The eleven young men, thin and ill, were released.

A while later a meeting took place in the bush somewhere between Angola and Namibia. Uaromine's headman, his father and a number of councillors came to see Headman Tjihange and Tako. They demanded blood money. A life for the life of Uaromine. The life of a young man. A young man's life, or sixty head of cattle. After lengthy deliberation, the families of the eleven young men each contributed a few head of cattle and paid Uaromine's father the blood money. Uaromine became a rich man after all.

The dog

The trouble started when Shane got the dog. "Palmwag has a dog now," he said when he arrived with the small black bundle. He called the dog Baloo, after the bear in Kipling's story. I thought it was a shitty name. A black dog should be called Satan. After a few weeks I was forced to admit, though: with his oversized paws and droopy eyes, he was unmistakably a bear.

Shane was going to turn him into an inn dog. He would lie on the stoep all day, eat leftovers from the kitchen and get fat. He would drink water from the pool and befriend the tourists. That was what Shane thought. The dog had different ideas.

His father had been half Labrador, half sheepdog. A good combination. But his father had been spoilt. He'd been the previous inn dog at Palmwag. Fat, lazy and friendly. Vigilant, nevertheless. His mother was a lively, pedigreed Rottweiler.

Gert and I lived in a house in the hills above Sesfontein. The house, slightly dilapidated, stood among mopane and thorn trees. On the slope below us was a fountain surrounded by large wild figs, where the baboons came to drink every afternoon. From the house, we overlooked a wide desert plain and ancient weathered mountains in the distance. The house was surrounded by hills and had the feeling of a mountain fortress. It was a good place to return to after a week in the veld.

When I was home, I followed the footpath through the hills every afternoon to have a beer at the Fort Sesfontein Inn. A few years before a rich German had had the old colonial fort restored. He had turned it into an inn for the safari convoys passing through on their way to Kaokoland. It was an oasis of palm trees, half-cold beer and a murky swimming pool. The dusty travellers, overcome by the desolation of the landscape and far from home, didn't complain about the poor service.

On my arrival, the young dog would charge at me and welcome me by wrestling with my leg. A proper little bear cub. At the bar Shane and I would make small talk over a few beers, before I walked back at nightfall. It wasn't long before the dog began to follow me. I let him be. Gert's cross-breed fox terrier, Flenters, would fly at the newcomer and the young dog, already bigger than Flenters, would cringe apologetically. Then he would empty Flenters's food bowl and crawl in between my feet. The next morning I would take him back to the fort.

There was a reason why I didn't have a dog. I had been in Kaokoland for only two years and was enjoying it there. Still, I sometimes felt it was time to leave, in search of new places and adventures. After another year, perhaps two, I would load my bakkie or shoulder my backpack and travel on. A dog tied you down.

One afternoon I stopped at the Fort in the bakkie. I lowered the tailgate to unload a few things and went inside. When I returned, the dog, which was growing fast, was waiting for me on the back of the bakkie.

"I'm telling you, Shane, I'm not taking responsibility for your dog."

But after that day, whenever the bakkie pulled away, the dog was in the back.

The dog was unsuited to his surroundings. He was pitch-black. Under his short coat there was a fluffy layer to protect him from the cold in the northern countries where his forefathers had lived. Though he suffered in the heat, it didn't curb his enthusiasm. From his lookout post on top of the long-distance diesel tank on the back of the bakkie his lively brown eyes took in the world as it flashed by. When we passed a herd of springbok or gemsbok, he would jump up and whimper with excitement.

When we explored the veld on foot, he chased after lizards and meerkats, only to lose them among the rocks. When we came across a herd of springbok or a troop of baboons, he was off in a flash. Fortunately he was still young and stupid and didn't get close to them. But I had seen what baboons could do to a dog once they had cornered him. Not a pretty sight. I don't like a dog that hunts, so whenever he came trotting back, panting, I would break off a mopane switch and thrash him. Rottweiler blood flowed strongly in his veins and he didn't learn.

One afternoon a herd of ostriches suddenly appeared from behind a dune and ran beside the bakkie at full tilt, determined to get away from us. It was too much for the dog. From the cab I watched his shadow jump onto the roof. Then he launched himself at the ostriches in a flying leap. He hit the ground with an enormous impact, bounced and rolled a few times in a cloud of dust. When he got up, he was winded and his mouth was full of sand. Dazed, he staggered back to where I had already stopped and got out. I smacked him soundly with my open hand.

Months passed and the dog grew big and strong. Wherever I went, the dog followed me like a shadow. He wasn't the kind of dog that would jump up against me or lick my face as I lay sleeping in the mornings. He kept his distance, watched my every move and followed as soon as I got up. When I was sleeping, he would lie down a few metres away, his head resting on his paws, and stare at me with gentle eyes. At camp and at home he was a good guard dog. If anything approached, he would give a short warning bark. His loyalty touched me and a firm bond developed between us. Whenever I returned to Sesfontein, I stopped at the Fort so that the dog could enjoy some leftovers.

White people don't stay at Sesfontein for long. Gert was an exception. He had been a policeman there for nearly ten years and he showed no sign of wanting to leave. After a year Shane resigned as manager of the Fort. He was returning to the Cape. It was the end of the year and I was going to spend Christmas in Swakopmund with my friend Mike Hearn, who was doing research on the black rhinos of Damaraland. Some friends of his from England would be meeting us there.

The new manager arrived at the Fort and Shane showed him the ropes before he left. It was late in December and I was on my way to Swakop. Gert had already left to visit friends in Otjiwarongo. I asked the new manager to look after the dog while I was away. He was the Fort's dog, after all.

The holiday in Swakopmund was a resounding success. The women amongst Mike's English friends were cute. Jack Daniel's No. 7 Tennessee whiskey only made them cuter. I broke hearts left, right and centre and lost my own several times. After New Year my heart, my liver and the rest of me were in need of rest. I found that I was missing the dog. I returned to Sesfontein with sweet memories of my holiday. In the desert the first rains had begun to fall.

At the Fort there was no sign of the dog. I found the new manager in his office. "Where's the dog?"

The fellow couldn't look me in the eye. "I gave him away."

I said nothing. Anger welled up in me, but I managed to stay calm. "Who did you give him to?"

"Asser Ganuseb. He needed a dog for his cattle post."

The new manager tried to explain. "Look, the tourists complained. He bothered them while they were eating. He jumped into the pool and dug up the flower beds."

I sighed. "All right. You have just forced me to take responsibility for the dog. From now on Baloo is my dog. My dog. Understand? No one except me goes near that dog."

I walked out, got into my bakkie and drove the sixty kilometres to Asser's cattle post to fetch my dog. The dog whimpered softly and almost jumped into my lap when I crouched next to him. He was thin and his coat was dull and dusty. When I opened the tailgate of the bakkie, he didn't hesitate for a moment before he jumped on.

At home I fed him on dog food that I had bought in Swakop. The next day we went camping in the veld. It rained intermittently and the outing was wet and unpleasant.

One morning a week later I was driving back to Sesfontein. The day was overcast. At Warmquelle I was stopped by a few young Herero men. "Morning, Chris. Please help

145

us. The Skelm River is in flood and Meintjies's car has been swept away."

"Where's Meintjies?"

"Over there at the shop."

I pulled over and drove to the shop. Meintjies was wet and dazed. "Chris, can you help me get my bakkie out of the river?"

"Get in. Let's go."

The young men joined us and jumped on the back. We drove to the Skelm River, halfway between Sesfontein and Warmquelle.

The Skelm River begins high up in the mountains east of Sesfontein and flows into the Hoanib. Like most rivers in Kaokoland, it is dry for most of the year. Though it very seldom rains at Sesfontein, the rainfall is higher in the mountains. It is therefore not unusual for the floodwaters of the Skelm River to reach the Hoanib River while the skies are clear at Sesfontein.

"I was driving from Sesfontein to Warmquelle. I was distracted and might have been driving too fast. It was only when I reached the drift that I realised the Skelm was in flood. It was too late to brake, so I accelerated and tried to get through," Meintjies said. Halfway through the river the water swept away his bakkie. He and a Herero passenger managed to get out of the cab. Three passengers on the back were trapped by the railings. The bakkie rolled once before the railings gave way. One girl reached dry land, but two young men were swept downstream and were still missing.

"How long ago did it happen?" I asked.

"An hour and a half. People are out searching for the missing men."

Meintjies was a storekeeper who operated a number of cuca shops in Kaokoland. He drove his loaded bakkie all over Kaokoland, carrying supplies to his shops, and then back to Windhoek to fetch more supplies. We found his bakkie a hundred metres downstream from the main road. It was lying on its side, half submerged in the flooded river. On the opposite bank Gert's police bakkie appeared through the bushes. It was loaded with people taking part in the search. So far they had not found any sign of the missing men.

The Hereros and I tied a rope to the railings of Meintjies's bakkie. The water tugged at our legs. Using my vehicle, we hauled the bakkie back onto its wheels. Then we tied the rope around the bullbar and pulled the wreck out of the water and up the bank onto dry land.

We proceeded to search in the bushes on the bank. We ran all the way to the confluence of the Skelm and the Hoanib. Where the floodwaters spilled out of the smaller tributary, the broad Hoanib River ran level with its banks. The water was strong. I decided to fetch the bakkie. The dog trotted along.

I crossed the dry bed of the Hoanib above the confluence and drove downstream until I saw the search party. Still no sign of the missing men. The terrain became rough and I left the bakkie behind. The Hereros, the dog and I continued the search on foot.

On a flat rock in the middle of the river we found the first body. The face was turned up to the sky and the arms flung wide. The four Hereros and I waded into the churning brown water. The dog followed fearlessly, went under, was swept along, reached a rock, climbed out and jumped in again. We reached the body. We grabbed hold of the arms and legs and one man held the head with the gaping wound. We struggled back through the water. The dog followed and reached the bank some distance downstream.

We laid the body on the bank. I had known the boy well. A good-natured dimwit with enormous feet. Just a few months earlier I had given him a pair of my old boots. The Hereros fashioned a crude stretcher and we carried him back to the bakkie. Eight kilometres downstream Gert's search party found the broken body of the other young man.

The weather cleared and I continued with my visits to the rangers at the outposts. My bakkie was due for a ten thousand kilometre service, so I returned to Swakop, this time in an official capacity. As I wouldn't be staying long, Gert de-

cided to accompany me. His fox terrier, Flenters, sat in front
and Baloo rode on the diesel tank at the back. It was a long
journey south, a large part of it along the Skeleton Coast.

Swakop was considerably quieter than during the holiday
season a month before, but the permanent residents hailed
us in the streets. Gert and I left the bakkie with the agency
and took the dogs to the beach. Baloo had never seen the sea
and at first he was timid. I walked into the shallows and he
followed. Soon we were running through the waves and
across the beach with Gert and Flenters in tow. We returned
to our rented room, showered and dressed to go out.

In Fagin's bar there were familiar faces. Jenny, the pretty
English barmaid, greeted me warmly.

"Come and meet our dogs."

She came out from behind the counter. Her wire-haired
mongrel was with her, as usual. She greeted Baloo and he lay
on his back with his legs open wide for Jenny to scratch his
tummy. Her mongrel approached and began to play with
Baloo. They were both young dogs.

Gert and I were tired after our long trip and we made short
work of a bottle of whiskey, having kicked off with steak and
beer. It became a late night and Gert grew quiet. A few people decided to move to the club next door, but Gert wanted
to go to bed. I convinced him to have one last drink.

We sat in the club, both very drunk by that time. Afterwards I could only recollect fragments of what happened
next. The rest would be filled in by other people.

Gert was a loner and noisy clubs did nothing to improve
his frame of mind. He had heard someone say something
about guys who lived in the bush with their dogs and thought
they could take over when they came to town. The dogs were
a nuisance to everyone. I demanded to know who had said
it. Gert pointed vaguely.

Next to a pillar stood a guy involved in a heated argument
with a girl. From my seat at the bar, I launched myself at
him. My right hand closed around his throat. I pushed him
back and pinned him against the pillar.

"That's right. Donner him!" the girl said.

I pushed the elbow of my short arm into his face. "Stop talking shit, man!"

Greg from the parachute club intervened. "Chris! Relax, man."

I came to my senses, let the guy go and walked out. Greg, Gert and the guy and girl followed. The guy wanted to know why I had acted like that. He was livid. I really couldn't say what had got into me. He grabbed me by the collar and I let him carry on. Then he calmed down. I tried to explain that someone had insulted my dog. He swore he'd had nothing to do with it. We went our separate ways.

"Actually, that *was* the wrong guy," Gert said as we walked back to our room. Baloo walked by my side.

It was late when I got up the next morning. I felt terrible. Baloo was lying next to my bed, watching me. What the hell had been the matter with me the night before?

I showered and went to find out if my bakkie was ready. "Only this afternoon," the mechanic said.

I maintained a low profile for the rest of the day and slept off my hangover. Gert went his own way.

When the bakkie was ready, I drove out to the parachute club. Greg and Jenny were packing parachutes in the hangar. Baloo and the wire-hair rediscovered each other. "What exactly happened last night, Greg?"

"Not much, man. I was just scared you'd tear the guy apart. But you might as well have moered him. He's a doos."

"Someone talked shit about my dog. I thought it was him."

"Everyone thinks you're a hero. They think you grabbed him because he was being rude to the girl."

Jenny's eyes were laughing. "Being rude to a girl is nothing. But if someone is rude to your dog, he deserves to be clobbered."

I found Gert and Flenters at a restaurant. We went back to our room and loaded our stuff onto the bakkie. My dog took his place on the diesel tank and we drove back to the bush where we belonged.

Experiment

I was leading an expedition on foot along the dry bed of the Ombonde River from Kowareb to Kamdesha, heading upstream from west to east.

The Desert Research Centre had asked us to make an estimate of flood and elephant damage to the ana trees in the river bed. They had given us formulas to apply and piles of forms on which to record the data: height and circumference of each tree; percentage leaf cover; percentage damage to the bark; number of dead branches; root damage. Each and every tree over a distance of 90 kilometres in an extremely inhospitable landscape had to be evaluated. It could only be done on foot. The ana tree is one of the chief food sources for wildlife in the barren Kaokoland: a vital link in the ecology.

We would need a large group of volunteers and we had only one bakkie. On completion of the task, most of us would have to walk out. In an office in Windhoek someone would capture the data on a computer and draw conclusions that would mean very little to most people. The elephants and the ana trees had been coexisting for thousands of years.

The technical details were of little consequence to me. Any excuse for an expedition would do. On this occasion two extreme worlds would be brought together. With consequences for both parties.

In Britain there is an organisation that works among the youth. They take unemployed, underprivileged youngsters from the city streets and bring them to Africa on an adventure. Here they get involved with community projects and nature conservation or research projects. The idea is to motivate them, to try and give them direction, even if it is just by showing them another world. It might just change their lives.

The members of the expedition would be made up of such a group. I was to be in charge. I was familiar with the area. My task would be to lead the expedition, look after the members and make certain that the data was recorded correctly. There were 17 in the group: two team leaders, a medic and 14 youths between 18 and 25. The leaders were usually people with a military background. It was expected of them to play a motivating role and maintain discipline. In this group the leadership element was somewhat different. An experiment. Paul, one of the team leaders, was a fire chief from Merseyside in Liverpool, in his early thirties, enterprising and energetic. We became friends immediately. He was also a deep-sea diver, who led diving expeditions to Scapa Flow in his free time.

Lucy was the medic. A long-legged girl, a nursing sister at a hospital in Liverpool. I fell in love with her, though she did not return the sentiment. She had pledged her troth to Jamie, a medical doctor, who was waiting for her in England. Ruth, another member of the expedition, fell in love with me.

Jason, the second team leader, was the guinea pig. He was a rehabilitated heroin addict. In the clinic he had attended he had shown promise and a desire to be cured. During his stay he had worked among drug addicts in the streets of Liverpool. After his release he had volunteered to carry on. The youth movement had heard of him and approached him. Would he be interested in becoming a team leader? In developing his leadership qualities? It could be an escape from unemployment and his miserable circumstances. More than willing, he agreed.

He was a skinny Englishman covered in tattoos. On his shoulder was an enormous bouquet of roses with a banner underneath on which there had once been a girl's name. An attempt had since been made to erase the name. Jason was enthusiastic and led by example. We became friends too.

The group was divided into two teams, one for each river bank. I moved back and forth between them, making certain that they recorded the data properly. I was accompanied by my assistant, Uakututwa, and, of course, my dog, Baloo. Gert van der Linde drove the bakkie. He supplied us with drinking water from Kowareb fountain or Otokotorwa borehole. Every evening he would meet us at a prearranged spot in the river bed, where we would set up camp.

Five days before the expedition began the buckles on the girth of my saddle snapped while I was riding down the Kowareb Schlucht at an easy gallop. I fell heavily in the sand. I suspected I might have cracked or broken a rib. For the next month it hurt abominably, especially when I was sitting or lying down. Besides, sleeping in a river bed was painful at the best of times.

It was the beginning of November in the Kaokoveld. It had not yet rained. The mopane leaves were a dry orange colour. It was sweltering in the river valley and there was a lot of dust. The sand was loose and made walking difficult. The work was monotonous. Where the stands of ana trees were dense, at the eastern mouth of the Schlucht, for instance, we sometimes covered no more than five kilometres a day. At times we would walk for half a day without seeing a single ana tree.

It took the group a few days to acclimatise. Before we started, I took them on a few half-day excursions, just to give them an idea of what to expect. It wasn't much help. They toiled and panted under their packs, complaining of pain and heat and blisters. Paul, Jason and Lucy encouraged them.

Suffering turns people into comrades, and eventually something kicked in. Smiles appeared on faces, despite the suffering. The group began to realise that they were involved in something unique. Gert and his bakkie under a tree in the late afternoon became a welcome sight, which was greeted with a cheer. Baloo became the mascot, everyone's friend.

Large herds of springbok and gemsbok that had come to

seek shelter against the heat under the trees on the river bank fled in clouds of dust when we arrived. To break the monotony, the group and I stalked giraffes at dusk.

The condition of the game was poor. It was not unusual for the time of year. Animal carcasses lay strewn on the river bed. In Kaokoland dead things don't decay. They die and simply dry out. Like mummies. Gemsbok and springbok lay in the sand. Bones covered with skin, heads thrown back, empty eye sockets. Dead baboons, an elephant calf, a fully grown giraffe cow.

At one of the last fountains in the Schlucht we found tracks and remains where hyena had lain in wait for the kudu that came from the mountains to drink. Here and there an African wild cat jumped out ahead of us. There were lion tracks up and down the river bed.

At night we built a large fire. Sentry duty was a precautionary measure. Two persons per two-hour shift were required to keep the fire burning high, and to be active but quiet in the camp.

Gert, Uakututwa, Baloo and I slept near the bakkie, slightly away from the rest. I was in pain and slept very little. I was aware of everything around me. A beautiful moon came up and spread its soft light over the wilderness, bringing relief after a relentless day.

Baloo's rattling bark woke me from my half-sleep. In a single movement I was out of my bedroll and on my feet, revolver in hand. When he barked like that, something was wrong. An unsuspecting elephant bull stepped out from behind a stand of leadwood in the moonlight. Baloo charged at him, and stopped him in his tracks metres from the campfire, where Lucy and Amy sat petrified.

Baloo's furious barking had made everyone sit up in their sleeping bags. The elephant made a wheezing noise. Baloo scolded furiously from the ground. I positioned myself between the girls and the confrontation and ordered them to move away. The elephant bull recovered from his surprise and retreated. He made a wide detour around the camp and disappeared quietly along the river bed in the moonlight. Once again Baloo was the hero of the day.

The youngsters on the expedition were slowly coming into their own. When it was time for siesta in the afternoon heat, Mattie took his pencil and sketchbook and drew the mountains and ana trees surrrounding him. Don took out a mouth organ and played Beatle tunes. Delia and Doris sang along. If these people had nothing else to be proud of, at least they were proud of the fact that their gloomy city had given the world the Beatles.

As the expedition progressed, I grew fond of this group of strangers with their crewcuts and dreadlocks, their tattooed bodies, their slogan-bearing T-shirts, their strange accents. I was fond of them like a lieutenant of his troops.

I was most attached by far to Paul and Lucy. Paul liked to tell me about his deep-sea expeditions at Scapa Flow. He knew the history of each of the wrecks that dotted the sea-bed there. His tales took me from my own desert world to a desert under the sea, the graveyard of a once proud fleet, sunk by its own crew at the beginning of the century rather than surrender at the end of a great war.

The night after Baloo's encounter with the elephant, Ruth crawled into my bedroll and snuggled up against my back. She had waited for Gert's snores to rise to a crescendo. She wasn't Lucy, but she was young and pretty and had firm breasts and strong legs and this happened so seldom in the wilderness that I couldn't refuse.

After that she came every night to relieve my pain. Before dawn she crept back to her own sleeping bag. Some mornings Gert sat up in his bedroll, lit his first cigarette, smiled and winked. Gert had been in the wilderness for a long time. He knew.

Some days when the ana trees were few and the road was long, Jason would walk beside me with his stringy body. He was a strong hiker and was enjoying the expedition. His conversation transported me to another world.

"Every day away from it is a small victory, Chris. But it

haunts you. Every day. Some days more than others. I can only hope that if I stay away from it long enough it will one day leave me for good. It's so easy to forget about it here. There are so many other things to take in. The beauty and the ugliness. The hard and the easy sides of nature. The wilderness. It broadens your mind. It cleanses your body. Here it's easy, Chris, but in Liverpool I have absolutely nothing to live for."

Sometimes we walked side by side in silence for a long time. One day he put his hand out to stop me. He turned and looked at me as if he had just had an epiphany. "You're one too, Chris."

"Huh? Pardon?"

"One like me. You're one too."

He stretched his arms wide and looked around him at the scorched wilderness that threatened to engulf us. "This. Here. This is yours. You can't and you won't go away from it. Heroin is mine. But I *must* get away from it. Do you understand? In a sense we are the same."

He looked at my disfigured body. "Yours is better than mine. Undoubtedly. But it can also destroy you."

On any expedition someone cracks at some time or another. This time it was Sofie. She collapsed, crying. She couldn't go on, she wanted the bakkie to come and fetch her. We called a halt.

The rest stood waiting in the shade as Jason crouched beside her. He helped her to her feet and led her into the shade of an ana tree. They sat down. We couldn't hear what was being said, but Jason spoke deeply, urgently, sympathetically. Sofie shook her head. She couldn't. Jason persisted. He spoke calmly and at length. Sofie began to listen. She wiped her tears. An hour dragged by and she calmed down.

Jason got up and shouldered his pack. He took Sofie by the hand and helped her up. He picked up her pack and slung it across his chest. Now he was carrying two packs. Hand in hand they came walking towards us.

Someone began to clap. It was taken up gradually by the rest of the group. It grew to loud applause. The group stood aside and made way for Jason and Sofie. Paul was standing next to me. He shared my thoughts: Jason at his best. The experiment was working.

It was a lean, sunburnt group that arrived at the veterinary control point at Kamdesha. Every ana tree in the Ombonde and the lower reaches of the Otjivasando had been accounted for.

They swam boisterously in the cement reservoir. They were comrades. They all felt they had triumphed over something inside themselves.

The next day we would start walking back on a double-track road through the veld. Those with the worst blisters, aching legs and worn-out shoes would be allowed to catch a ride on the bakkie with Gert. He would take them to the base at Kowareb. Then he would return to fetch the next group of stragglers along the way. The strongest members would walk all the way back.

An interesting phenomenon emerged. Besides Paul, Jason, Uakututwa, Baloo and myself, it turned out to be almost exclusively girls who completed the journey on foot. Sometimes I hung back on purpose, just to admire Lucy's long legs and Ruth's muscular ones as they made short work of the distance. It's true what they say: they *are* stronger than we are.

Back at Kowareb, we bought all the beer in the cuca shop. It was against official policy. Expedition members were not allowed to drink. But no one gave a damn. We were going to have a farewell party.

The party was loud and lively. Addresses were exchanged. My CD player went through two sets of batteries. Ruth and I went for a walk in the moonlight and made out at the waterfall under the fountain.

The truck arrived the next afternoon to take them to Windhoek.

"You're my hero," said Lucy, embracing me, and I hugged her more tightly for a moment.

"I love you," said Ruth.

"This expedition has changed my life, Chris," said Jason. "When things get unbearable for me over in Liverpool, I'll always remember our days of battling through the bush in the sun. I'll never forget you."

"I'll never forget you either, Jason."

Paul and I shook hands. Delia and Doris had trouble saying goodbye to Baloo. Sofie held on to Gert's large body for a long time. The truck left in a cloud of dust, filled with waving people.

After a while Ruth stopped writing to me. Lucy wrote regularly. She and Jamie were happily married. They planned to leave Liverpool and open a practice in Australia. She told me about the others. They met occasionally for a reunion.

The last time I had a letter from Lucy was about three months ago. Jason. Late one night he had returned to his father's house from a bar. They found him on his bed the following morning. They had to break down the bedroom door. The needle was still stuck in his arm.

Gatvol

It was the ugliest time of year on the Kwando River flood plains. The air was filled with a dirty brown haze. The grass on the plains had been burnt, and grey dust devils whirled across the black earth. The Caprivi people brought their cattle from the river to the kraal swathed in solid sheets of dust.

I was standing on a wooded hummock beside a lily pond and my immediate surroundings still held some of the enchantment that the flood plains usually had for me. At my feet lay a pile of elephant dung dropped there by a lone animal the night before. Not even the proximity of elephants helped raise my spirits. I looked at the dismal flood plain and decided. I was gatvol. I was utterly and completely fed up.

On a leafy island in the distance, under an African mangosteen, was my camp: a few tents and a bakkie on a scorched plain. It was an afternoon in late August, the end of the dry season. The time of fires on the grassy plains of Africa. I walked back to my camp in the setting sun. Why I was here, I didn't know and what I would accomplish here, I didn't know either. One thing I did know: I was fed up.

It had started with a request from my boss to come from Kaokoland to lend a hand with a lion problem in the Eastern Caprivi. I had loaded my bakkie with Herero lion hunters, .303s, spring traps and camping equipment and driven from one godforsaken wilderness to another. And found myself at the centre of a dispute.

My first stop had been at Sangwali on the edge of the flood plains in the Eastern Caprivi. The induna and his Kuta had given me a hearing. They were so glad to see me. Now that I was there, all their problems would be solved. The

Hereros and I were welcome to stay as long as we wanted. Nature Conservation was not at all concerned with their problem and refused to help.

I hadn't been misled by their stories, so from there I had gone to Katima Mulilo, to the offices of Nature Conservation. There was only one white game ranger still in the service of the government. His initial cold reception soon made way for an outburst. Why hadn't his ministry been informed of the matter? I mentioned a letter and a report that one of my colleagues had sent him three months before.

Then he launched into a tirade against the local communities that played off different conservation organisations against one another. While he was carrying on, my irritation grew. I had already been annoyed when I had heard that after an exhausting hunting season in Kaokoland I was to come to the Caprivi to "evaluate the lion problem".

When I left the ranger's office, I realised I'd had enough. Of the ranger, my boss, Hereros, Caprivians, Kaokoland, Caprivi. Everything. My boss liked to be seen as a crusader implementing a new kind of community-minded conservation in Namibia. The last of the old school game rangers clung jealously to their game reserves and legislation and refused to believe that others could look after game too. They saw every new idea as a threat. Then there were the local communities, who were exploiting the situation for their own benefit.

And fools like me did the dirty work. What for? Just to be able to live in the bush?

Well. Here I was in the Eastern Caprivi to "evaluate" the problem. Fed up or not. It was actually quite simple. You didn't have to be a genius to sum up the situation. Two national reserves were situated about forty kilometres from each other. Both bordered on the eastern bank of the Kwando River. Wedged between the two were a number of villages, where the inhabitants planted muhango and let their cattle graze on the flood plain. The game reserves were unfenced and lions left them whenever they felt like it to stalk the cattle.

We were camping about five kilometres from the Mudumu National Park at a place called Lianshulu. We heard the lions roar on the first night. With me were six Hereros, all of whom had formerly been troops with Koevoet or in 101 Battalion. They lived on the western boundary of the Etosha Game Reserve and knew all about lions killing cattle. There was also a Caprivian assigned to us by the induna. He was the community's lion hunter.

That night the lions struck. In the early morning we found the carcass, but someone had been there before us. What was left of the cow had been collected by its owner for personal use.

Filemon Kapi, my second-in-command, admonished: "Leave the carcass as it is. We can set traps around it."

"These lions don't return to the same carcass," the owner answered sullenly.

We followed the lions' spoor through the bush and across the flood plains. It looked as if there were three youngish males. They were heading straight for the boundary of the reserve. The Hereros and I were armed with .303s. Lister, the lion hunter, carried a .375 Brno

It soon became clear that the lions had long since made their way back into the game reserve. I told Filemon to fetch the bakkie and meet us at the cut line.

My prediction had been correct. The lions' tracks were clearly visible on the sandy cut line that formed the boundary of the game reserve. They were safely back in the reserve. We walked along the cut line for a while and saw a herd of elephant.

Filemon arrived with the bakkie and we drove back to camp. Why didn't these Caprivians keep their cattle in a kraal at night? he asked me.

At a village we bought a goat and slaughtered it at camp. Over a mug of tea around the campfire I tried to explain to myself why I was so fed up. I had been working on the project in Kaokoland for two years. It had been a wonderful new beginning for me. A vast, arid wilderness to explore. New peo-

TOP, LEFT: Chris as a sixteen-year-old boy on a hunting trip with his father, Commandant Cas Bakkes.

TOP, RIGHT: Military patrol in 1989 on the Kwando River in the Caprivi, where the Namibian, Angolan and Zambian borders meet.

ABOVE: Camping with fellow student ranger Steven Dell at Kwaggavoetpad, 1987.

ABOVE: The crocodile hunters of Kwamhlanga: From left to right Daniel Koen, Chris, Petrus Sepogwane, John Peba and Josef Mokoa. KwaNdebele, 1990.
RIGHT: Wilderness trails ranger in the Kruger National Park, 1993.

OPPOSITE PAGE
ABOVE: With colleague Filliosse Mula in the Kruger National Park.
BELOW: Lions from the Guweni pool feasting on a buffalo carcass.

TOP, LEFT: With Venomambo, son of Ozohavera, on a visit to the Himba settlement at Otjivaurua.

TOP, RIGHT: Tako, a Himba herder from Omuramba, close to the Kunene River.

ABOVE: Attending the burial of Himba chief Kazetaura in August 2003, together with the Himba game rangers Ngeve, Karonganga and Nanisire (left to right).

TOP: Black rhino (*Diceros bicornis bicornis*) cow and calf at the Uniab River.
ABOVE: Christmas in the desert: with bosom friend Mike Hearn.

ABOVE: Baloo.
ABOVE, RIGHT: Tier.
RIGHT: A one-armed
man and his one-eyed
dog on the Rooiplaat
plains after the rain.

OPPOSITE PAGE
ABOVE: Watching
elephants with clients
in the bed of the
Hoarusib River.
BELOW: Skeleton Coast
camp, 2002: helping
clients through the
flooded Khumib River
to reach the airstrip
in time.

TOP: Rhino Camp, Damaraland.
MIDDLE: A tent called home.
RIGHT: Emsie Verwey in her
"office" at Rhino Camp.

ple and animals to get to know, undreamed-of freedom. In a way Kaokoland was the last remnant of the old Africa, where man and beast toiled together in a relentless wilderness. It had been a lonely two years so far, with Hereros and Himbas my only companions, and one or two white refugees, like myself. It had been a hard two years of nomadic living and nightly camping in the desert. I had had heat, thirst, dust storms, flash floods, wild animals and wild people to contend with.

The top brass in my organisation consisted mainly of idealists, people whose goal was to put the management of natural resources into the hands of the local communities. My boss, who had done groundbreaking work in this field, had needed someone with a game ranger background to handle the more practical aspects of conservation management.

I had to train community rangers. Soon it became in-service training. I found myself permanently in the veld with the rangers. On patrol, counting game, pursuing poachers. When the elephants raided the mealie fields, I was there with the rangers to chase them off. My boss and the local communities increasingly depended on my assistance with similar problems and I travelled from one problem area to the next.

During the hunting season that year, a Herero headman had made me his hunter. Hunting is hard work, and I had asked Gert van der Linde to come from Sesfontein to help. Across desert plain and through mopane bush we hunted prolifically and shot numerous gemsbok and springbok. After a month's hunting we were exhausted and in need of distraction.

There was little distraction to be had in Kaokoland, and getting drunk at Fort Sesfontein was the only recreation available. In Kaokoland you led a pioneer's life. You had to be careful. Anarchy could easily prevail. To occupy your mind, you read every book you could lay your hands on. You positioned yourself at the Fort Sesfontein bar counter in search of passing tourists. Just to see a different face and have a conversation and a beer with another human creature, before you disappeared into the desert again.

Perhaps my boss had noticed during a visit that I needed a change. Because I was the only one of his staff with experience of lions, he had sent me to the Caprivi. Actually I had been pulling high revs for a while and needed a holiday, not a lion hunt.

Though I had experience with lions, I was certainly no expert. For three years I had tracked lions on foot, showing them to tourists without anyone getting hurt. In that time I had shot two lions.

Shooting the first lion had been a strange experience. A young male, a three-year-old downy-beard, was bitten in the foot during a fight with another lion. Though the lion was able to walk, the wound became septic. The lion began to hang around a rest camp. Tourists saw him and reported it. The game ranger in that section was worried that he might enter the camp in search of easy food and attack a tourist. Because the ranger was busy elsewhere, I was assigned to track and destroy the lion.

It had been a time of high ideals and a rosy future. A time that was over.

A Shangaan ranger and I had gone into the bush after the lion. About three kilometres from the camp we found him. He had joined up with a pride of six lionesses and older cubs. They were lying in a clearing. It was a late summer's afternoon. The veld was green and there were clouds in the sky.

At a distance of a hundred metres I stopped the bakkie and got out. I wasn't about to shoot my first lion from a vehicle. We stalked the lions through the ghwarrie bushes. I had come face to face with many lions on foot and I knew that they would either challenge us with a flick of the tail and a growl, or run off into the thickets.

That afternoon it was completely different. There was something sad about the occasion. I stepped out of the ghwarrie thicket and the lions saw me. I was scarcely thirty metres away. The injured lion was lying among the others and I couldn't fire immediately. They all got up. For a while they stood looking at each other and at me, sniffing here and there, as if they were coming to a decision. It was time to say goodbye. The pride of six walked away, into the veld. The injured male stayed behind. He looked at me and gave a low growl in the direction of the pride. One lioness stopped and turned and then carried on walking. The male didn't look at me again. He averted his head slightly as if to say: "I'm ready. Get it over with."

It was an easy shot. The .458 bullet entered behind the shoulder and pierced the heart. The second shot, fired as he was lying on the ground, was a mere formality.

I shot my second lion during a wilderness walking trail. When I heard the growl behind the bushes, I knew something was wrong. I left Filliosse, my Shangaan assistant, with the clients, walked in the direction of the sound and cocked my rifle. She charged without warning, only to fall down helplessly in the dust. Frantic, she gathered herself up to lunge. A few metres further she fell down again.

It must have been an altercation with another lion. Her left foreleg had been ripped from the shoulder and was dangling uselessly from a strip of skin. She kept trying to get up to vent her fury and despair on me. A single bullet through the head released her from her agony.

We received a message that a lion had killed two head of cattle at Sangwali and decided to move our camp. We drove along the dirt road through bush country, my mind still on the restless feelings that were threatening to overwhelm me.

When I embarked on my career as a game ranger ten years before I'd had only one thing in mind: Adventure. I was determined to honour the pioneering spirit of bygone days. I wanted to explore unknown wildernesses and make them my home. The meagre salary and limited opportunities for promotion did not really concern me.

And there *was* a lot of adventure. I came as close to the lifestyle of my heroes of old as was possible for a city boy from Pretoria in the late twentieth century. But what did I have to show? I had less now than what I had set out with. I had no house or wife or child. I had been wandering for so long that I didn't fit in anywhere any more. All I had was a story to tell.

Sangwali was a dusty, dirty, cheerless place. The lions had caught two cows and the remains had already been eaten. Lister, the lion hunter, scolded the residents. How often had he told them to leave the carcass in the veld? The lions might return. They stared at us sullenly. Then someone produced the heads, hides, stomachs and feet.

Now the Hereros gave the Caprivians a demonstration of how to set a trap. Using branches of a buffalo thorn, they built an impenetrable stockade with two entrances. At each entrance sticks were positioned crosswise, over which the lions would have to jump to enter the kraal. Then came the delicate task of setting the spring traps. It took four men to force open the dreadful jaws. The traps were carefully placed in shallow hollows inside the stockade, just behind the cross-bars. They were lightly covered with soil and sprinkled with the stomach contents of the dead cattle. The Hereros work-ed carefully. Finally the remains of the cattle were placed in the middle of the stockade, between the spring traps.

We made camp for the night on the edge of the flood plain.

All night the drums sounded in Sangwali.

At dawn we inspected the traps. One set of lion tracks led around the stockade. At the entrance the lion had stood for a long time, right next to the crossbar. He could just have leaped over. He didn't. He had turned and disappeared into the bushes.

"These lions are clever. They're not going to let them-selves be caught in a trap," said Filemon Kapi. We followed the tracks until they entered the Mamili reserve. For the rest of the day we drove from kraal to kraal, enquiring about inci-dents. There had been none.

Beside me in the bakkie Filemon Hungwa started to com-plain. He was unimpressed by the Caprivi. He saw lean cattle, mangy dogs and listless women. Before we came I had warned all the Hereros that Aids was a big problem in the Caprivi. I told them to leave the women alone.

"Caprivi is not a good place. The cattle, the dogs and the women are all ugly," said Filemon Hungwa.

He was one of my most capable game rangers in Kaokoland. Together with Filemon Kapi, Stefanus Kavetu and Simeon Virerako, I couldn't have wished for a better team in the Caprivi.

Filemon Hungwa's wife had given birth to a baby girl a week before our arrival here. He had asked me to name the child. All I could think of was my mother's name. Filemon and his wife had been very pleased. When immediately afterwards, however, I had ordered him to stay at home to look after his wife and baby, he was up in arms. There would be no lion hunting in the Caprivi without him. His other children could lend a hand at home.

On our way to the Caprivi I had stopped at the Hoba Meteorite at Grootfontein. It is the biggest known meteorite ever to strike the earth. Fifty tons, consisting of nickel and other metals. The Hereros all climbed on top of the meteorite and I took photos. Especially Filemon Hungwa was deeply impressed.

That night we set up camp beside the main road between Grootfontein and Rundu. When things had quietened down around the fire after supper, Filemon Hungwa, who hadn't spoken much after his visit to the meteorite, made an announcement. Overhead the stars were glittering brightly. "Today I was in heaven. I stood on top of a star."

He looked up at the sky. "I climbed up. Kuva ronda," he repeated in Otjiherero. Then he looked at me. "My daughter's name is Margaret Kuva Ronda Hungwa."

I drove through the Mamili game reserve near Sangwali with the Hereros. I stopped beside the river and the Hereros saw hippos for the first time in their lives. They were also amazed at the huge herds of elephant. In one place we counted three

hundred elephants on the flood plain. In the barren Kaokoland thirty elephants make an extraordinary herd. Deep
inside the game park we found a herd of cattle.

During the next few days the lions were quiet. The Hereros became surly. They missed their wives. At least you've
got wives to miss, I thought.

Then the lions began to kill cattle from the kraal at Malengalenga. When Filemon Kapi saw the kraal in question,
he nearly burst out laughing.

"So many trees here in the Caprivi. Many more and
much taller than in Kaokoland, and this is the kraal they
build! This thorn shelter won't protect the cattle against anything."

In Kaokoland, on the edge of the Etosha game reserve,
the Hereros walk for kilometres to cut mopane posts to build
an impenetrable stockade. A Herero detests manual labour,
but no sacrifice is too big for his herd. His cattle are his
wealth.

On our last day in the Caprivi I had to address a large
meeting and share my findings with the indunas, their Ku-
tas, members of the community and members of Nature
Conservation.

The previous night the lions had caught three cows in the
bushes outside Malengalenga. The tracks were fresh. There
were three lionesses and one big male. We followed them far
across the flood plains. Their tracks led to the river, but not
to the game reserve.

The morning sun was beating down, but we remained
hopeful that the lions would not enter the game reserve.
With me were Lister the lion hunter, Filemon Hungwa and
Simeon Virerako. I had left Filemon Kapi and Stefanus
Kavetu at Sangwali to address the meeting if I was late in
returning.

We reached the Kwando River. In front of us lay a dense
reed bed. The tracks led in there. We hesitated on the bank
beside the reeds. Suddenly I was uncertain. I didn't want to
go in there. The cattle belonged to strange people and the

lions belonged to a strange place. I turned to Filemon and Simeon. I thought of Filemon's baby daughter.

"We're not going in there," I said.

Lister looked disappointed. He challenged me with his eyes. Then he cocked his rifle and stepped into the reeds alone. We gazed after him from the bank. I cursed to myself.

"Stay here," I said to Filemon and Simeon. I swung my .303 from my shoulder and followed Lister into the reeds.

The reeds were incredibly dense. The tracks wound along a narrow footpath. Soon I caught up with Lister. The reeds towered above us. We could run into the lions at any moment. My heart was hammering. The vegetation was so dense that I hung my rifle across my shoulder and pulled out my revolver.

It was only afterwards that we realised what had happened. On the bank Filemon and the lion must have caught sight of each other simultaneously. Filemon and Simeon were on a slight rise, and they noticed a lion at the edge of the reeds some distance downstream. But the lion became aware of their presence and slipped deeper into the reeds. It joined up with another one and they headed for denser terrain.

The lions made straight for the reed bed through which Lister and I were making our way. Then we saw them, and Lister took aim. The lions were coming in our direction, but they had not yet seen us. Two lionesses. I put my revolver back in the holster and raised my .303. I was still taking aim, when Lister's rifle roared.

The lionesses froze for a moment when the shot was fired from in front of them. It went over their heads. They made a left turn and disappeared into the reeds. Filemon and Simeon saw the entire pride moments later, exiting from the reeds in the distance and racing towards the game reserve.

I addressed the meeting at Sangwali. A crowd had gathered under a giant sausage tree. Several indunas were present, as well as members of Nature Conservation.

"The problem is simple, but not so the solution. For years the lions have been hunting cattle on the flood plains of the Kwando River. The lions cross the river from Botswana and the Western Caprivi. They find a safe haven in the Mudumu and Mamili game reserves. If we succeed in getting rid of these lions, other lions will take their place.

"During our short stay in the Eastern Caprivi the lions have caught eleven head of cattle. Sometimes two or three in a single night, and the unhappiness is understandable. In the time that the men of Kaokoland and I have been here we have, however, seen many things that compound the lion problem. Most of the cattle that were killed were in the veld outside the kraal at night. The kraals themselves are of poor quality and offer little protection. There are enough trees in the Caprivi to build proper kraals that will withstand the lions. Furthermore, the laws of the land are ignored and large herds of cattle graze inside a proclaimed national reserve. It is a certain way of tempting lions to hunt cattle. There is also a distinct lack of cooperation between the community and the Nature Conservation authorities. To such a degree that it borders on open animosity. Neither group is prepared to give in.

"To me and my colleagues from Kaokoland the problem and its solution don't really centre around how many lions there are and how many cattle are killed. The problem and its solution centre around the attitude of the community. There is a reluctance in the community. I propose that you mobilise your young men and work out your lion problem yourselves.

"Now you'll have to excuse us. The Hereros want to get home. Their wives and children and cattle are waiting. I want to drop them off and go to Swakopmund for a few days, where I'll visit the night clubs and bars and all the places where young people hang out at night. Perhaps she'll be there. The girl who has been evading me for more than ten years, because I've been too busy walking through the bush in search of elephants and lions."

A dog without a master is a dead dog

It's true what people say about dogs: he was my best friend. He chose me, and I deserted him.

All he wanted to do was explore the desert with me. It was he and I in the veld. He followed me like a shadow. His only desire was to be close to me. To please me. He thought it his duty to hunt buck for me. He was young and failed time and again. I tried to thrash it out of him.

My cousin, who understood dogs better than I did, explained the whole thing to me later. I had never realised it. She explained it like this.

"It was what he was bred for. It was in his blood. He had to find meat for you. If he came back to you without a springbok or an ostrich after a hunting attempt and you thrashed him, he was just going to try harder next time. He thought you were punishing him because he hadn't caught anything."

By the time my cousin explained it to me, it no longer mattered.

I was a game ranger. My dog wasn't allowed to hunt. I had shot many Himba dogs for killing springbok. In my short-sightedness I thought I could thrash the hunting instinct out of him. I knew I'd have to shoot him the day he caught something.

At Okongwefontein there was a black rhino cow that the rangers at Purros had named after him. It was the first black rhino he had ever seen. He just couldn't control himself. With a whining bark he jumped out from behind the milk bush beside me and went after the rhino.

When she became aware of the black beast charging at

her, she sped off, panic-stricken. He stayed on her heels until she gained momentum and disappeared into the ridges. He returned with his head down, cringing.

One night he chased a leopard from the camp at Omatjingumafontein. We had bought a goat from the Himbas and slaughtered it. We'd hung the carcass in a mopane tree beyond the dry stream bed and the leopard must have smelled the meat. When its raspy growl came from the mountainside above the camp, Baloo charged without hesitation, barking, into the night. I thought: Goodbye, Baloo.

A while later he came creeping back. He must have found it strange to be praised this time instead of thrashed.

When we arrived at a Himba kraal, he never looked for a fight. Head held low, he would brush against my legs, while four or five Himba dogs circled him, growling. Until one got up the courage to tackle him. Then he would explode.

With a bark like that of a baboon he would throw himself upon the nearest dog, grabbing it by the scruff of its neck and flinging it aside. Like a black demon, he'd fly in among the other dogs and seize them one after the other. Until they made off in every direction, howling and bleeding.

Soon he had a reputation among the Himba and Herero. If he ever had sons, I should bring them one, they said.

The day came that he made his first catch. I was shattered. He had cornered a kudu heifer after a long chase through the mopane bush. Held her by the throat. Not killed her, just held on. It was his big moment. He stood holding the kudu by the throat, waiting for me to join him. To see what he had caught for me.

I kicked him away from the petrified animal. The kudu was so shocked that she just lay there. I had to keep the dog away from her until she had trotted off, shaken and dazed.

I held the barrel of my revolver to the dog's head, my thumb on the hammer. He blinked his soft brown eyes. Expectantly. I released the hammer, pushed the revolver back into the holster and walked away. We were alone in the veld. No one needed to know about this.

Baloo jumped up and joined me, asking, "Must I catch you something bigger? What? Just tell me. I'll do it for you. What am I doing that's not right? I'll do better next time."

Then I left the Kaokoveld. My employers and I were no longer seeing eye to eye and I found another job in Botswana. I would be driving Oom Eben Els's safari trucks through the Kalahari. The dog couldn't go along. Dogs aren't allowed in game reserves.

Gert van der Linde would look after Baloo. Gert loved him and he loved Gert. The day my bakkie drove away from Gert's camp, I didn't look back. Gert was holding Baloo. I could feel the dog's questioning brown eyes burning into the back of my head.

Baloo went to call on the mongrels at Kowareb. There was a bitch on heat. It must have been there that he picked up the rabies.

The Damaras came to report to Gert: The dog was running around in the mountains at night. They had seen him in the moonlight, etched against the calcrete ridges. Barking and whining at the same time. Howling for the moon.

Gert went looking for him. With his kierie and police boots and his large frame he climbed the slopes. When he reached the place that the Damaras had pointed out, two black vultures flew up.

171

Ecotone

I was back at the Ombonde. Gerhard Thirion and Thys Cronje were with me. A year had passed since we were last here with clients. Safaris on the Skeleton Coast and in the Western Kaokoveld didn't leave me much time to revisit my old stamping grounds.

This time Horace had been unable to come. I had been summoned from the northwest to lead the safari here because I was familiar with the place and the people.

Gerhard and Thys began to set up camp. They made certain the clients were happily settled in canvas chairs in the shade of the ana trees. Beer in hand. They knew I was going to break away for a while.

We had come from the Ongava tented camp through the western part of the Etosha that morning. The clients had been impressed with the eland and black rhino we had seen. We had exited at Galton gate. From there we had travelled along the Hobatere fence to the Kamdesha veterinary gate. There we had left all fences and gates behind.

In the dry bed of the Otjovasandu the loose sand had begun to suck at the wheels and I had had to step on it to pull the trailer through. We had seen large herds of springbok, gemsbok and two giraffes. At the confluence of the Otjovasandu and the Ombonde we stopped to set up camp under the ana trees.

The game path led up the bank, through the riverine mopane and camel thorn, to the mopane thickets at the foot of the rise. Dry bushman grass stood bright yellow. In the late afternoon sun the young mopane leaves shimmered in the breeze. Soon the well-known Ombonde feeling was back in my heart.

I saw the gemsbok in the shade of the mopane thicket ahead of me. Through my binoculars I counted eleven. I wasn't going to disturb them. I left the game path and ducked through the mopane bushes, giving the gemsbok a wide berth.

After a while I came across a pair of steenbuck nibbling at the bushes, completely at ease. The sun gave their coats a golden sheen. The little ram looked up and stared at me for a while. Then he lowered his head and carried on browsing.

I crouched when I saw the elephants. I knew these two old bulls with the broken tusks. In the past seven years I had met them regularly on the river banks. I left the trampled game path. It was their path. I watched them from the bushes. In the river bed the grey hornbill gave its whistling call from the leafy canopy of the ana trees. I drank in the scene.

I had tried hard to convince my employers to become involved here. To build a bush camp or something similar. They had not been keen. It was a marginal area, my boss had said. We already had two camps beside the Etosha pans and three camps in the dunes of the Namib, as well as the camp in Damaraland and my camp at the Skeleton Coast in the Kaokoveld. This place was neither bush nor desert.

It was true. My boss was right. This was a transition area between bushveld and desert. In scientific terms it is known as an ecotone. The area between two ecosystems. Betwixt and between. That was why no one had wanted to get involved here. Until now.

But that was exactly the fascination the place held for me. It was a modest wilderness. A migration route for the small population of elephant. Thanks to good rains and effective conservation efforts, in which I had played a role, there was a growing population of giraffe and eland here. Large kudu bulls inhabited the surrounding ridges. A few years ago a black rhino had walked in from the south, stayed for a few days and gone back again. From time to time lions came from Otjovasandu, but the Hereros shot at them.

It was I, in my capacity as nature conservationist, who

had convinced the local population of the importance of this place. Effective conservation could be to their advantage. It had been my secret dream to establish a bush camp here one day for the sake of conservation and for the benefit the safari industry could bring to the community. I had even identified the place where I would build my tented camp. At a bend in the river, hidden among mopane trees on the bank.

Now everything was going to change. And it was my fault.

For a while I kept watching the elephants. Then I left them behind. Under a camel thorn on the bank I found leopard droppings. I walked back to camp in the last rays of the setting sun.

Back at camp, my old friend Filemon Kapi and the game rangers had arrived. They were driving two brand-new Toyota Hilux bakkies. Under his uniform Filemon's stomach had expanded. We greeted each other like the friends we were, though the heartiness was slightly strained. We hadn't seen each other for a long time and things had changed.

"I see you're driving a bakkie nowadays," I said, and Filemon laughed. "It's time we did a few foot patrols, like in the old days."

Early the next morning, before we left for a tour of the conservation area, Filemon led us up the ridge. The granite mound dominates the landscape and from above you have a beautiful view of the confluence of the Otjovasandu and the Ombonde.

"Soon we are going to build a rest camp here," Filemon said.

I said nothing. How could I oppose him? I had started it, after all. But I knew: A rest camp *here* would destroy this unique location. The knowledge weighed heavily on my mind.

When it became clear that my employer had no interest in this area, Filemon was approached by another group. This group had close ties with the Swapo government. It was a group with plenty of foreign money. They were planning an ambitious project at the Ombonde. They currently faced two charges of corruption.

We left on our tour. The river bank where I had come across the elephant bulls was deserted now. Further down-river we drove past the mopane thicket where I had dreamed of building my camp. Horace had agreed that it was a good place. We had both tried to convince Filemon and his group. A camp should be unobtrusive.

We left the river and drove over the Otokotorwa plain. We reached the foot of a granite range. Here we got out and climbed the ridge to the base of a hollow cliff.

I knew this place. Filemon and I had found shelter here one stormy night. Around us the rain had fallen in drifts, and lightning had streaked the sky and lit up the plains. Below us, at the foot of the hill, a herd of elephants had formed a laager. Fearful calves in the inner circle. Adults worried about the lightning and the proximity of men. It had been an unforgettable night in the wilderness.

The morning was bright and sunny. In the distance the plain ran out against the hazy mountains. Behind those mountains the desert began.

Filemon looked at me. "Nice place for a rest camp, don't you think?"

I made no reply. I knew it was my last time here.

Mountain zebra at Okondekafontein

They spotted me from a distance and I spotted them as they fanned out. My bakkie had been crawling up from the river valley and had reached the mouth of the basin. They shimmered golden, sliced in half by the short-legged bushman grass.

There were many of them and though I knew they were found here, at first I mistook them for gemsbok in the distance. But only for a moment. They are unique and won't allow themselves to be mistaken for anything else.

The approach of the bakkie blocked their only natural escape route. The only way out for any *other* creature.

A group of eight broke away to the north, to where the basin formed its widest curve. Behind them the tear streak of the fountain glistened on the cliff face.

Closer but still distant, on the eastern slope, a group of thirteen thundered past. For a few seconds they halted on a ledge. To regroup and spur each other on. Then they picked the nearest exit, a mere excuse for a path, and toiled up the heights. True to form. Around them the basalt cliffs were bleeding in the dying day.

It was the group of five, closest to me, that decided: Make or break. They came straight at the bakkie. Determined, with powerful necks.

I wasn't aware of the exact moment when I stopped and got out.

They clambered up the southern slope and faced the threat head-on. Fatalistic, defiant. They filed past the bakkie, outlined against the sun. The sounds of stones clattering against the rock face and hooves on basalt stone reverberated through the earth, through the soles of my feet, through my very being.

I perceived it all with crystal clarity. The clattering rocks. The day at its most beautiful in the throes of death.

On the slope they came to a halt. They gazed at me, as if to ask: What are you going to do?

And I knew: Even if I left this place, I would never leave.

Rainy season

Rain makes me uneasy. I'm not a Free State mealie farmer or a Lowveld fruit farmer. I live in the Namib, the oldest and driest desert. Here organisms have adapted over millennia to make do with a minimum of moisture. We don't need rain.

In wilderness areas with a higher rainfall, where I have lived and worked before, the rainy season brings a lot of things. Game migrating and scattering so that you can't find them anywhere. Undergrowth so thick that it restricts your view. Gnats, flies and mosquitoes. Bakkies getting hopelessly stuck in swampy ground. Tick fever and malaria. I was struck down twice by malaria in the Kruger National Park, once in Zambia and once in the Caprivi. Malaria is no fun.

In the desert the rainy season is a nuisance. Short, but a nuisance. No one in the desert is prepared for rain. In the Kaokoveld we revel in ten and a half months of beautiful, sunny, rainless days. In January we start watching the eastern horizon as the anvil-shaped clouds build up in the distance. At night lightning flickers behind the mountains and thunder rumbles dimly.

The Hoarusib usually comes down in flood before the rains reach us. It is a large river and its catchment area is in the north-eastern highlands. Once it starts to flow, we are cut off from the outside world and our movements are restricted.

The river is a long, linear oasis with tall riverine trees, like ana, camel thorn, leadwood and dense groves of makalani palm. In the dry season it supports a healthy and growing elephant population. If you drive downriver between Epako and Leylands Drift, you can see elephants almost right

178

through the year. During the rainy season it is wise to stay away from the Hoarusib.

The Khumib, where we had our camp, is a small river. It has a small catchment area in a region with a low rainfall. Last year there was a trickle of water in the Khumib on four occasions. This year it came down strongly six times during the first two weeks of March. When the Khumib comes down, you know: it's raining in the desert.

During this time I had to fetch staff from Sesfontein. It meant I had to cross the Hoarusib in flood. It meant I was looking for trouble. Every year the river claims vehicles. I'll never forget Meintjies's crumpled bakkie and the two broken bodies we took out of the Hoanib in 1998. When it rains in the Kaokoveld, I don't sleep well.

I left the camp on the Khumib in the morning and reached the Hoarusib River at Purros, sixty kilometres further. The Hoarusib had subsided considerably and we found a place north of Purros where the main stream branched into three smaller feeders. Phineas, Filipus and I waded through each of these cautiously. Then I drove through from one island to the next. The first hurdle was behind us. The heat was oppressive. Above the ridges to the east clouds were gathering. Dark and sultry.

The Gomatum, another tributary, flows down a valley that one has to pass through on the way to Sesfontein. The Gomatum had already come down and in places the road was washed away. We struggled through the kloof and reached the wider valley on the way to Tomakas. The veld was dotted with puddles of water. Clouds were lowering ahead.

On the Giribes plain we drove into the first heavy rains. We also had our first flat tyre. The rainy season has never been a joke to me.

Another flat tyre later we reached Sesfontein. Wet and miserable. It was Saturday afternoon. To find anyone to repair a wheel at that hour was difficult. Everyone was on the stoep of Efraim's cuca shop, half drunk. Phineas and Filipus quickly made their way there. Filipus had come along for the ride – something for which I would later be thankful.

At last Petrus Ganuseb's sons agreed to repair the tyres for me, while I went in search of Fly and Samora. They were to return with us.

We set out on the return journey of 160 kilometres under a cloudy sky. It was after three o'clock and I was eager to cross the Hoarusib before dark. Filipus had found it difficult to tear himself away from the cuca shop. He had enjoyed more than a few drinks.

Soon it began to drizzle. The rocky ridges with their stunted mopane growth slowed us down. We crossed the Ganamub and the terrain evened out. Sheets of water lay on the Giribes plain. At Tomaka the rain caught up with us again. It had rained heavily in the catchment area of the Gomatum and I knew the river was going to trap us somewhere ahead.

We arrived at the kloof in the Gomatum at the same time as the rain. Where I had crossed the river earlier through a washed-away but dry river bed, I was now confronted by a churning mass of floodwater. At the far side of the kloof the setting sun appeared through a rift in the clouds.

Now I was in a hurry. Filipus was still drunk and Fly and Samora were in a festive mood. Unconcerned, they gazed at the churning water. In the fading light I took note of the muddy tyre tracks on the opposite bank. I aimed the nose in that direction, put the bakkie in gear and stepped on the accelerator.

The old double cab Toyota bakkie was our workhorse at camp. I used it for driving to Sesfontein to spare the more temperamental Land Rovers.

The bakkie was making headway. Halfway through, we reached a sandbank, where the water was shallower. I saw my chance and put my foot down.

On the other side of the sandbank the nose plunged deeper into the water, pushing up a large bow wave. Water washed over the hood and I kept my foot down.

We reached the opposite side. The water had hollowed out the bank and the front wheels disappeared into an underwater gully. It broke our speed. The front wheels bounced out of the gully and the nose jumped up the bank. But the momentum was lost and the front wheels sank into the soft, sandy bank.

We came to a halt. The back of the bakkie was completely submerged, and the rear wheels were stuck in the mud. The front wheels had ploughed into the muddy bank and the vehicle lay buried up to its diff. The sun had just gone down and under the overcast sky it was growing dark rapidly.

A feeling of helplessness overwhelmed me. Desperately I changed to donkey gear and tried to drive us up the bank. I only succeeded in digging us in more deeply.

I knew it was still raining behind us and that the water would get stronger. I groaned despondently and lowered my head onto the steering wheel. It was at times like these that I wondered what on earth I was doing in this godforsaken desert.

It was Filipus who rallied first. He jumped from the back of the bakkie, landing in waist-high water. He retrieved the spade from the half soaked load on the back. The beer had suddenly changed into fuel.

"Men, we have to dig. This water is going to take our bakkie."

He went into action, dived deep into the cold water and began to dig out the diff. I left the engine to idle and got out. Around us night was falling.

Phineas, Fly and Samora also ventured into the water and started to dig. I took off my shirt and sank down in the cold rainwater, my arm underneath the bakkie. The drive shaft and axles lay deeply embedded in the wet, sandy gravel. I laughed wryly and began to dig. Around the vehicle the men were doing the same. Filipus was urging them on as he worked with the spade. I could feel the current tugging more strongly at the rear of the bakkie.

Filipus was pleased with our progress. "Come, let's push it out now. We'll have to push it back. Back to the sandbank. It's the only way."

The idea sounded totally absurd. Going back through the floodwater in reverse was looking for trouble.

"No, let's try going forward first," I protested. Filipus let me have my way.

I got in behind the wheel and the men took up their positions behind the bakkie. I gave a signal. They pushed and I put my foot down, with the bakkie in donkey gear. All our efforts were undone as the vehicle settled back into the soft mud.

"Let's dig again, men," Filipus said stoically. He was a Damara, born in these parts. He had dug out many vehicles.

Again we lowered ourselves into the dark, cold water and began to dig. It took a long time, but after a while it seemed as if the force of the water was diminishing. I stopped and waded through the water. Yes, indeed. The sandbank in the middle of the river was visible now. Still, there was no time to waste. The Gomatum could come down again at any moment.

Filipus had convinced me of the wisdom of his plan. We freed the axles and diff from the mud. This time the men stood in front of the bakkie. We were going to push it back through the water to the sandbank in the middle of the river.

The men leaned against the bullbar and I put the vehicle in reverse. Amid a chorus of grunts and groans I let out the clutch slowly, not allowing the wheels to roll. Miraculously, like a cork from a bottle, the bakkie shot free of the bank.

I ploughed through the water and up onto the sandbank. I stopped and felt the compact sand slowly giving way under the weight of the vehicle. Filipus was still filling up the tracks in the bank with the spade, but I shouted to him that I couldn't wait. I slammed the gear lever into first and stepped on the accelerator.

I charged through the water, heading for the river bank.

With a painful crunch the front wheels made contact with the slope and I almost ground to a halt. Then the bakkie bounced up the bank and out of the river. I kept my foot flat until I was certain that I was on firm ground. The men gave a rousing cheer.

We resumed our journey, but our suffering was far from over. Ahead of us the river had washed away the entire road. We were forced to drive through fast-flowing water. I did not feel at ease. It was pitch-dark. I knew more floodwater was bearing down on us from somewhere behind.

Slowly, painfully slowly, the bakkie laboured through the water and across the stones. I took my bearings from the sandbanks looming in the headlights. At the mouth of the kloof I found a place where we could get away from the river. I was getting too old for this type of adventure.

At Purros the Hoarusib was low but the men convinced me it would be better to stay the night.

"At-ta-ta. The Hoarusib at night is a different story," said Samora.

I knew he was right. I was tired. Everyone was tired. We spent the night at Purros.

The settlement of Purros lies near the confluence of the Gomatum and the Hoarusib. I lay beside Phineas's hut in my wet bedroll, mosquitoes buzzing around me. In the small hours I was awakened by the rushing noise of the Gomatum coming down in flood.

At dawn I inspected the Hoarusib and saw it had risen during the night. We were forced to wait for four hours after sunrise before the river subsided sufficiently for us to go through.

Tired, hungry and wet we arrived at camp. The next day was the beginning of my last safari before I would go on leave.

My clients were two photographers of a well-known geographical magazine. The Frenchman was pleasant, but the American was demanding. I'd been on safari non-stop for almost four months and I was fed up. Moreover, it was the rainy season.

The photographers wanted shots of the Himbas. The only route to Kamathitu's kraal was up the Khumib River. Day after day we were forced to postpone the excursion, because the river was in flood.

By the third afternoon the Khumib had gone down. We loaded our camping equipment and drove along the muddy river bed. I introduced the photographers to the Himbas at Otivaurua. Kamathitu welcomed them. I left them in the kraal to take their late afternoon photographs while I got the fire started and pitched camp.

That night the weather was kind and it didn't rain. The mosquitoes were a nuisance.

The next day we were back at camp in time. I packed my bag in record time. The plane landed on the runway and took me away to Swakop for a fortnight's leave. I was delighted to have survived another rainy season.

Why did I always allow myself to be talked into something?

After four months on safari, all I had wanted to do was party late and sleep late. Now, after a mere five days in Swakop, I was going camping again.

Ilse and Jojo managed a wilderness school for local children at the Ugab River. Ilse's husband, Paul, a good friend of mine, was out on safari. There was no one to help the two girls. Would I please go along to act as guide and helping hand? Certainly. No problem.

We took the coastal road out of Swakop, heading north past Henties. Before Mile 108 we turned off on the gravel road to Uis. In the distance I saw that it was raining in the Brandberg. My heart sank into my boots.

"Tonight the Ugab will be coming down," I told the girls. They didn't believe me.

It was almost dark when the Ugab overflowed its banks. Waist-high in water, Jojo and I walked back and forth, carrying trunks and camping equipment to higher ground. Ilse was struggling to keep the little band of children together. God. I hoped this would be the end of it.

Back at Swakop I felt unwell. I ignored the feeling. It couldn't be. On the third day I was racked by fever. Must be something I ate.

A friend dragged me, protesting, to the doctor. There was blood in my urine. The doctor confirmed my fears and hospitalised me. It was malaria.

The rainy season had won again.

Gemsbok near Ogamsfontein

I found him just south of Ogamsfontein, among the granite hills. From a distance he appeared to be injured. He allowed me to approach. I lifted the binoculars and studied him.

Until very recently, perhaps even yesterday, he had been in his prime. Now he stood forlornly at the foot of a hill, staring out over the desert plain that ran out hazily against the Etendekas.

The tip of one horn was broken off and the keratin was splintered and fibrous. The other bull's rapier horns had gouged deep gashes into his muscular back. There was a gaping wound above his shoulder, where his opponent's horns had found their mark.

He stood with his face away from the sun as I tried to establish through the binoculars whether his eyes had been injured. The side of his face was swollen and there were visible scars across the white and black pattern of his nose and forehead. Tears streaked down his face as he raised his head and looked at me.

What a battle it must have been! A clash of two champions, where only one could be victorious. Had he been the dominant bull that had been forced to yield to the challenger? Or had he been the upstart, too light for the older bull?

I tried to imagine the pounding hooves sending dust and dirt flying. Saw them in my mind's eye, lunging with lowered heads, striking and dodging, striking and dodging. Watching for a chink in the other's armour. Then the crunch as the horns locked and they leaned in with all their might. Searching for a sign of weakness. Who would give in first?

It seemed to have been a lengthy fight. Lasting through the night, perhaps. Judging from his scars, he hadn't just broken away and fled after the first contact. No. In this battle there had been resolve. Or obstinacy. I wondered about the condition of the other bull.

For a while he kept staring in my direction. Then a visible change came over him. He looked away and walked purposefully to where a dollarbush grew among the stones. He began to rake deep furrows in the ground with his hooves. He sank down on his knees and crushed the succulent shrub to a pulp with his forehead. He mashed the plant into the ground. Fat round leaves and plant sap stuck to the base of his horns and his face. The glands between his horns and in his cloven hooves left his scent on the churned-up ground and the crushed dollarbush.

A message. A challenge to any contender. Come if you dare. Then he got up and walked into the ridges without looking back.

Ozohavera

Kamathitu and I had been walking the road together for more than seven years. It had been a good road. We addressed each other as "omukwetu" – it is Otjihimba for "comrade". He was with me when I saw giraffes in the Khumib River for the first time. It was he who took me to Okondekafontein high in the Entendekas, where the zebras drink.

His first wife was Kavitikitorwa, sister of Kauroorua the drifter. She had been missing for a long time. I hadn't seen her here at Otjivaurua since my return from Botswana two years earlier.

Kamathitu's second wife was Ozohavera. A beautiful woman with an infectious laugh. She pulled her weight in the household and took on the role of first wife in Kavitikitorwa's absence. Kamathitu and Kavitikitorwa's eldest daughter, Kuangara, was her friend.

Kavitikitorwa's absence did not surprise me. She and her brother Kauroorua were Tjimbas from the Kunene River. The Tjimbas are known to be wanderers. Kauroorua sometimes went across the river, into Angola, and disappeared for months. Once he came back with an AK over his shoulder that he tried to sell in Opuwo.

The Tjimbas were the first inhabitants of Kaoko. Traditionally they were hunter-gatherers. Their origin is unknown. When the Himbas and the Hereros came here with their cattle in the fourteenth century, they found the Tjimbas here. One only had to look at Kauroorua. He didn't look like a Himba. Himbas and Hereros are tall people with Nilotic or even Semitic features. Kauroorua was short and sturdy, like a pygmy from Central Africa, with an open face and lively eyes.

Traditionally Tjimbas did not own cattle. It made the Himbas and Hereros look down on them. During an expedition in the Otjihipas in the 1960s, Ben van Zyl came across a group of Tjimbas who were still making use of stone implements.

Through the years the Tjimba girls were quickly snatched up by the Himba youths, and soon the distinction between Tjimba and Himba was very vague. Today, referring to someone as Tjimba is considered an insult. Everyone is Himba today. But the free spirit of the Tjimba still flowed strongly in Kauroorua and Kavitikitorwa's veins.

When I stopped at Otjivaurua one morning, Kamathitu greeted me with a sombre expression. We squatted in the shade of his kraal.

"Omukwetu," he began, "I have to go away for a while. To Otjinungwa. I don't know how long I'll be gone."

"Is something wrong?"

"I got a message from Wapenga in Onjuva. My wife Kavitikitorwa has moved in with another man. I must go and fetch her."

"I understand, Kamathitu."

"Ozohavera and Kuangara will stay here with the children and see that all goes well."

I gazed after him as he rode north on his sturdy white stallion. It is a two hundred kilometre journey up the Khumib, past Onjuwa, into the Marienfluss, to reach Otjinungwa on the banks of the Kunene River.

In the following weeks Ozohavera kept things running smoothly. She understood that my clients found the Himba lifestyle interesting. When the Land Rover stopped at Otjivaurua on the Khumib River with a tour group, she and Kuangara would be watering the cattle at the wells.

Lean muscles were chiselled on their backs and arms as they bent down to draw water from the well and pour it into the trough. The well was one and a half metres deep and surrounded by a stockade. There was one opening in the kraal and inside there was a wooden trough, carved from the trunk of a makalani palm.

Either Ozohavera or Kuangara would stand in the well, knee-deep in the water. The boys would herd the cattle, which were frantic to get to the water. Skilfully they'd manoeuvre four head of cattle through the entrance of the kraal. The trough was filled and the cattle drank. As soon as Ozohavera decided that their thirst had been slaked, she would strike them on the nose with a stick. The boys would chase them out and let in the next four.

"A lesson in water conservation," I explained to my wealthy clients, standing around the well.

Back at the kraal, Ozohavera would crush ochre rocks to powder, while Kuangara blended the powder with butter fat. They smeared the red mixture on their bodies, their legs, faces and hair until they gleamed with a red sheen. Now they were beautiful. The colour of cattle.

Ozohavera would exhibit her wares. Milk urns carved from the soft wood of a corkwood tree, baskets woven out of palm leaf, bead necklaces made from the shell of an ostrich egg. Everything painstakingly handcrafted. She was eager to please. She enchanted my clients with her laughter and clapped her hands delightedly when they handed her money after a transaction.

A cash economy had been introduced to the Himbas only during the bush war. Many Himba men had joined the South African forces and brought home their pay. The local South African Defence Force shopping facility at Opuwo had been filled with the wonders of Western civilisation. Today, with the influx of tourists to Kaoko, cash was easy to obtain.

At an appointed time I would collect Ozohavera and her family and drive the 160 kilometres to Sesfontein. There they would buy blankets, pots, knives, tobacco, salt, sugar and gin with the money they had made out of my clients. Kamathitu had already used some of the money to enlarge his herd.

When the time approached for Kamathitu to return, Ozohavera gradually became quieter. I understood her position. Who had kept the household going the entire time that Kavitikitorwa had been away?

And then one morning Kavitikitorwa was back. Dressed up and pretty, she sat in front of her hut, which had been closed up for a long time. She smiled complacently when she saw me. On my arrival I had seen Kamathitu's stallion in the yard.

Kauroorua was also there, this time without an AK. We greeted each other warmly. We hadn't seen each other for a long time. He was wearing the ondumbo headdress of a married man.

Kamathitu appeared in the entrance of Kavitikitorwa's hut. He laughed self-consciously as he greeted me.

"What happened to you, omukwetu?"

"A wasp, man."

I took antihistamine ointment from my medical bag and applied it to the eye that was swollen shut. I took my leave.

At the Khumib River, at the wells under the mopane, Ozohavera was waiting for me. I could see she was upset. She asked for medicine for her swollen hand. Where a wasp had stung her.

Magic safari

From the word go things had gone well on this safari. It usually depended on the clients. A British honeymoon couple, an Italian fashion designer and his much younger wife from Milan. An American travel agent.

With the British, you had to watch your step. Test them first. They're unpredictable. Keep them where you can see them. They can sometimes be your best clients, but they're the most erratic.

"I come from a family with a proud history of shooting Englishmen," I once said to a British client, tongue in cheek. My remark was reported and became the subject of discussion at a council meeting.

Fortunately my managing director, an English-speaking South African, was a man with a sense of humour. Apparently he exclaimed: "That's the kind of man I want for the Skeleton Coast."

Italians from the north are known for the generous tips they leave. They usually come from Turino, Parma, Milano or Bologna. Moreover, they are wonderful people. They show sincere appreciation for everything you show them and do for them.

Americans who take the trouble to come and explore the Skeleton Coast are some of the best clients you can ever hope to meet.

The British honeymoon couple were carefree and in love. He was an economist and she an attorney. Young and successful. The Italian, his beautiful wife and I clicked immediately. (Neither was I blind to the way she was looking at me.) The American travel agent had been all over Africa. He knew the industry and helped to make things easier. We became instant friends.

August is a rough month in the safari industry. There is very little respite. It was the end of August and I was having a tough time. As a plane landed to fetch the one group of clients, the next group would get off the same plane.

On the first afternoon we drove to the coast, where Mathias Koraseb died a hero's death and lies buried among the driftwood on the beach. It was 45 kilometres from our camp, past Sarusasfontein, through the roaring dunes.

The ice was broken when I led my clients up a dune and let them slide down slowly. Deep out of the belly of the dune rose the voice of the earth during its creation. At the foot of the dune my clients got up, breathless and amazed. The Namib had sung them its welcoming song.

We cruised through low dunes covered with ganna bush. From behind one of these a brown hyena jumped up and raced across the salt pan. I stopped and we watched him until he grew small on the horizon. To the west the cold ocean roared.

I stopped the Land Rover on the beach and we paid tribute to the brave Mathias Koraseb. Through the waves we saw the remains of his Walvis Bay tugboat that was wrecked here in 1942 when he had rushed to the aid of another boat. I placed a pebble on his grave. The safari had begun.

When the sun broke through the fog the next morning, we came across a herd of giraffe in the Khumib, upriver from our camp. Tourists from abroad who have travelled extensively in Africa are always pleasantly surprised to find giraffe in this stark landscape.

This herd was extraordinarily productive. In the past three years five calves had been born, the latest arrival only two months old. They were outlined against the red quartzite ridges in the morning sun. We stayed for half an hour and unique photos were taken. The bond grew stronger.

At Otjivaurua the Himbas welcomed us warmly, as usual. No matter how I tried to play down a visit to the Himbas, the clients were always amazed by what they saw. The sophisticated traveller from Piemonte or Massachusetts stepped into another world as soon as he got out of the Land Rover at Otjivaurua.

When we left an hour later, it was with exclamations like "magnifico", "stupendo" and "fucking fantastic". Then there was a long silence in the vehicle.

We crossed the Etendekas, passed Ohorondanomanga peak, and ate lunch under an ana tree at Epako. Now began our search for the elephants.

At Okanguma the Himba children came running from the cattle post. They pointed excitedly at the tamarisks downstream: "Ozondjou, ozondjou!"

I gave them the fruit left over from our lunch, and the Italian woman caught my eye.

We found them in the thickets: the tuskless cow with her tuskless daughter and the bull calf with the good ivory. The large bull, the second largest ivory bearer of the Hoarusib, was also there, and was showing interest in the toothless daughter. The mother felt it was a family matter and charged after the Land Rover as we drove away.

We found the cow with the crooked tusk, her calf and three young bulls at Okongombe Thembe vlei, where they were drinking in the company of a herd of cattle. There were also springbok and ostriches. On the slope was the cattle post and I pointed out the children walking through the veld with their dogs. In the setting sun, the elephants passed close to the Land Rover, the cattle filling in the background. This is the real Africa, I told my clients.

We spent the next day exploring the desert and the coast. The Land Rover sailed over the rolling dunes. Once a barchan dune caught me off guard and I had to dig us out.

Springbok and gemsbok grazed all around us as we drove across the endless plains. I told my clients about the Strandloper hunters and we got out of the vehicle to view their round shelters. We drove on, across the salt pan, crossing Agaatberg to Cape Frio. At False Cape Frio we ate lunch.

The day was windless and the sun glittered on the waves. The guests were relaxing noticeably. The British couple took a long walk down the beach and the others sat on canvas chairs, staring at the ocean.

At Cape Frio we walked among the fur seals. Fifty thousand of them lay on the beach, waddling into the waves at our arrival. Jackal patrolled up and down the beach.

When we drove back that afternoon, I knew: the safari was a success. I was looking forward to my tip when the plane took off the next afternoon. Italians give generous tips. Americans too. With the British you can never be sure.

Back at camp, I found my friend and colleague Chris Greathead, who had flown in to help with the next safari. That night we sang and read poetry around the campfire. Across the flickering flames my eyes locked regularly with those of the Italian woman.

It was the last morning of the safari. I was a man with a mission. For a few weeks I had been tracking them. I had lost them every time just before they disappeared into the undergrowth. I knew where they were. Today I was going to find them.

Heavy fog lay across the desert as we headed south. It grew light as we began to descend into the Hoarusib valley. The broken desert landscape made for a magical atmosphere.

We drove down the dune mountain. Below us lay the Hoarusib poort. The sun lay in streaks across the tamarisk thickets, the dry watercourse and the sea of dunes on the southern bank. Something caught my eye. I stopped and got out. Raised the binoculars. And there they were.

We drove on, down into the valley. I drove slowly, for the diesel engine was noisy. Now we were close enough for the clients to see them too. The mist was disappearing in the scorching sun.

One of the males was still feeding on the gemsbok. The other two lay sated and bloody-mouthed in the river bed. Then I saw them for the first time: under the tamarisks on the bank two cubs lay next to their mother.

The last lion pride in this area was exterminated by the Himbas in 1989 for attacking their herds. Last year, for the first time in twelve years, lions ventured into this area again. Three young males and one female. They had apparently been driven out by the dominant animals of a Damaraland pride in the Aub and Barab valleys. They had walked for two hundred kilometres to reach the Hoarusib River. The first thing they'd done had been to kill Daniel Karotjaiva's stud bull.

The lions would learn quickly. They remained inside the Skeleton Coast Park and in the rainy season, when the gemsbok left the Hoarusib, carried out raids at Purros. Eight head of cattle had already bitten the dust. The Himbas grabbed their rifles and followed the tracks, but the lions always slipped back into the park in time. Somehow they knew they were safe here.

These were timid lions, however. They knew their lives were in danger. I had only seen them on two previous occasions and then I had been tracking them on foot, alone. Once I walked for ten kilometres to see them for only five seconds, as they disappeared up a ravine.

Festus had been lucky enough to see them twice in the company of clients. Chrisjan Liebies had seen them once, also with clients. I had begun to feel that I compared unfavourably with the other guides.

Four months ago, the female disappeared. Only the tracks of the three males lay in the bed of the Hoarusib. I had my suspicions. When the female's tracks reappeared, accompanied by two smaller sets, my suspicions were confirmed.

This morning I became the first person to see the cubs. Thrilled, I pointed them out to my clients. The Land Rover reached the bank and the lions scrambled to the safety of the thickets. I drove parallel with the bank. The lioness was confused and misjudged the denseness of the tamarisks. She led her cubs around a bush and came out in a clearing right beside the Land Rover. For a moment they stood frozen to the spot. The flustered female led a short charge up the bank. Growling, she kicked up sand before breaking away and leading her cubs into the thicket.

We drove into the river bed and found two males watching us from the tamarisks. They had beautiful pure blond manes. We watched them for the next half-hour. We caught another glimpse of the female and her cubs as they slipped away downriver.

The mood in the Land Rover was cheerful during the return trip. I could see the admiration in the Italian woman's eyes. It had been a successful safari. Hemingway spoke of "the unresponsibility of victory". How does one say that in any other language?

At the back of my mind I was speculating about the size of my tip. At least 300 US dollars from the Italians. 100 US dollars from the American, for sure. Perhaps about R300 from the British couple.

Back at camp the clients gave Greathead and Festus an excited account of our excursion. In two hours the plane would be there to fetch them and to bring the new clients.

I was exhausted. I wanted to lie down for an hour. It was my eighth safari in a row. I drove to my wooden hut beyond the ridge. I put Valiant Swart in the CD player and lay down on my bed. Content that another safari had gone well. All that remained was to bid the clients farewell. And then we would start all over again with new clients.

Half an hour later Greathead arrived in a flurry of noise. With him were the four Himba youngsters who kept the tents in order. Greathead shoved them into the hut and closed the door. Valiant was singing "Donkerpad".

"Money has disappeared from the clients' tents. A lot of money."

The four youths stared at me expressionlessly in the sudden darkness of the closed hut. I got up slowly. Three days' hard work down the drain.

"I want that money," I said calmly.

I studied them. There was Rateras, Daniel Karotjaiva's

son. I had known him for seven years. He was with me when I spotted my first black rhino in Kaokoland. Just the other day we followed a spoor on foot for eighteen kilometres. In a while he would be helping me during the hunting season. It wasn't him.

There was Alfons Hambo. Titus, his elder brother, had been my personal assistant for years. For months Alfons had begged me for this job. Not him either.

Samora. His father was a game ranger. It couldn't be him.

Ambrosius. It was him. He knew he was on borrowed time. A skollie from Sesfontein. Liked to pick a fight in the staff quarters, and we'd been suspecting for some time that he was stealing booze. But how could we prove it?

"I want that money, guys."

Greathead took the lead. "Meeting. I want everyone – all the staff members – at the staff quarters in five minutes. That plane will be here in an hour. Rateras, fetch Johannes Kasupi and tell everyone at camp. Ask Festus to keep the guests calm."

Everyone met in the staff kitchen. Chris Greathead spoke earnestly. He was at head office now, but he had got to know everyone here when we set up camp two and a half years ago. He and I had come a long way together. Fourteen years ago we were in the army together. After that, game rangers in the Lowveld. Now, after many years, colleagues again in the wilderness.

"The man who took the money didn't steal from the clients. He didn't steal from Chris and me either. He stole from you. When that plane lands in Windhoek, the company will compensate the clients for every cent that was stolen. The money will be taken from your annual increases and Christmas bonuses. That man has stolen from *you*."

Johannes Kasupi stepped forward. He was the old man of the group. He'd started to work here as a young man – under Karlowa, the first game ranger at the Skeleton Coast.

"Sir, let's settle this thing the Himba way. Let the diviner point out the guilty party."

I agreed immediately. "Filemon or Filipus, one of you, drive to Okongombe Themba immediately and fetch Tjihuri."

"There's no need, sir," Otto Kasaona spoke up. "Gideon here is a trained diviner. Both he and his sister. His mother taught them."

Tjihuri was a great female healer and diviner in this part of the Kaokoveld. Her son Gideon had a part-time job at camp. He washed dishes. I didn't know he was also a diviner.

We stood around the snooker table in the staff kitchen. Two ten rand notes were circulated and the men took turns holding them in their fists. Gideon sat on a chair. He took the crumpled notes and unfolded them. Stared at them intensely. His hand began to shake. Then his entire body. He closed his hands over the money, raised his arms over his head and uttered a short, shrill cry. Next to me, Greathead jumped in alarm.

Slowly Gideon opened his eyes. Now he was someone else. A dignified diviner with a direct line to the spirit world had taken the place of the submissive dishwasher.

He spoke in a language that wasn't Himba. Apparently only Johannes Kasupi understood. He acted as interpreter for the other Himbas. Otto Kasaona interpreted for Greathead and me.

The four suspects stood at the head of the snooker table. Gideon was seated opposite them. He spoke in a strange voice. He said: "Four men entered the tents. One by one. One swept. Another cleaned the bathroom. Another one put clean linen on the beds. The last one brought clean towels. That one stayed in each tent for a long time. He opened the guests' bags and searched through their clothes. He found their wallets and took their money. Not everything. He wanted to mislead them. Then he concealed the money. Somewhere. I can't see clearly where."

While he was speaking, I watched each suspect. Rateras, Alfons and Samora stood without expression. Ambrosius stood with a sneer on his face, his hands scornfully on his hips. As if he found the whole affair ridiculous.

Gideon looked straight at him. In the strange voice and language he pointed him out. Johannes Kasupi translated: Ambrosius. Unnecessarily Otto translated: Ambrosius.

Ambrosius grunted. "If it's me, Gideon, why can't you see where I hid the money? Show me where the money is."

Gideon answered in the strange language: "We'll have to send for Tjihuri. She'll find the money."

Filemon and Gideon left to fetch Tjihuri. I returned to my clients. I apologised. Explained that it had never happened before.

The Italian fashion designer assured me that his loss had not detracted from a wonderful safari. His wife was wearing a close-fitting woollen blouse without a bra. She had exquisite breasts. She, the American and the British couple assured me that it was nothing. I was grateful, but I couldn't shake off my disappointment.

The plane landed and we said our goodbyes on the landing strip. The new clients got out; there was work to be done. The Italian couple shook my hand and mounted the steps to the plane. The American followed.

The British couple looked almost embarrassed as they pressed something into my hand. "It's all we have left."

It was eight hundred rand.

That night Tjihuri found the stolen money behind the staff toilet.

Confluence

It was while I was climbing onto the roof of the Land Rover to untie the camping chairs that the feeling overwhelmed me. So intense that I felt a physical pain where my heart was. I continued to fumble with the knots while I leaned back against the jerry cans. Was *this* how love felt?

On the roof I was closer to the overhanging branches of the ana tree under which we had stopped. A gnarled branch drew my attention. Not a remarkable branch. Rough bark and knots and a bare patch where an elephant tusk had scraped off the bark. What was wrong with me?

Around us gemsbok and giraffe fled from the shade of the ana trees, out into the river bed. An elephant bull beat a retreat, while another took no notice of our arrival. Unperturbed, he carried on picking up pods with his trunk and stuffing them into his mouth.

We had left the Schlucht earlier and had just reached the Ombonde River when Thys's bakkie got stuck. The sand was too loose for the trailer. We unhooked and hitched up my Land Rover. Slowly the trailer had come out of the sand. The wheels of the Land Rover had found traction in the sandy tracks.

Horace and Gerhard had continued ahead. Their wheels would compact the sand. I would bring the trailer, while Thys would follow in his bakkie. I had to focus on keeping the trailer in the tracks and maintaining momentum, especially over the sandy ridges in the winding river bed.

It had been almost two years since I last drove up this river. I remembered a time when I had walked the entire length of the river.

It was late summer. Dry season. The orange mopane leaves fluttered from the trees on the river's edge and settled in the tracks. The ana pods hung in ripe clusters. The banks had been washed out steeply by last season's floods. The roots of trees were exposed. Here and there a mopane leaned steeply. Next season it would be driftwood.

The old feeling settled in my body. The only rivers I saw nowadays were the Khumib and the Hoarusib in the northwest. I had been away too long.

From the roof of the Land Rover my gaze followed the gemsbok and giraffes. They cantered up the bank and across the flood plain, disappearing behind the mopanes for a while. Then they reappeared on the slope. I counted fourteen giraffes. Lazily they browsed up the ridge.

I untied the camp chairs. As I worked, I thought of the girl who had been mine until recently. We met in the Fish River Canyon. It was a good place to meet. It was May and there was a lot of water.

For a year and a half we kept the relationship going. Every three or four months I went to Pretoria to see her. But the city was just as alien to me as when I had gone to school there. I still didn't feel at home. The nights I spent with her were good, but after a while I got bored with the parties. What did you say to people who had never been in the desert?

Last December she came on a visit to the Skeleton Coast. All very beautiful, but not much of a life, actually, she said. She had a good life in Pretoria. An important position, a good salary, a comfortable flat and a car.

For a while I enjoyed spending my leave at her flat. But one morning during my last visit I woke up beside her and told her I was going back to the desert. Our relationship was going nowhere. She cried.

Her photograph was still on the bedside table in my wooden house beside the Khumib on the Skeleton Coast.

Gerhard had taken the clients for a walk. Thys was making the fire. Horace and I sat in the shade on the camping chairs. We looked out over the confluence of the Ombonde and the Otjovasandu. The ana trees in the river bed might have been part of a landscaped garden. The stream bed was wide here, the trees tall. Six metres from the ground the leaf canopy began, cropped to precise dimensions by giraffe and elephant. The elephant bull had now moved further away to the shade of another tree.

Horace stuffed his pipe. The few days together in the veld had brought us closer again. Sometimes you forget how much you like someone. His health was deteriorating. Cancer of the lymph glands. Apart from the beard that was greyer and the purple spot on his cheek, he looked much the same to me. A weather-beaten old pioneer.

"This place changes a man, Horace. During my last leave in Pretoria I was impossible. Out of tune with everyone. You don't notice how much you have changed until you go back to civilisation."

Horace lit his pipe. Drew deeply.

"A woman doesn't want to know that you love anything more than you love her. That's why my wife left. You come here to find peace. Before long it drives you mad. Your freedom becomes your prison cell."

For a while we sat in silence. The elephant moved further away, in the direction of the Otjovasandu. He found some more pods and lingered in a patch of shade.

There was no place in Africa more enchanting than this confluence.

The Etendeka mountains

I feel at home in these mountains. I often come here, for a variety of reasons. They're not easy mountains. The loose torras underfoot have caused me to fall on my face. The afternoon heat can make the valleys seem like an oven in hell. Here you sweat and you bleed. They are hard mountains.

The early morning light and the late afternoon sun make these mountains beautiful. In the gorges there are hidden fountains with the sweetest water. The mountain takes a long time to befriend you. To make you his own.

The mountain makes you tough. He puts you through the mill. Hunting zebra here is one of the greatest challenges a hunter can take on. A mountain zebra is a child of the mountains. The mountains look after him. They don't let go of him easily. First the hunter is put to the test.

These mountains look after the rhino too. A poacher has to be very determined to go after rhino in these ravines. On the south side the same lavas have sheltered the precious rhino population for many years.

In summer the rhino leave the fountain in the valley and move up the slopes in search of the cool southwesterly breeze at the top. At great inconvenience to the game ranger on rhino patrol.

Yes, the mountain and I understand each other. He has seen me return time after time. Now he makes life easier for me. He shows me the zebra paths that point to the quickest route up the mountain. He teaches me to step between the stones and shows me where his fountains are hidden. He has accepted me.

He is a youngster himself. A mere 130 million years. Much younger than the granites and schists over which he erupted. When South America began to break away from Africa, the tectonic effect stretched the crust of the earth thin. Deep rifts appeared in the earth's crust and basalt lava flowed from them like blood. Like any young mountain, he is a proud mountain. A wild mountain.

Today I am back on the mountain. Not a single zebra is in sight on the slopes. Sweat burns my eyes and soaks my shirt. I walk as fast as my legs can carry me. I stopped jogging a kilometre back, when the slope became too steep.

Today I'm not sure whether I want to be on the mountain. Today is different because I don't know what I'll find on that final ledge just below the plateau. I still have a long way to climb. Up above, high above me, a column of smoke rises up and the remains of the burnt-out plane glint in the sun.

Two days ago two Cessna 2-10 aeroplanes brought the Italian clients. Festus and I drove from our camp at the Khumib to fetch them at Purros. There were eight of them. Four men and four women, four in each plane. Attractive, enthusiastic people from Bologna, on the last leg of their Namibian safari. Only one woman could speak decent English; two of the men could barely make themselves understood.

We showed them the elephants of the Hoarusib and the furry seals of Cape Frio. In the evenings around the fire they sat back in their canvas chairs, staring at the starry desert sky, and sighed, "Bellissimo." The two young pilots camped with us too.

At noon today we took them back to Purros where the two small aircraft were waiting on the deserted airstrip. While the pilots were completing the preflight procedures, Festus and I served them a cold lunch under a camel thorn. The day was warm and windless.

Farewells were said and handshakes exchanged. The clients went on board and then the pilots. One after the other the engines spluttered and roared into life.

A safari guide taking leave of clients is expected to stay at the landing strip until the planes are safely in the air. In these forsaken regions of Kaokoland it is especially appropriate. While the Cessnas were taxiing slowly to the other side of the airfield, Festus and I agreed that I would watch the take-off while he would take what had remained of the lunch to the Himbas at Purros.

On the other side of the airstrip the revolutions of the engines increased. Then the first one approached. The take-off run was long. The pilot used the entire runway. The wheels passed low overhead, the engines screaming in the thin air. The aircraft made a wide turn in the west and head-ed north. Destination: Epupa Falls. After taking painfully long to gain height, the plane slipped through a large gap between the Etendeka mountains and the lower quartzite hills.

Then came the other plane. It also struggled to gain height. It made a wide turn, and I lost sight of it. I got back into the Land Rover and switched it on.

As I drove down the bank of the Hoarusib River, I saw Festus's Land Rover in the broad, dry stream bed some dis-tance ahead. He drove up the northern bank and disap-peared from view. I followed him up the bank and took on the powdery dust of the flood plain.

Festus stopped at a Himba cattle post beside the road. I looked up at the Etendeka mountains diagonally ahead. High up, near the summit, I noticed a puff of black smoke, tiny in the distance.

I accelerated and pulled up next to Festus. I pointed it out to him and took the lead. Like maniacs we raced across the gravel plains to the foothills.

Almost as soon as we reached the rocky scree, I had a flat tyre. I grabbed the first-aid kit and water canteen and got in the Land Rover with Festus, who had stopped beside me just long enough. On the radio we contacted Ian back at camp.

The terrain was so rough now that the Land Rover was making very slow progress. "Festus, take the Land Rover as close to the cliff as you can. We're taking too long. I'll go faster on foot. Radio the camp."

I slung the medical kit over my shoulder, grabbed the canteen and tried to open the door. The handle was stuck. I lost my temper. "Fuck! Piece of British shit!"

I kicked the door so that the catch was flung far into the veld. I tumbled out and began to run up the slope, carrying the first aid bag and the canteen.

I had just returned after a week's leave, where I had feasted on beer and red meat, and I felt it in my body. My lungs were burning and I was panting and sweating. I was forced to slow down.

Now I am walking up the mountain, wondering what lies ahead. Charred bodies, perhaps. I look back. Below, Festus has stopped the Land Rover. He is following on foot.

A figure appears on the mountainside ahead of me. The pilot has taken off his shirt and the blood has dried around his nose. His body is pale, like that of a ghost. I give him the canteen. He drinks deeply.

"How many have survived?" I ask.

"Everyone. They're all up in the mountain." He drinks some more.

"Injuries?"

"The women are all right. The men can't come down by themselves. But they're OK too."

I point him in the direction of the vehicle, take the canteen and carry on.

I am tired and agitated. Someone calls my name from the cliff. I fall and nearly, damn nearly, break the canteen on a rock. I begin to climb.

I reach the women halfway up a gully. They fall upon me, sobbing.

"It's going to be fine," I comfort them. "Everything is going to be OK."

They point at the men high up on a ledge. Festus has caught up with me and he is consoling the women now. We climb up the cliff together and reach the men. One has a few gashes on his face and arms and an injured ankle. The other one is complaining of a sore back. We make them comfortable in the shade of a rock. Festus bandages the man's ankle and I treat the cuts on his face.

Then I tackle the final stretch to the wreckage. Apart from the wing and tail, everything has burned out completely. No personal belongings to save. How could anyone have survived this?

I return to Festus and the men. We proceed to hobble down the mountain. The women help where they can. Somewhere on the slope I dish out painkillers.

"Bellissimo," one of the men smiles at me, and I know he means it.

Lower down Ian MacCallum's rescue team reaches us. They have water and cool drinks and food. There are Damaras from the camp and Himbas from Purros. Their solicitousness touch the Italians anew.

The rescue team takes over and the clients are taken to the vehicles. Filemon and Elias tell me that they have already changed my tyre. Everyone is laughing now. The relief is enormous. A rescue plane circles overhead. It has just reached us from Windhoek.

I lag behind and wait until I am standing on the mountainside alone. Then I turn round to the mountain. The sun has just disappeared behind the tallest peak. Late in the afternoon these mountains are beautiful. Peace has settled over everything. For a while I gaze at the rugged cliffs.

"Thank you, mountain," I say.

Steppenwolf

The whole thing began when Leti and Karen came to visit.

"What can we bring along?"

"Six Duracell batteries and a bottle of Jack."

The batteries were for listening to music.

The desert grabbed them immediately. On that first windy, misty afternoon we headed into the dunes. The bakkie sailed across the sand to the accompaniment of "Riders of the Storm" by The Doors.

Just before they left, they presented me with a second bottle of Jack. Not just any old Jack. They made me promise to save it for a special occasion.

Not just any old Jack, indeed. Like that of the well-known Jack No. 7, the bottle was square, though shorter and squatter. The neck was longer, thicker and fluted. It had a wooden cork top. The label read: *Jack Daniel's Tennessee Whiskey Single Barrel No. 1.*

A booklet hanging from a string around the neck of the bottle told the story. Jimmy Bedford was Jack Daniel's master distiller in Lychburg. While the whiskey was aging in the barrels, only Jimmy was allowed to decide which barrel's whiskey was the best quality. Taste and character were the defining factors. In the end he selected the best barrel and the bottles were filled. Whiskey from other barrels was never mixed with it. Every bottle from this single barrel was marked with the number of the barrel and the date. The bottle that Leti and Karen had given me was number 2-0979, the date 5-15-02.

On the first night of a safari I never used to sing at the campfire. It was too soon. I would use the first evening to size up the clients. I would keep my distance and be formal and polite. In the course of the second day – after we had slid down a roaring dune, called on the Himbas, seen our first elephants and giraffes, and had to dig ourselves out of deep sand a few times – the clients began to become friends. The constraints disappeared as soon as the wilderness grabbed them. Then I would sing.

This group had been different from the start: a few colleagues from head office and their friends on a half-price safari. All young people. The only bona fide clients were a middle-aged couple from Hamburg. Early on the first afternoon the younger people began to make short work of the beers in the cooler at the back of the Land Rover. I wasn't sure how the Germans would react, but they took it in their stride.

When we stopped at the granite hills to admire the sunset, I could see in Wolfgang Hof's eyes that the desert was beginning to settle inside him. There was awe on his jovial face.

At camp there was no stopping my colleagues and friends. They wanted to party. From early evening their boisterous laughter echoed around the campfire. Wolfgang and his wife, Marita, were also there. They looked happy.

I decided to take the chance and kicked off with my favourite: "Hotel California" by the Eagles. The applause was overwhelming and the stage had been set.

A colleague launched into Golden Earring's "Radar Love" and where he got stuck, the others jumped in to help. Someone followed up with Creedence's "Bad Moon Rising" and everyone joined in the chorus. A girl fetched a guitar in her tent and strummed the chords of Deep Purple's "Smoke on the Water". The booze flowed freely. Wolfgang's face became more radiant and his smile broader.

Chrisjan Liebies, who knew only country 'n western, gave a faultless rendition of "The Devil Went Down to Georgia". When things began to quieten down, I picked up the pace with The Grateful Dead's "Friend of the Devil". A fellow from Johannesburg, dressed all in black, pitched in with Black Sabbath's "Paranoid".

Then it was Wolfgang's turn. Without hesitation, he sang the words in his heavy German accent:

Get your motor running
Head out on the highway
Looking for adventure
Or whatever comes our way.

When he came to:

Like a true native tribe
We were born, born to be wild

there was chaos around the fire. Everyone roared the climactic words in unison:

Born to be wiiild!

The middle-aged Wolfgang was applauded tumultuously and patted on the back. On the spot he was renamed Steppenwolf.

The next morning we explored the Hoarusib River. We found two male lions feeding on a gemsbok. We stopped at the clay castles and got out. With his stout figure, Steppenwolf was keen to clamber over rocks and climb up every cliff and hillside. Occasionally he would cause a rockfall, and I would warn: "Watch your steppen, Wolf."

At the Hoarusib mouth he dived into the cold Atlantic with Chrisjan Liebies and me. He took in the stark desert coastline around him. He was alive. Marita noticed, and relaxed along with him.

To Steppenwolf it became a hallowed experience. At sunset he would distance himself from the group and go off to appreciate it in silence. Later on he would join enthusiastically in the rock concert around the campfire.

Our travels through the desert rewarded us with encounters with mountain zebra and bat-eared fox. After a long search we found the elephants. But it was the overpowering landscape that touched Steppenwolf most deeply. The golden dunes creeping across the red basalt plains. The wide salt pans, once part of the sea, on which the figure of a man grew small.

As we stood on the rocks at Cape Frio looking at the thousands of Cape fur seals, Marita told me confidentially that it was Steppenwolf's birthday.

In a sandy spot at a quicksand fountain I got seriously stuck. We had to dig out the Land Rover and place sand plates under the wheels. Chrisjan Liebies's Land Rover was on firmer ground and he brought out the tow rope. Steppenwolf kept up with the younger men and dug and pushed vigorously. To him it was part of the adventure.

We made steady progress and an hour later we were free. Soaked with sweat and exhausted. Steppenwolf wiped his brow and commented drily: "Get your motor running."

Back at camp it was the last night of the safari. The group had become a close-knit unit. It was Steppenwolf's birthday. The occasion was right, Leti and Karen would have agreed. I went to my room and fetched the bottle of Jack Daniel's Single Barrel No. 1.

Tonight the people around the fire were quieter. They were tired and a bit sad about the safari being over. I sent the bottle round. In the glow of the fire the golden liquid was rich and smooth. It soothed the palate and went down smoothly. It settled snugly in the body. Not just any old Jack, after all.

Steppenwolf raised his glass. "I have been on safari everywhere: Kenya, Tanzania, Uganda, Botswana. Never have I experienced a safari like this one. The Skeleton Coast is the Jack Daniel's Single Barrel No. 1 of safaris."

The other day a parcel arrived for me in the mailbag. It was a heavy, rectangular box. I opened it and out came a short, squat bottle with a fluted neck, filled with golden liquid.

There was a note with it. It read: *Keep your motor running.*

Afrikaans must stop

"Afrikaans must stop." My boss spoke fervently. "It's against company policy."

I was once again in his office in Windhoek.

"Come on, Chris. They regard you as their leader."

I gave his statement some thought and found it ungrounded. In my opinion they merely regard me as eccentric. A one-armed, tousle-headed loner, apparently blissfully happy in a godforsaken wilderness. They were young. Their best years lay ahead. Sometimes I could see them wondering about me.

The serious note in my boss's voice got through to me. "I have sent two circulars to the northern camps – they just ignore me. Our clients are complaining. If you are within hearing distance of clients, you have to speak English, or else they'll feel excluded. English is the official language. The majority of our clients are English-speaking. Why won't you speak English? What's so difficult about it? I don't understand."

Driving back to camp in my bakkie across the plains and mountains of the Kaokoveld, I reflected on my boss's words. I agreed with him. My English-speaking clients, mainly American or British, were my bread and butter. They were the reason for my being here.

English is a universal language by means of which I was able to communicate even with my Italian clients, albeit through an interpreter. The Dutch clients and I would get a kick out of making conversation in Afrikaans and Dutch. It would soon become tedious, though. The Dutch would remember that they used to oppose the Apartheid government and they'd become unresponsive. I'd begin to find their pronunciation annoying. Take the Coke bottle out of your arse, I wanted to say.

Anyway, it was Englishmen like Charlie Bolton, Horace McAllistair and Colin Bell who had been prepared to give me a second chance. Not the National Parks brotherhood. It was ironic that those very Broederbond appointments were the ones who managed to retain their posts in spite of affirmative action. The traditional old school rangers were given the chop. My boss was right.

I discussed the matter with Liebies while we were working. Liebies was digging sand from underneath the Land Rover's front wheels and diff. I was working the lever of the high-lift jack and placing stones under the wheels. The sun beat down mercilessly and we were sweating.

The elephant herd surrounding the Land Rover was getting restless. The cow with the crooked tusk shook her head and flapped her ears. A grey dust cloud rose from her flanks. Her calf hid behind her legs. We tried to make ourselves invisible against the wheels of the Land Rover, while our clients sat huddled together inside the vehicle.

Here you had two Boere in a grave situation. We knew that cow. But we were supposed to address each other in English, so that our clients wouldn't feel excluded. It was a ludicrous idea.

"Would you be so kind as to pass me that rock, Liebies, old man? There's a good fellow."

Liebies's perspiring face was caked with dust. His eyes and teeth gleamed white in his sunburnt face as he laughed.

Some time earlier Douw Steyn and I were stranded on the open plain between the Sechumib and the Khumib in a similar situation. Douw had broken the front end of the wheel spanner and neglected to swear in English when he landed flat on his back.

I had just broken the head off my spanner too, while trying to loosen the same wheel nut. The Damara in the workshop at camp had been a bit overzealous the last time he changed this wheel. Moreover, the misty sea air causes things to rust.

Liebies radioed Thys back at camp and asked him to bring us another wheel spanner. Our clients explored the dunes while we were waiting. They knew only one language. They presumed English came as naturally to us as it did to them. They didn't realise we had been forced to learn English in order to survive in the safari business.

A happy day: Windhoek radioed to let us know there would be no clients at our camp for the next four days. We sprang into action immediately. With a cooler full of beer and Valiant Swart in the cassette player we jumped into Liebies's bakkie. We travelled two hundred kilometres through Hartmann's Valley to Serra Cafema, where we camped on the banks of the Kunene River.

There is something about perennial water flowing through a thirstland: it's a solace for the soul. For the next few days we sat on deck, drinking beer and braaiing. We took the boat and travelled up the Kunene. We anchored it on the opposite bank and walked about in Angola. In the evenings we sang around the campfire. Douw played the mouth organ.

One morning Kobus and Sakki took us across the towering dunes on quad bikes. We flew over sandy mounds and sailed down treacherous slopes. Below us lay the meandering river and on the other side there were panoramic views of Angola. Back at camp we lit a fire, drank beer and fished.

On our last evening we sat around the big table on the thatched veranda. We were surrounded by the rushing of water. In the light of the lantern I looked at the people around me. There was Chrisjan Liebies – Christiaan Liebenberg. Stubborn as a mule, with a fearless sense of adventure. Even though he was ten years my junior, he was one of the old hands here. There was no duneland on the Skeleton Coast that Liebies and his Land Rover had not conquered. The minute the Hoarusib receded, he was ready to take it on in a four-wheel drive. Sakki van Rooyen, a scatterbrained,

madcap girl, who had twice covered the distance from Sossusvlei to the coast on foot. Kobus Pienaar, son of a big
game hunter. Douw Steyn and Daleen, Emsie Verwey, Thys
Cronje from Botswana, Sheryl Bester. Most of them in their
early twenties, a few slightly older.

The backbone of our industry was present at this table.
The girls ran the camps. Made the beds, cooked and baked.
In the kitchen they conjured up dishes learned from their
mothers on farms near Grootfontein or Okahandja. They
taught the Himba and Damara staff new skills and took care
of cuts and burns. They were mostly alone at camp. Far from
home – a more isolated location than the Skeleton Coast or
Serra Cafema wasn't easy to find.

The men spent all day in the veld with clients. They explained geological features, tracked elephant and taught their
guests to fish. They covered kilometres on foot, in Land Rovers
or on quad bikes. Every day they changed tyres and dug vehicles out of the sand in the sweltering heat. Their knowledge
was exceptional and no task ever got them down. When a
driveshaft or a halfshaft broke, Thys would go out in a support
vehicle. After the guide and the guests had left, he would
remain behind with his Damara helpers to repair the vehicle.

The night wind sighed through the makalani palms and
the abiekwas yellowwoods. We sat and talked. How many
white people had we seen come and go here? Few stayed
long. How was it that all those present here tonight were die-
hard Afrikaners? The men were too young to have known
national service. (I think it bothered Liebies; he was trying
to make up for it through his intrepid behaviour.)

These guys were the new generation and, God, they gave
me hope for the future. Everyone knew that the days of the
big white game ranger were numbered. You had to carve a
niche for yourself.

We had made ourselves indispensable to the company. We
manned the outposts. Foreigners didn't last long here. They
left for the Hollywood camps of Botswana. Without us the
company would suffer.

Camaraderie glowed in the lamplight. More whiskey was poured. We were all in agreement. We honoured the name of the company. We would continue to serve it well. As we had always done.

And we'd do it in Afrikaans.

Detour

The clock on the dashboard of my bakkie showed half past two in the morning. The desert lay clear in the moonlight. I left the gravel road and turned off into the river bed. A few metres further I stopped and got out. For several minutes I stood in the quiet of the night.

Then I took out the shovel from under the tarpaulin and began to cover the tracks of the bakkie. Where I'd turned off the dirt road, I scattered stones. I replaced the spade and got back into the bakkie. I switched on the engine and drove on without headlights.

Now I had to drive carefully. I'd already had a flat tyre and changed the wheel, using my only spare. The stream bed was rocky and I made slow progress. Ten minutes later I passed through the quartzite ridges, leaving behind the plain with the gravel road leading across it.

I had planned the whole thing carefully. It had been long after dark when I'd driven through Sesfontein earlier. No one had seen me. I'd driven into the night, into the desert. A lone traveller in a vast landscape.

Without difficulty I recognised the stream bed into which I turned. The moon was bright and I knew these parts well. Been exploring them on foot for years.

The incline became steeper as I descended into the river valley. The quartzite ridges made way for granite and schists. The stream bed widened into a small basin and soon broken cliffs were towering above me. In the dim moonlight the folds and clefts cast mysterious shadows.

My thoughts wandered back to my recent visit to Italy. It had been a wonderful opportunity. Overnight I'd been transported from this forsaken desert wilderness to the glamorous world of the international tourism industry. At the tourism expo in Milan I was a resounding success. My presentations and slide shows featuring the Kaokoveld and the Skeleton Coast drew a lot of interest. The Italians were mad about me, just as they were on safari.

Afterwards I called on travel agents in Naples. In Bologna I spent time with people I'd rescued from the Etendeka mountains at Purros after a plane crash.

The previous four years in the safari industry had been golden years for me. Clients found my safaris inspiring. They raved about my energy and enthusiasm. My knowledge of the region, its wildlife and geological features left them amazed. My relationship with the Himbas moved them.

I'd soon become well known. My bosses in Johannesburg and Windhoek realised my market value. My photograph appeared in travel journals. A suntanned, laughing man, with long, bleached hair. The desert man. Friend of the Himbas.

Travel agents began to insist on my services. At last I enjoyed the recognition I deserved. My good relationship with the local communities counted in my favour. I was drawn into my company's negotiations about expanding into new areas.

Now I was making my way through narrow canyons. I approached the river. The first abiekwas yellowwoods and mustard bushes became visible around a bend. I reached a thicket and stopped the bakkie. I was close to the dry river bed and I walked up a small ravine, through some mustard bushes and down the bank to the white sand below. I stood listening quietly. I had to be sure no one knew I was here.

I stretched my limbs after the long drive. I needn't have worried. The wilderness was deserted. Not a soul was camping on this river bank tonight.

This thing had been coming on for a while. Through the years it had appeared in many guises. First I'd been the outsider at school. I preferred to spend my weekends alone on the farm, rather than with friends on the sporting fields or at parties. Always somewhere in the veld, exploring.

Being alone had never been hard for me. As the years went by, it had only become easier. I'd never had trouble saying goodbye. It wasn't that I didn't love people; I just couldn't live among the masses. I couldn't share their living quarters. I wasn't alienated from society; I'd just never belonged there.

I had been in the Kaokoveld for the best part of a decade now. This place had supplanted everything I'd left behind. Could you love a place more than a person?

I went back to "civilisation" less and less often. Long-distance relationships had become less important. Short-term friendships with my clients were easier. A firm bond for three or four days, a warm farewell, a short-lived exchange of letters and then we disappeared from each other's lives for ever. There was never any sadness and disappointment at having been hurt. Yes. That was the best kind of relationship.

The change had begun to take place long before I arrived here. At first I'd been blind to it. Everything was new to me. I laughed when the embittered old game rangers and hunters spoke of the good old days. When, over their sixth whiskey in Kamanjab's pub, they railed helplessly against everyone and everything that threatened and destroyed their Kaokoveld.

Until my eyes were opened. I saw the tidal wave of four-wheel-driven convoys rolling through the area every time an adventure magazine published an article describing this place as the last wilderness. Fully equipped with the necessary road maps and GPS coordinates. Everything was being destroyed.

I'd been part of the team that undertook an impact study for the proposed Epupa hydroelectric scheme in the Kunene River. I'd helped obtain the opinion of the Himba communities on the building of the dam. Seldom before had I come across such strong opposition.

The Himbas saw the dam as a threat to their entire existence. In the first place, the dam would flood their sacred places, their ancestral burial grounds on the river bank. The graves of their ancestors were their birthright, their title deeds to this land. If their ancestors' graves were destroyed, they would lose their claim to the land.

Futhermore, their pastures would be flooded. The palm forests on the banks would disappear. The palms were used for food and for weaving baskets.

Horace and I sat under the omborombonga trees at Okaua and listened to the Himbas. Everyone was there. Ozonkongombe Tjingee, Tjikombamba Tjiambiru, Kapika, Katjira and the strong Matjuimbiku Mutambo. When Matjuimbiku got up to speak, there was fire in his eyes.

"The government wants to build a dam. A dam means job opportunities. To build a dam you need skilled labour. I am a cattle farmer. It's the only work I know. The government is not going to appoint me to build its dam.

"To build this dam, you first have to build a road. A road through the Kaoko. Along that road three things will come to my people: alcohol, crime and disease."

He stared hard at the Himbas, and there were nods and murmurs of agreement.

At a Himba meeting the headman speaks last. When Headman Tjingee began to speak, everything had already been said. He got up and extracted a snuff spoon from his ondumbu headgear. He looked at the Himbas long and earnestly. Then at the rest of the company: the government officials, the dam builders, the legal representatives, the anthropologists, and Horace and me.

With the snuff spoon he drew a line. From one ear, across his throat, to the other ear. Then he spoke: "Build the dam. Slit my throat. It's the same thing. Opuwo."

Apart from all the valid arguments the Himbas had voiced, it was also a fact that one of Africa's most beautiful waterfalls would disappear. I realised during the impact study, however, that all these arguments wouldn't make the slightest difference. The dam would be built.

Subsequently the mines in the Skeleton Coast Park were reopened. My company had succeeded in establishing a profitable safari business on the Skeleton Coast within three years. With a low-impact high-cost operation, money was being paid into the government coffers for the first time in the history of the park – a lot of money. Tourism was Namibia's fastest growing industry. However, no one took any notice, and the Skeleton Coast was being mined. Tom Cumming and his fellow conservationists had been cautioned and threatened: they were not to oppose the mining activities in the park.

I squatted and drank the clear, running water of the fountain. I got up and walked back to my vehicle through the bushes on the river bank.

No one cared anyway.

The changes that were going to take place here and the changes taking place in my heart had met. Flowed together. Crystallised. Come to life.

I was saying farewell.

I switched on the bakkie and drove into the abiekwas thicket. A few weeks ago I'd come here and made a small clearing in the bush. The tamarisks stood dense in a cleft in the rocks. No one would find the bakkie here.

I retrieved my .303 and my revolver from behind the seat. I slipped the latter into its holster. I took some cartridges from the ammo chest under the tarpaulin and put them in the side pocket of my backpack. Then I picked up the ammo chest and placed it on the floor of the cab. It would be safer there.

Most of my earthly possessions fitted into this bakkie. They would be safe here. I drew the tarpaulin over the back. Then I opened the hood and disconnected the battery. I closed the hood and locked the cab. I pushed the keys into my pocket.

I shouldered my backpack and rifle and set off up the gorge. I would come back here from time to time, but my plan was to stay on the move.

From time to time I'd shoot a springbok. There was plenty of water in the river and I knew where the fountains were in the mountain. My safari camp was one and a half days on foot from here. I'd carry out nocturnal raids after the plane had brought fresh provisions. If I stole judiciously, no one would notice a thing.

From the ridges I'd fire at the tourist convoys. Just to harass them. They'd get the message that this place was no longer safe. I'd pay nocturnal visits to the mining camps and sabotage their machinery. Cut hydraulic pipes, disrupt their work.

I wasn't quite sure how I was going to stop the work on the dam, but I was sure I'd be able to muster a hundred Himba warriors when the time was right. When the construction on the harbour at Angra Frio began, I'd hide in the dunes and wait for my chance. They'd never catch me.

Daybreak found me on the summit. Beneath me lay the deserted river valley. An endless wilderness stretching as far as the eye could see. I stood there for a while.

It would have been so easy. Simply to disappear. For several minutes I relished the thought. Then I shook my head and smiled at myself. Perhaps some day.

I walked down the mountain. Back at the bakkie, I connected the battery to drive back to my camp on the Khumib River. There was work to be done.

The day of the cats

Emsie is a cat girl. The walls of her flat at Swakopmund were covered in pictures and paintings of cats. Miniature cat figurines – made out of wood, ceramics or glass – adorned every tabletop and shelf. Even I, her boyfriend, was born under the sign of Leo.

That's why she found it so difficult to leave her two stray cats behind the day she decided to make a living in the wilderness. Her landlords, a German couple, were kind enough to agree to keep the flat for her. They would look after her cats in the periods between her two-monthly visits.

After a year in the wilderness the longing was too great. She borrowed my bakkie and drove down to fetch her cats. For the cats and herself it was a gruelling trip. The grey cat with the green eyes reacted negatively to the tranquilliser Emsie gave her. She behaved like a wild animal and tried to squeeze through every gap in the wire cage. A scorching southeaster began to blow and it was hot as hell. To the cats, accustomed to the misty, cool Swakop weather, it was a baptism of fire.

When I returned from an exhausting eastwind-ravaged safari in the Kaokoveld, the cats were there. Between tent, canvas and shade netting they sought shelter from the heat. Stretched out between the ceiling canvas and the roof canvas, they slept off the aftereffects of the sedation and the journey. Clearly unhappy in their dismal new surroundings.

The white cat with the large blue eyes recovered first. She had a calm temperament. She found herself a cosy spot in the tent: on top of the wardrobe in the bathroom tent, or where the shade netting formed a natural hammock under the tent roof. There she whiled away the days. She jumped down only to eat and to go for a short walk around the tent in the early evening. She was an affectionate cat and was constantly brushing against Emsie and me.

From the word go the grey cat decided that she was not going to make the tent her home. During the day she was missing. At night she would pay a brief visit to the tent. She would paw Emsie until she woke up for a bit of cuddling. Then she would eat the food that had been put out for her, curl up on the bed for a few hours and, at first light, disappear into the veld again.

Early one morning Emsie and I followed her. She ran ahead, but stopped frequently to look back at us. Almost as if she wanted to say: "Don't follow me. I don't want you to know where I live." We found her hide-out in a series of hollows in the calcrete bank on the river's edge. Sheltered against the east wind.

I have never been keen on the idea of domestic cats in a wilderness area. They breed successfully with the indigenous African wild cat. In more densely populated areas of South Africa the African wild cat has disappeared completely. It is rather ironic: three thousand years before Christ the Egyptians bred the domestic cat, *Felis domesticus*, from African wild cats, *Felis lybica*, that they trapped and tamed.

In some nature reserves domestic cats have wreaked havoc among indigenous birds and small mammals. Years ago some of my varsity friends went to Marion Island to help eradicate the imported domestic cats, which were threatening the endemic bird species. I remember how jealous I was when they returned six months later, long-haired and bearded. They had exciting stories to tell of chasing after cats in the polar nights, armed with shooting lamps and shotguns.

Emsie got her cats from the Animal Welfare Society. Their animals are neutered before the new owner is allowed to take them, therefore inbreeding would not be a problem. She also assured me she would keep them well fed on cat food so that they wouldn't be tempted to catch larks or gerbils.

It does not take me long to become fond of any animal,

and soon I enjoyed having the cats around. Each had its own character.

One day Anton Esterhuyse arrived at our camp from Wêreldsend. His semi-tame African wild cats had had a kitten. He didn't want to keep it, because the male had killed the previous litter.

Emsie's face lit up. There is always room for another cat in her life. After a cup of coffee, Anton promised to bring the kitten as soon as it had been weaned off its mother. The mother was very protective. She lived in a dense curry bush with her kitten and allowed no one to approach. Anton showed us the scratches on his arms.

Then the white cat disappeared. One evening we watched her jump through the window of the bathroom tent and walk off into the night. The next morning she had not returned. That night the grey cat came in as usual; the white cat's food remained in her bowl, dried out.

Every evening we heard the spotted hyenas calling and the black-backed jackals howling around camp. She was a white cat. She stood out at night.

Emsie was brave. During the day she managed the camp. There were breakfasts to be served and tents to be tidied. Supplies to be ordered on the radio. The drinks had to be chilled. Water had to be pumped. When the clients and I returned from the veld covered with dust, the bucket showers had to be filled. The meals had to be ready. In the evenings she fulfilled the role of hostess at the campfire and the supper table. After the guests had gone to bed, she would walk around outside, calling her cat.

One evening she was overcome by emotion. I pulled her close and held her. Tears rolled down her cheeks, over my chest and into my shirt. I comforted her: "Never underestimate a cat. They're independent animals. They can go without food and water for a long time. It's not for nothing they're said to have nine lives."

We heard the call of a spotted hyena in the dark, and my words sounded hollow.

A week later Anton brought the kitten, a terrified grey bundle. We put him in Emsie's cat cage and moved the cage around so that he could watch our movements and get used to us. When we approached, he spat and growled and flattened his little ears. I felt sorry for him inside the cage. I used the chance to study him closely. When I noticed the rust-coloured fur behind his ears, I knew he was a full-blooded African wild cat. The red colour behind the ears disappears as soon as the wild cats breed with domestic cats.

Three days later we decided to let him out of the cage. I felt sorry for him, and Emsie still missed her white cat. She found the new kitten too wild and strange. She didn't feel that there would ever be a bond between them. It was evening when we let him out. The grey cat had just returned from her hide-out at the river. The two cats sniffed each other inquisitively outside the tent. Then the grey cat came in to eat and the wild cat walked uncertainly into the dark wilderness.

I was just setting out on an extraordinary safari. My guests were American yacht owners who had navigated all the oceans of the world. It was their first safari in Africa and they had brought along their own guide. Gavin Ford was an ex-ranger and elephant hunter from the Zambezi valley. At present he was a specialist guide in Botswana. He had an intense love for and knowledge of the veld. He had an aura of dignity, something so often absent in people who have worked as safari guides for any length of time. It had been a long time since I'd found myself in such inspiring company. Gavin was a gentleman of the wilderness. The safari became a magnificent experience.

The first day began quietly. We explored the Agab River and picked up the spoor of a rhino cow and calf. A few scattered showers had fallen. The east wind was drying out the new grass quickly. In the distance we saw isolated herds of springbok, gemsbok and ostrich. It became a morning of tracking, and a balancing act to remain downwind of the rhino. We covered a considerable distance on foot. It was a hot day.

Towards afternoon we caught up with the rhino. We saw them in the distance on the open, rocky slope. I brought the group to a halt. One last time I repeated the safety procedure.

Now we were walking slowly across the rocky terrain. The rhinos had lain down in the shade of a witgat tree. It was open country, with little safe ground. Something was bothering the calf and he got up. His mother woke up too. Now they were both standing, looking in our direction. I signalled to the group to sit down. They obeyed.

For the next ten minutes the rhinos tried to figure out whether they had actually seen something or not. We sat motionless, scarcely daring to breathe. There was no shelter. The patch of milk bush where we had been heading would have afforded some shelter, but it lay out of reach now. Minutes felt like an eternity.

Then the cow decided that the calf had been imagining things and lay down again. For a few more minutes the calf stood around, then lay down too. We sat in the sun for another quarter-hour – sixty metres from the black rhinos. I wanted to be certain that they were sleeping soundly. Then I motioned to the group to get up. Quietly I led them away.

Where the Land Rovers stood parked under the shade of a witgat tree, we enjoyed a cold lunch. The Americans talked excitedly about the encounter – a first of its kind for them. Gavin was clearly impressed with the trackers and me and our approach. I spoke enthusiastically about our involvement with a conservation project in collaboration with the Save the Rhino Trust.

That night the wild cat returned to the tent. He rushed at the white cat's food bowl and gobbled down its contents. When he noticed us watching him, he fled into the night.

The next morning we found him crawling out from under the deck of the lapa tent. Emsie threw him a piece of cold meat. He grabbed it and disappeared under the floor again. Minutes later he was back. Emsie put down a plate of meat and a saucer of milk. Cautiously he crept closer and began to eat. The guests watched him quietly. I looked at Emsie. The wild cat had come to stay.

Early that morning we found rhino. After an easy walk across hilly terrain we found another cow and calf north of the Uniab River, browsing at a milk bush. The east wind blew strongly into our faces. We sat watching them from the safety of a ridge. They were unaware of us.

From a valley higher up another rhino appeared. A bull this time. Browsing, he came walking in our direction. Some distance from the other two he also stopped at a milk bush. In the morning air we could hear him chew. The guests took numerous photos. We left the rhinos after they had found a place to lie down.

We travelled further north in the Land Rovers. In the Aub and Barab valleys it had rained more copiously. We looked at bottle trees and welwitschias. Gavin Ford saw a Burchell's courser for the first time. The mood was cheerful. Large herds of mountain zebra ran alongside the vehicles. Gavin and I discussed history and geology. To the Americans everything was new. They gazed at the giraffes in astonishment.

At the fountain at the foot of the mountain pass between the Aub and the Barab Rivers, we encountered the lions: a lioness with her three young sons. They jumped up out of the rushes in front of the Land Rover. They trotted up the slope and stood watching us. Another excellent photo opportunity for the guests.

The lion population around here had shown a healthy increase with the good rains of the previous nine years. In this area big cats were a rare sight. Although they could be found around here, they remained timid. It was seldom that lions allowed people to photograph them like that. I explained all this to the guests while the lion family strolled calmly up the slope.

We drove across the rocky mountain pass and into the

Aub valley. We stopped to admire the big basalt canyon. Lower down we found a cheetah female. She was heavily pregnant. Meekly she watched us from under a ringwood tree, barely forty metres away.

"This is unheard of," I said while the Americans were taking photos. "There is a healthy cheetah population here, but usually we see them only when they dash off to put the nearest ridge between us and themselves."

The cheetah stretched out in the shade. She stared at us nonchalantly, waving her tail.

The sun began to set and the basalt of the Hoekberg foothills turned red. We descended deeper into the Aub valley. A feeling of contentment nestled inside me. It had been a remarkable day. My clients had appreciated it and were worth it. They sat in silence, transported by the beauty of the landscape.

The next moment I saw another rhino in the dry watercourse of the Aub. He was unaware of us. I swiched off the vehicle. Gavin watched him through his binoculars. His hand fell on my shoulder. With barely suppressed excitement, he whispered: "Leopards."

My binoculars shot up to my eyes. "Where?"

"In line with the rhino, in front of him. Among the rocks on the bank. Into the sun."

The binoculars found the leopards. A large male and a smaller, younger female. Clearly in love. Kapoi and the trackers in the Land Rover behind us had also seen them. It took Gavin and me longer to point out the leopards to our guests. The spotted cats blended perfectly with their surroundings.

One after the other the guests spotted them. The male jumped from rock to rock in pursuit of the female. Together they drank from a pool. The female arched her back as the male rubbed against her. She jumped at him playfully and they rolled in the sand affectionately. Then they were up on their feet once more. Together they disappeared into the abiekwas thicket.

Gavin, the guests and I agreed: it had been the day of the cats. In the fading light, we drove back to camp.

"You know, if we see *one* of these cat species in a month, we count ourselves lucky," I said excitedly. "Now, on one safari, in one day, we see a lion, a cheetah *and* a leopard."

"Don't forget the African wild cat," a woman said from behind.

"Yes," the others agreed.

Evening – the end of a perfect day. I had just stepped out of the shower. Emsie was busy in the bedroom. Soon we would meet Gavin and the guests at the campfire for drinks. She was in evening dress and I was wearing a clean shirt and long trousers. It's nice to look decent after a long day in the veld.

I pulled the brush through my hair and heard something at the bathroom window. I turned.

"Emsie. Come and have a look."

Emsie came into the bathroom tent. In the window sat the white cat. Starved, bedraggled, with a wound on her cheek. Her large blue eyes gleamed brightly.

Emsie came running and gathered the cat in her arms. She buried her face in the dirty white fur. She was laughing and crying at the same time.

Delighted, I stood back. A perfect day. The day of the cats.

Veteran I

The rain caught us at Koabesfontein, ten kilometres from camp. It may sound close but ten kilometres is a long way across Damaraland's rocky terrain in a Land Rover. Especially if the rain is falling as it did then. I stopped and handed out ponchos to the guests.

As usual, the rain was coming from the east; there wouldn't be much rain west of Koabes. I tried to avoid the storm by choosing the westerly route. I hoped the shower would be over by the time we turned east to our camp. Why do I always have to be the one who gets caught in the rain in the desert? I wondered, slightly disgruntled.

When we turned east at Salvadora, the rain was coming down more heavily. Within seconds the ponchos were drenched. They offered no further protection to the elderly Americans. I could see the uncertainty on their faces.

It was a strong easterly wind that was bringing the rain. Now we were forced to drive right into it. It was still five kilometres to camp. The drops struck us like buckshot pellets. Every stream and drainage line coming down from the hills was brimming with reddish brown water. Within minutes the Salvadora was flowing strongly. Around the Land Rover everything had turned liquid.

The uncertainty on the faces of the ladies made way for naked fear. One old gentleman allayed their fears by pretending that it was a trifle – "Hey, this is Africa!" The other gentleman clenched his jaw and glared at me as if the rain was *my* fault.

To reach camp, we had to drive a kilometre up the dry stream bed of the Salvadora. The Salvadora can hardly be called a river; it's a shallow stream bed that holds water once every two or three years. Now we were confronted by a churning mass of brown water pouring in from everywhere, looking more like lava than water. From the east the rain was still peppering us mercilessly.

"Don't worry, we're nearly there. It'll soon be over," I placated the guests. My words sounded hollow. I knew that the irate gentleman had already decided I was an imbecile.

It was impossible to venture close to the Salvadora. I made for higher ground and drove up the rocky slope of the northern bank. My plan was to weave across the ridges and come as close as possible to our camp. Almost immediately the Land Rover got stuck. The earth was so wet that the basalt torras gave way under the wheels. We were stranded.

Fortunately Steven Kasaona was with me, an able young man whom I was training as a guide. The two of us jumped out. Swiftly we hoisted the Land Rover out of the stones with the high-lift jack. The vehicle was carrying a heavy load, but it was too wet to ask the guests to get out.

In the end we got stuck four times. That is when a safari guide's work becomes difficult. In the pouring rain Steven and I worked the jack like madmen. Laughing and joking, we comforted the despondent guests, who sat huddled together, soaked to the skin.

The jack slipped and a knuckle lost its skin – it was nothing. We'd soon be there. Cheer up. I was gripped by a helpless rage that I dared not show. To hell with this godforsaken hellhole where I live. Why am I still here? No. To hell with it.

Then we were out again. Slowly the Land Rover crawled forward. Through drifts of rain the camp became visible, a mere two hundred metres away. Only the churning Salvadora lay between us. Again the Land Rover sank into the mud. So near yet so far.

Enough was enough. I'd carry these people through the river myself if I had to.

"Stay here," I ordered. Not that they could go anywhere, I realised as soon as the words were out.

I jumped out and walked to the river. I waded into the water. The current tugged at my legs, shorts and sandals. Carefully I placed one foot in front of the other. I waded in deeper.

The water was strong, but surely not *that* strong. If you can't walk through, you can't drive through: that is the rule. The water plucked at my shirt, and I felt for the pebbles and placed my feet carefully on the dragging bottom. At one place I sank in to just below my armpits. Then the water became shallower. I walked out on the opposite bank. I turned round and walked back. It was almost easier.

Steven had already lifted the Land Rover with the jack. He's the kind of guy I want on my team.

I could see in the eyes of the disapproving gentleman that he was convinced he was dealing with a crazy person. I looked at him and smiled. "To hell with you, old man," is what I meant when I said: "Hold on, we're going through."

The rain stopped. I got in behind the wheel. Changed to donkey gear and hit the gas.

The Land Rover pushed up a brown bow wave in front of us. I made certain that the wheels maintained traction on the rocky bottom. Without difficulty we reached the other side. I turned to the guests triumphantly. They looked impressed, despite being wet and miserable.

At camp Emsie and the team were waiting for us. She welcomed the guests with sherry and steaming coffee. Ingrid, Brown and Fly stood by with blankets and towels. Magnus was already struggling to get the smoky campfire going with paraffin. The tents had survived the windstorm. It had rained in and the groundsheets were under water, but Emsie and her team had succeeded in keeping the bedding dry.

Hot bucket showers were fetched from the donkey. Magnus was getting the better of the campfire. The skies cleared and the sun broke through.

An hour later we were all sitting around the fire. A breathtaking sunset broke through the clouds. The mopane trees glistened with drops. The whiskey tasted good.

234

The guests had managed to find dry clothing in their luggage. Slowly they recovered, still slightly stunned by the experience. Emsie told them that the rain meter at camp had measured sixty-five millimetres – in an hour and a half.

The irritable gentleman looked at me across the fire. He gave me a dry smile and said: "You know, son, we've been coming to Africa for twenty odd years. This is the first time we've experienced a storm in the desert. You did well."

It became a good safari. The next morning we found three black rhino near camp. The desert was washed clean and fresh.

The old man and I understood each other. He had seen the last month of the Second World War as a lieutenant in the engineering corps.

"Yesterday brought back a lot of memories," he said to me. "The engineering corps had to build bridges where the Germans had blown them up as they were retreating to Berlin." He laughed wryly. "We were too slow. Those damned Russians got to Berlin before us."

Everyone in the back of my Land Rover has his own story to tell.

Veteran II

Everyone in the back of my Land Rover has his own story to tell.

Randall Bachman had been on safari with me before. Twice on the Skeleton Coast, and now we were here on Damaraland's rocky plains. He was keen to see the desert elephants. Both previous visits to the Skeleton Coast had been during the rainy season. The Hoarusib had been in flood and impassable, and the elephants had sheltered somewhere in the gorges. On neither occasion were we able to find them. However, Randall and I had taken a liking to each other. Now he was back on a rhino safari. As before, he was alone. We were going to try for the desert elephants again.

Randall Bachman was a formidable figure. He intimidated the other clients. In his late fifties, he was still lean and muscular. His short hair was salt-and-pepper grey. He had a brusque way of speaking. But it was his eyes that the other guests found disconcerting. His pale blue eyes stared right through you. It was the thousand-yard stare of someone who had come face to face with death. On his neck there were scars that disappeared under his shirt, almost like those of Captain Ahab of the *Pequod*. Moreover, his six foot two frame towered over the other guests and he seemed to look down his nose at everyone. For some or other reason he liked me.

He had been involved with the American nuclear weapons programme as an engineer – that was all he was prepared to say about his profession. He was on early pension. He attended every Formula 1 Grand Prix in the world. Between races he came on safari to Botswana and Tanzania, and now also to Namibia. He supported Ferrari, and Michael Schumacher was his hero. He also admired Coulthard and Montoya.

It took us a long time to find the rhino. The trackers had to prove their mettle. There were large herds of zebra and gemsbok, and several giraffes on the open plains. Kudu here and there. Only in the afternoon, after a long hike across the plains, did we find a rhino cow and calf. We stayed with them until sunset. The guests were happy. But Randall Bachman wanted to see desert elephants. It seemed as if Randall, the elephants and I didn't go together.

The other guests didn't socialise with Randall. He was curt and withdrawn and they avoided him. That evening round the campfire under the starry sky I told my crocodile story for the thousandth time. My sophisticated guests listened, horror-struck and visibly shaken. Randall was hearing the story for the third time. He sat beside me quietly, staring into the fire.

I finished my story. People asked questions and expressed their astonishment. It was quiet for a few minutes, then Randall began to speak. His gruff voice and brusque delivery caught the other guests by surprise. After a while they began to listen.

"It was 1968. I had reason to feel good. Three days before I had shot down my second MIG over North Vietnam. That night we had orders to destroy a bridge. We were a squadron of four Phantom F4 fighter planes. Just before sunset we took off from the aircraft carrier. When night fell, we were over North Vietnam. Ahead of us lay the target. The planes made their approach in single file. I was number four. One after the other my comrades launched their rockets. By the time it was my turn, the Vietcong's anti-aircraft missiles were ready. I launched my rockets. Flying past, I was struck by a ground-to-air missile. My flight engineer was either dead or unconscious; I got no reaction from him. I myself was badly wounded. The plane was on fire and I struggled to keep it under control. At last I succeeded in gaining height.

Fortunately I still had radio contact with my comrades and the aircraft carrier. I took my plane higher and higher in the general direction of the ocean. My fellow pilots talked to me, encouraging me. The plane began to stall and I was losing height. When I reached the ocean, I was able to fly to where I saw the lights of an American patrol boat. I gave myself a shot of morphine and ejected. When I woke, I was on the hospital ship, with 63 pieces of shrapnel in my body. I never flew again."

Around the fire it was quiet. A few guests shifted uncomfortably in their canvas chairs. Most were Ivy Leaguers from New England. They had hardly ever seen blood. They had always avoided conversations about Vietnam.

The next morning at the breakfast table I noticed a quiet respect for Randall Bachman in the manner of the other guests. Some of the women smiled sympathetically in his direction.

The safari came to an end. We left camp and drove out of the wilderness. At the Karkapi River, ten kilometres before we reached the main road that would take us to the airstrip, we came across the herd of elephants. They were browsing among the mopanes and bathing in the dust. They paid little heed to our presence. A cow walked right past the Land Rover. Under her belly walked her two-week-old calf.

I turned and looked at Randall Bachman. He returned my gaze. Around the corners of his mouth there was the trace of a smile. For the first time I noticed a softness in his eyes.

Piet Renoster

I watched Piet as he came riding up on his mule. He was wearing shabby boots and khaki trousers. Over his long-sleeved cotton shirt he wore a threadbare waistcoat. His wide-rimmed felt hat was sweat-stained. He held his rifle across the pommel. The hair protruding from under his hat was snow-white, as was his forked beard. He sat easily in the saddle. He looked a bit like a Bittereinder returning from commando.

Piet dismounted stiffly. A blanket, a hessian bag and a water canteen were tied to the saddle. He had been in the veld for a few days, but we had arranged to meet at his cattle post this morning and Piet was a man of his word. I had come to hear his story. From his own lips.

I had already heard it from others. Actually, the story belonged to Piet *and* Neil McGregor. Neil had told me his version, but Piet was the central character, after all.

While I'd been waiting, I had made a fire and boiled water for tea. I had left my camp early that morning and brought along a freshly baked loaf of bread. After Piet had put his rifle and blanket in his hut, unsaddled his horse and stretched his legs, he sat down in the camping chair facing me. I handed him a slice of bread and a mug of sweet tea. We sat and we ate.

After the meal he began to talk. He was a dignified man. He spoke quietly.

"My name is Piet Hizerako. My father was a Herero and my mother a Damara. I was born here. I have lived here all my life and I'll die here. I farm with cattle and goats. My wife and family live in my house at Warmquelle and this is my cattle post at Otjiperongo. Some people call me Piet Renoster. I used to be a poacher.

239

"I shot three black rhinos and four elephants before I was caught. Mister Neil caught me. He is a clever ranger. I was sent to jail in Windhoek. I was inside for seven months. Mister Neil knew only about the three rhinos and two of the elephants. But he doesn't stop once he begins; he knew I was hiding something. While I was in jail, he searched the area. He found the other elephant carcasses. And my spent cartridges. I had just got back to Warmquelle when the police arrived. I got another four months at Otavi."

While Piet was talking, I thought of Neil McGregor's version of the story. He had followed the tracks of the mysterious poacher for more than a year. He developed an obsession with him. It was in the early 1980s and Damaraland and the Kaokoveld were in the grip of a severe drought. It was estimated that eighty thousand cattle died in the Kaokoveld. Himbas and Hereros who had lost all their livestock committed suicide.

Neil told me how one night he had shot fourteen starving lions at a cattle trough. "There was no more food in the veld. So they came to the cattle posts, but the cattle were already dead. The lions were nothing but skin and bone; it was tragic to see.

"In the Hoanib River the elephant calves began to die. Some of the elephant cows aborted. No rhino births were recorded and the condition of the animals was poor. Besides the drought, they were now also at the mercy of an unscrupulous poacher. I was determined to catch the scoundrel. I watched the big game of the Kaokoveld being exterminated and I was determined to do all I could to prevent it. But this poacher was a clever old fox; you could see he knew the area like the back of his hand."

Piet Hizerako filled his pipe with the tobacco I had brought along from Palmwag.

"Why did you shoot elephants and rhinos, Piet?"

"My cattle were dead and my goats were thin. What could I do? My children were small. They had to live. The rhinos and elephants walked on the land where my cattle used to be; I knew where they walked. There was nothing else I could do."

"Who bought the horns and ivory from you?"

"A Herero came to me. He said his boss would buy them from me."

"Who was his boss?"

"A white man. A farmer from Kamanjab."

"How much were you paid, Piet?"

"With the money I got for a tusk or horn, I could buy fifty kilograms of mealie-meal."

Neil McGregor began to close in on the poacher. All the evidence suggested that the unlawful hunter was operating from the cattle post at Otjiperongo. He suspected Piet Hizerako, but he wanted to catch him red-handed. For weeks Neil hid in the hills around Otjiperongo. He had already found two rhino carcasses and two elephant carcasses. Next to each carcass he'd picked up a single cartridge shell; they were all of the same calibre. He sent them away for forensic testing. The results came back – they were from the same rifle.

"What did you hunt with, Piet?" I asked.

"My 303." He pointed over his shoulder at the hut, where he had put away his rifle.

"How many shots for each animal?"

"One."

"A 303 is a light rifle for elephant and rhino, Piet. I myself have shot eight elephants, all with a heavy calibre – 458. Five of those elephants fell at the first shot. One got up and I had to shoot him again. The other three needed several shots before they fell."

"An elephant sleeps during the day; he stands under a tree. A rhino lies down. If you're alone, you stalk him downwind. You can get close. You shoot an elephant just above the eye; a rhino behind the ear. It's people who are scared who fire so many shots."

Neil McGregor saw the lappet-faced vultures circling in the distance and watched them until they settled. He went in. The rhino had been shot the previous day. The vultures could not pierce the hide yet and were waiting patiently. Neil picked up a single spent cartridge.

He found Piet Hizerako at his cattle post at Otjiperongo. In his hut were two rhino horns and a 303 rifle. The shell that Neil had picked up next to the carcass was a 303.

When I asked Neil McGregor what he had done to Piet when he caught him, Neil didn't answer. Now I asked Piet Hizerako the same question.

Piet looked into the fire. He picked up a live ember with his thumb and forefinger and put it in the bowl of his pipe. He sucked furiously and clouds of smoke whirled around his head. He coughed. He screwed up his eyes as he looked up at the sky. "This year we're going to get a bit of rain."

About certain things a man doesn't speak.

It was when Neil McGregor had found the other two elephant carcasses and realised that Piet had lied to him that he'd had the idea. But first Piet Hizerako would have to be punished suitably. When he had Piet put away for the second time, he struck a deal with the magistrate.

I made more tea. Piet was puffing away smoothly at his pipe now.

"The day I walked out of the cells at Otavi, Mister Neil was waiting for me. He said nothing. He looked angry. I got into his bakkie. He drove back to the Kaokoveld. All the way he said nothing. I knew what his plan was – it was the old days. I knew he was taking me to the veld to shoot me. There were stories that he had done the same thing to poachers in the Caprivi. I was very scared and began to think of a way to escape.

"Mister Neil stopped the bakkie here at Otjiperongo. We got out; his revolver was at his side. He stood in front of me beside the bakkie. He said: 'Piet, you are a sly devil.' Then he drew back the tarpaulin. On the back of the bakkie were two fifty-kilogram bags of mealie-meal. Also a large bag of sugar and a large bag of salt. There were blankets and a new pair of boots. Then Mister Neil said: 'You are the most cunning poacher I know. From now on you work for me. I'll bring your food and your wages every month. From now on you're going to use your skills as a poacher to help me catch other poachers.'"

Piet sipped some tea and stared into the fire. Then he said: "That was twenty years ago. Since then Mister Neil and I have caught many poachers. We catch them and then we train them to work for us.

"All the poachers around here work for Nature Conservation now. The drought comes and then the rain comes. Sometimes our cattle die. But our children are not hungry any more. There are plenty of elephants and rhinos now."

Rhino watcher

It was late afternoon when we began to descend into the valley. We had driven along the old mountain pass, getting as close as we could in the bakkie. After a while the terrain had become too rocky for the vehicle. Soon we found a zebra path down the mountainside. We tackled the last three kilometres on foot.

Kapoi Kasaona led the way; he had a sturdy bush knife in his hand. Behind him followed Mike, his faded backpack on his shoulders. A knife had been pushed into his belt. Between Mike and me walked Emsie. She was carrying the camera. I brought up the rear. The long-handled axe rested comfortably on my right shoulder.

Around us towered peaks and flat-topped hills. We were entering the foothills of the Etendekas. From the slopes we were being watched by mountain zebra, etched against the yellow winter grass. There were several scattered herds. The average number in a herd is seven: a stallion and three mares, all with foals of varying ages. As we approached, the nearest stallion stepped protectively in front of his herd. He snorted restlessly in our direction. They were on their way to the fountain too.

A herd of kudu were watching us from a mopane thicket on the floor of the valley below; further along stood a herd of gemsbok – all intending to drink at the fountain sometime tonight. Now they would have to wait for us to finish. Booted eagles soared in the cobalt blue sky overhead. I drank in the scene. Never would this world cease to enchant and move me.

Emsie looked back and smiled. She understood.

On the floor of the valley, near the fountain, Piet Hizerako was waiting for us. He had been waiting all day. I passed him the water bottle. He drank and motioned for us to follow him. We wove through the mopanes.

Under a mopane bush some distance away lay old Grog. Nine years ago I had seen him for the first time, not too far from here. Mike, Theuns and I were together. We had picked up his spoor at Kleinfontein early in the day. He'd led us deep into the hills. We crossed a ridge and suddenly he was in front of us. We flattened ourselves against the rocks. For a long time we watched him. Theuns managed to take a few photos, while Mike jotted down data on a form. It was my first black rhino patrol; Mike and Theuns were old hands. I lay there, admiring Grog. He was in his prime then. I noticed that the tip of his front horn was missing – it was too symmetrical to have been a natural fracture.

We lay watching Grog until he became sleepy. He left the brosdoring and found a shady patch further along under a ringwood tree. For good measure, he sprayed a milk bush with urine one last time. After that his eyelids began to droop. His head sank lower and lower; his large nostrils puffed up clouds of dust. Then he slumped down. First the hindquarters and then the heavy forequarters. With a final sigh, he fell asleep. Mike, Theuns and I left him there.

On the return journey I asked Mike about the short horn.

"Grog was one of the first black rhino to be dehorned in '89. He was fifteen at the time."

I remembered it well. Simon and I were in the Caprivi then. Rhino poaching was reaching alarming proportions in Southern and East Africa at the time. Simon and I had our own hands full with the ivory poachers in the Caprivi – it was open warfare.

It hit the headlines all over the world: Namibia was dehorning its black rhino in the desert areas. It was an emergency measure, for they were the only black rhino that existed outside a National Park.

In a way it was a deliberate deception. Not all the rhinos were dehorned; only a few. Nature Conservation played for time in a bid to get the poaching under control. The media published widely, however, that all the horns were being removed and the bluff paid off. Grog did his bit to throw dust in the poachers' eyes.

During the past two years we had often come across Grog on safari. He was tolerant of people; he was old now. His tolerance did not include his fellow rhinos, however. Everyone who had watched him over the years knew he was a fighter. In his younger years he regularly wiped the floor with the other bulls; he was king of these foothills. It seemed that his stubby horn made him more belligerent, though the other rhinos had the advantage. They regularly punched him full of holes. As his horn grew back, he slowly regained the upper hand. For a while he was champion again. But then old age began to take its toll.

In recent years he was dethroned twice. Once by Speedy and on another occasion by Ben. Ben was the dominant bull at the moment; even Speedy avoided him. But old Grog still kept coming back for more. His head was covered with warts and knobs. His ears were in shreds. Whenever we found him, he had a fresh bruise around his eye or a cut across his cheekbone.

It looked as if Ben and Speedy were taking turns to teach him a lesson. This valley became his retreat. He ventured out of here only to confront Ben or Speedy. After his umpteenth thrashing he would stumble back to recover.

It was here that we came looking for him on safari. While Speedy would charge at us furiously as soon as he became aware of us, and Ben would beat a hasty retreat, old Grog would get up and approach. He would turn his head left, then right, as if he was showing off his latest scars. Proudly exhibiting them to us. Sometimes he would get up out of his shady patch, browse for a while – just to make certain the people had a good view of him – and then lie down again. That evening his massive erection would be the main talking point among the safari-goers around the campfire.

Old Grog's horn was no longer blunt; it had grown out completely. Around here the rhino cows had longer horns than the bulls. A bull honed his horn on a rock or a tree trunk regularly to keep it ready for action. Old Grog boasted a powerful, short, sharp fighting horn – not that it was much help to him in his old age.

A while ago Karonda put in an appearance: an arrogant young bull from the eastern hills. Full of confidence, he came walking across the Rooiplaat plains. On safari we watched him with interest.

Speedy gave him his first hiding. After that Ben thrashed him soundly. Head over heels he fled to the mountains – straight into old Grog's valley.

Kapoi came to report: Old Grog was injured. He was dragging his hind leg. There was a hole in his right haunch. His condition was poor. We asked Piet Hizerako to watch Grog for a week or two; Kapoi would assist him when he wasn't on safari. The old man agreed. After all, he had known Grog for years.

Kapoi took food and water to Piet Renoster in the veld. He came back and reported: Old Grog was weak. His ribs were showing. He didn't leave the fountain. Piet refused to come out of the veld; he was staying on to watch Grog. Two old men alone in the wilderness.

During the first week the rhino showed no sign of improvement. Then he began to step lightly on his injured foot. After three days he was able to put his full weight on his right foot again.

I drove out myself to join Piet. Together we stalked Grog. He was slightly lame, but he was moving away from the fountain, plucking greedily at the milk bushes. The wound on his haunch had formed a scab. It looked as if he was gaining weight.

Satisfied, I looked at Piet. "It seems old Grog is getting better."

At the end of the second week Kapoi came back from the veld. "Piet says we must come. Old Grog died this morning."

Old Grog lay on his side at the base of a mopane trunk. Emsie took photos for the postmortem. With difficulty we rolled the heavy body out from under the bushes. With our skinning knives we cut through the thick skin around his neck and throat; we cut deeply until we felt bone.

I grabbed hold of old Grog's horns and twisted his neck. The bloody slit gaped wide. With a single accurate blow of the axe Piet Renoster severed the cervical vertebrae. Mike wrote in his notebook. Emsie took more photos. Kapoi cut through the last tendons. Piet took the axe and chopped a sturdy mopane stick. He pushed it in behind the opening in old Grog's throat and out through his mouth.

It was getting dark as we carried old Grog's heavy head up the mountain, taking over from each other in pairs. The next day Mike would take it to the research station at Okaukeujo. Grog's horns would be locked away in a safe. His blood and tissue would be used for DNA research; measurements would be taken of his skull.

That evening we sat around the campfire. We had already enjoyed a meal of meat and porridge.

Mike took a sip of his beer. "Old Grog was more than thirty years old. It was a good life."

Piet Hizerako stared deep into the flames. His snow-white hair contrasted sharply with his dark skin.

"I've known old Grog for many years. One day I nearly shot him." He was quiet for a while. "That day I had him in my sights for a long time. My finger was on the trigger. I had a clear view. He didn't know about me. I waited for a long time. Something inside me warned me; something spoke to me. I lowered my rifle. Shortly afterwards I was caught.

"I've never known why I didn't shoot him that day. Until now. Now I know why: Grog and I are brothers. We both paid a price so that the rhino could live. I was a rhino hunter who went to jail. Then I was given a second chance. Now I am a rhino watcher. Grog's horn was sawn off so that other rhinos could live. But those rhinos who owed their lives to him, killed him.

"Now I know why I didn't shoot him that day. Old Grog and I were both destined to become rhino watchers."

Christmas in the desert

"Chris."

"Yes."

"Let's celebrate Christmas in the desert."

"Look around you, Mike. We *live* in the desert. Let's celebrate Christmas at Swakop."

"I don't mean this desert. I know people with a farm that borders on Sossusvlei. They said I could camp there over Christmas. Some of my friends are coming from England. Why don't you come too?"

Mike and I were reclining against our bedrolls under a mopane tree in the Kowareb Schlucht. He always had these strange ideas.

He dragged deeply at a dagga joint. "Trust me, Chris. Come celebrate Christmas in the desert with me."

Mike was late again. As always. Yesterday, December 21, I arrived in Swakop from the Kaoko. Mike had arranged to meet me at The Tug on the quay today at one; it was half past one now. I was sitting on the balcony. Inside, the place was packed with foreigners and holidaymakers. I decided to take a walk on the beach. Mike could wait for me.

Half an hour later I was back at The Tug. I looked through the glass doors. No sign of Mike. But that was how I knew him. Still the same people in the restaurant. I sat down on the balcony again and ordered another beer. It was a sunny day at the coast.

A girl got up from one of the tables inside. She approached me uncertainly. "Excuse me," she said, "are you waiting

249

for a man called Mike? He said we should meet him here at one."

"I'm waiting for him too, yes. It's such a nice day. Why don't you join me outside?"

Mike's English friends moved to my table and I was introduced to Rick, Charlie, Claire, Sarah and Ron. The girl who had approached me was Henrietta, affectionately known as Henri. More beer was ordered. We chatted and made each other's acquaintance.

Their fears about Mike had been allayed. They were visibly relieved when I said: "Look, this is Mike for you. Always late, and usually very late. He'll be late for his own funeral one day."

Charlie and Henri were the only ones who actually knew Mike; the others had never met him. They had landed in Windhoek from the UK the prvevious day and arrived in Swakop that morning.

More beer broke down the barriers. The atmosphere was genial. "Yes," said Henri, "Mike told us to look out for a long-haired guy with one arm."

At three o'clock there was still no sign of Mike.

"Let me take you on a tour of the town's watering holes," I proposed. "Mike can look for us for a change." Everyone agreed enthusiastically.

At five Mike tracked us down in the Schutze Hotel, better known as the Boere Bar. By this time the Brits and the local bar flies had become sworn allies. Henri was playing snooker with Piesang Pretorius, who was paralysed on one side of his body after being wounded in the bush war.

Rick announced that he wanted to spend Christmas in the Boere Bar. "Who is this Mike chap anyway? Sod Mike. I'm staying right here."

At that moment Mike entered.

After he had greeted everyone, introduced himself and apologised profusely, he motioned for me to follow him. Outside the bar stood his bakkie, heavily loaded with supplies, camping equipment and paraphernalia.

"Chris, this isn't everything. There's more that we'll have to load onto your bakkie."

"What are we going to do with all this stuff, Mike?"

"Chris. It's Christmas, remember?"

That was Mike, always late for his own parties. It turned out to be an extraordinary Christmas. Mike never planned anything on a small scale.

It was late afternoon the next day. Our Christmas camp had been pitched under camel thorns beside the dry bed of the Aub River, in close proximity to the red dunes of Sossusvlei. Coarsely woven carpets with Eastern motifs lay scattered around the campfire. On the carpets were large cushions decorated with bells and tassels. Multicoloured kikoi cloths and wind chimes of bamboo hung from the branches of the trees – for atmosphere, Mike said. In a corner stood a plastic Christmas tree decorated with camel thorn pods and porcupine quills.

Besides the two-person tents for the girls, a mess tent canopy had been rigged to provide extra shade. Under this canvas roof stood a small battery-operated fridge and a fold-out table loaded with titbits and delicacies. Mike had spared no effort or cost. We smoked cigars and drank malt whiskey.

We read prose and recited poetry around the fire. Mike and I regaled the others with stories of our adventures in the wilderness. Every meal became a feast of potbrood and potjiekos. There was an endless supply of champagne. The English couldn't believe what had befallen them; it was their first visit to Africa. I felt guilty about my meagre contribution to the feast and tried to make up for it by acting as Mike's right-hand man.

It was Mike's pleasure to make the occasion special for his friends. He had a way of turning strangers into friends. On Christmas Eve we dragged our stuffed bodies up the red dunes. Charlie took along his didgeridoo and played it up there.

On Christmas day Mike prepared two Welsh turkeys. He

251

cooked them in an oven underneath the sand. The meat complemented the cold champagne. There were gifts and Christmas cake.

The feast continued during the return journey. At Solitaire we stopped for Moose McGregor's legendary coffee and apple tart. At a view site overlooking the Kuiseb valley we cracked another bottle of malt whiskey. I came to know the Brits and their histories. Claire was recently divorced. Ron suffered from depression and was battling with a drug problem. So, *that* had been Mike's plan.

It was late when we drove into Walvis Bay. Crazy Mama's kitchen was on the point of closing, but Mama said we could come in and eat. Afterwards we danced at La Plaza. It had been a good Christmas.

The next day we parted company at Swakopmund. There were tears in the girls' eyes. My new friends left, and Mike and I went for a beer at the Lighthouse.

We sat looking out over the sea while the draught beer took the edge off our hangovers.

"Mike. That idea of yours was a good one."

I caught my first glimpse of Mike Hearn from the shade of a mopane outside Khorixas. He didn't see me. I had just returned from Tanzania and was on my way to the Kaokoveld. On my way to a new life. I was almost there. Eight months through Africa had taken its toll. Malaria, diarrhoea, a broken hand and a lack of money. I was down and out. Horace McAllistair's message that he had a job for me in the Kaokoveld came as a godsend. I didn't waste any time in getting from the shores of Lake Victoria to the Kaokoveld. All night long on open trucks through Tanzania, Zambia, the Caprivi.

Under a mopane tree outside Khorixas sleep overwhelmed me. When I woke up, the Land Rover had almost passed. It was too late to draw the driver's attention. In the seconds during which the open Land Rover raced past, I got my first impression of Mike. An open-faced fellow in his early twenties. A hawk nose and shiny brown locks that streamed behind him. Suntanned arms and hands. His khaki shirt was faded and the back of the Land Rover was loaded with camping equipment and supplies. On the door was the familiar emblem of the Save the Rhino Trust.

In those few seconds I had seen enough. I recognised a man who was at home in his surroundings. In his bearing I read the confidence of someone who knew what he wanted and did what he wanted. Just as I used to. At that moment I knew: I wanted to be like that again.

A week later, driving along the banks of the Springbok River in a brand-new bakkie with an old .303 behind the seat, I met Mike in person. My first assignment was to help the staff of the Save the Rhino Trust with their annual census. I would never encounter a better friend in the Kaoko.

For the next three years Mike and I met regularly in the veld. Sometimes we'd work together on a game count or a rhino census. On other occasions we would stumble across each other's camp sites – Mike was stationed at Kowareb and I at Sesfontein. When we were both at home, we called on each other with a crate of beer, or a bottle of whiskey and a piece of meat. During the hunting season he would visit me at the hunting camp. Mike didn't actively oppose hunting; he just disliked taking part in it himself.

When my bakkie's engine seized on the Beesvlakte after an oil leak, I called on Mike to tow me in. It took us an entire day to get through the sand of the Kowareb Schlucht. Nothing was ever a problem for Mike. Those were difficult, lonesome times. It was good to know you were not alone. I spent many nights chatting to Mike around a campfire under the crystal-clear, starry sky of the Kaoko wilderness.

Mike came from a wealthy family in Kent, England. "Our house was next to a zoo – more nature park than zoo. A place with large open-air cages for the animals. At night I lay in my bed and listened to the lions roar. My dream of Africa began there. There were three black rhinos in the zoo. I was ten when one of the cows had a calf. The caretaker allowed me to feed him. I hung out there all weekend. During school holidays I volunteered my services.

"The zoo was also involved with fundraising for conservation projects. That's how I heard of the Save the Rhino Trust. I wanted to go to Africa. I suspect the zoo was fed up with me, so they sent me to Namibia – as their contribution.

"My first year was spent at the Windhoek head office. It was frustrating, but I learned a lot. I had to feed all the data that came out of the veld into the computer. I developed an extensive database. A year later I went into the veld myself. I learned a lot from the Damara trackers. Most of the rhinos are on computer now; my database is growing by the day. I've applied for a grant from the University of Kent. I hope to turn my field work into a master's degree."

Mike believed in camping in style. At first light he would be up, busy at the fire. When he saw I was awake, he would place a foaming, steaming mug of cappuccino next to my bedroll.

"It's the small things that make the difference," he always said. He spoke of his grandfather with pride. "My grandfather was in the Royal Camel Corps in the Sudan. He always said: 'Remember, Mike, any old sod can live uncomfortably.'"

It was during this time that we celebrated Christmas in the desert.

After three years I swapped Nature Conservation for the safari industry. I set up camp beside the Khumib River in the Skeleton Coast Park. Mike was also doing well. He had received his grant from the University of Kent. Thanks to funds being donated to the Save the Rhino Trust, he was able to replace his old Land Rover with a brand-new one. His studies meant that he had to spend at least three months per year in England. There were no rhinos where my safaris operated, so we saw less of each other.

After many months had passed, he arrived at my camp one day.

"Chris, I have a bright idea."

"Let's hear it, Mike."

"Let's get ourselves a place in Swakop. I'm looking for a place where I can write up my field work, and you can use it when you're on leave."

"You mean a flat?"

"Yes, or a house. We'll share the rent. I'll pay the water and electricity."

I thought for a while. "Have you got a place in mind?"

"Chris, you're going to be crazy about it. On the sea. A beautiful view. Three bedrooms, two bathrooms."

So it happened that Mike and I invested in the rent of a seafront manor. At first I was reluctant. It was terribly expensive. But in the end I had to admit: Mike had been right again. Mike did nothing on a small scale.

Heavy rains fell in the Kaokoveld that year. I was on leave and had just arrived on my first visit to the new house when I was laid low by malaria. Mike nursed me back to health in our new home. He made tea and ordered pizza. He drew back the curtains so that I could look out over the ocean.

"You were right, Mike. What a beautiful view."

"Chris, you know what my grandpa used to say: 'Any old sod can live uncomfortably.' "

We had good times. Our house became a haven to which I could return after two months of desert expeditions. Mike spent more time at Swakop than I did and built up a circle of friends. The safari operators who lived in Swakop and operated in the Kaoko became regular visitors at the house. Their lady friends too. Mike bought a mountain bike and joined a biking club.

Whenever I arrived at the house, Mike would be entertaining. It was a time of parties and late nights. We hung around in pubs and night clubs and slept late the following morning. It was great to wake up with the sound of waves in our ears.

There was also a healthy flow of girls. When Mike was in the veld, he was generous with his keys. I often arrived home to find two or three ladies occupying his room or the spare room. When Mike was home, he usually had a pretty young girl by his side. It was a lovely, lively house. There was always music and, in the mornings, the smell of cappuccino.

But the pressure of Mike's success was slowly taking its toll. His studies were demanding. There were also his responsibilities at the Save the Rhino Trust – he had since been promoted to Director of Research.

Furthermore, he enjoyed the status he had acquired among the young crowd in Swakop. He was their Renaissance man. The handsome, sporting hedonist. The successful academic. The devoted nature conservationist. He carried around him the aura of a Jesus figure: the mystique of the wilderness combined with long hair and green eyes, a tall, powerful frame and worldly sophistication. All these attributes made him a well-loved and popular social figure – a role he took on with enthusiasm.

Mike and I seldom met in the veld now. At Swakop we were always partying in a group. There was no more time for private conversation. I didn't realise the load was becoming too heavy for my friend.

One morning we were sitting on the sofa in the lounge. We were drinking cappuccino and staring out across the sea.

"Chris."

"Yes?"

"Let's celebrate my birthday in the desert. I'll be thirty this year."

"Damn. Have we known each other that long?"

This time Mike did it in style. We decided that Bloedkoppie was a good place for a birthday party. In the desert, but within reach of Swakop. A great many people were invited. Mike hired a caterer to make all the preparations before the time.

We drove to Bloedkoppie in the minibus Mike had acquired. It was a convenient set of wheels; he had taken out the back seats to create sleeping space.

A tented village had arisen at Bloedkoppie. No money or trouble had been spared. Mike and his mountain-biking friends showed off their bikes and skills on the granite slopes in the late afternoon.

I didn't enjoy the party. It wasn't real, like Christmas at Sossusvlei. There were many different characters and each tried harder than the next to impress. Mike played host and went to great lengths to meet everyone's demands.

I noticed something in him that I couldn't fathom: a restlessness and a hidden melancholy. I couldn't put my finger on it, but I knew Mike wasn't himself. Later that night I climbed Bloedkoppie alone in the moonlight while the party was still raging below.

The next morning the guests departed early; they were keen to get home. Mike and I stayed behind to help the caterer clean up. With Mike was Helen, an Australian girl for whom Mike had a soft spot.

We drove back in Mike's minibus. Helen was in the back. Around us the desert stretched far and wide. We wound down a stony ridge and then the road led straight across the rocky plain.

The minibus was gradually veering towards the side of the road. "Mike, stay on the road," I said.

"Mike, you're going off the road," I repeated.

"Mike, what are you doing?" Helen's voice came from behind.

I looked at my friend at the wheel. His hands had left the steering wheel and he held them clenched to his chest. His upper body was twisted round so that he was facing Helen at the back. His long hair had fallen over his face. I had no idea what was happening.

"Mike, stop fucking around!"

The next minute the minibus went onto the gravel verge. It ploughed up a bank, shot up in the air and landed on the road reserve. Ahead of us loomed a sandy ditch. Helen let out a scream. The minibus was heading straight for the ditch. Still Mike sat hunched up, facing the back. The ditch came nearer. My right hand gripped the wheel. I realised I had to keep the wheels straight.

The minibus lurched through the sandy ditch and landed with a crunch in a cloud of dust. Helen was flung against the roof. The wheels remained straight and the minibus ploughed on through the desert. The loose, sandy gravel began to suck at the wheels. The vehicle slowed down and began to stutter. We came to a halt.

Uncontrolled spasms jerked through Mike's body. I jumped out and ran round the front of the minibus. I yanked the door open. Mike's face was blue. His pupils were constricted. His lower jaw was slack. I looked inside his mouth – his airways seemed clear. Why was he blue?

The spasms were less severe now. I held him so that he was leaning out of the door. Saliva was dripping from his throat. I placed my hands under his armpits, lifted him out and laid him on the sand. The convulsions continued. I pinched his nostrils, put my mouth over his and blew. I compressed his chest. I repeated the procedure a few times. He coughed. His breathing seemed normal. The convulsions abated. He lay in the sand, unconscious.

In the meantime Helen had recovered. We had to get Mike back into the minibus. He was a big fellow and a dead weight. Damned heavy. The only way to do it was for me to place my hands under his armpits once more and drag him around the vehicle. We laid him in the back. Helen wiped his face with a wet cloth and got in next to him. His breathing was regular.

I stepped on the accelerator to get the minibus out of the sandy gravel. Moments later we were back on the dirt road. As fast as possible I drove to Swakop. Helen held Mike's head in her lap. She stroked his hair.

Slowly Mike came to his senses. "Oh God. Oh God," he mumbled confusedly.

"Howzit, bra? Welcome back. You gave us a fright."

Ten minutes later Mike had recovered enough to ask Helen to find his medication in his backpack. Back in Swakop we put him to bed.

Helen had to go home. I stopped her at the door. I looked

into her eyes. "Helen. Not a word about this to anyone. Right?"

"Right, Chris. I promise."

Mike slept for a long time. Late in the afternoon I took him a cup of tea. I sat down on the bed. I had never seen him so depressed.

"Why didn't you tell me, Mike?"

He pulled up the blankets and stared out over the sea. He sighed. "It's been such a long time. It never happened while I was tracking rhino alone in the veld. It's coming back."

"You work too hard and you play too hard. You must take it easier."

"When I was small, my parents took me to see a specialist. He said I should always live near a town or city – within reach of doctors and hospitals. That's when I decided it wasn't going to control my life. That's why I'm here. That's why I do what I do. If I was in England now, I wouldn't even be allowed to drive a car.

"I was a child when I got it for the first time. In an amusement arcade – the flickering screens triggered the attack. Many of my school friends were present, boys *and* girls. While I lay there jerking, I wet my pants. It was the worst humiliation. I think my computer screen is making it worse."

I thought for a long time before I spoke. My heart went out to my friend. I didn't want to see him like this.

"Mike, it's just your brake. Guys like you and me, we need brakes – I've got only one arm. If we didn't have brakes, we would conquer the world. But you must calm down. We need you. Your studies, your conservation work – they're invaluable. The black rhinos need you. Your friends love you. Don't live in denial. Tell us how you're doing. Tell us where you keep your medication. It's nothing to be ashamed of. No one thinks less of you."

Then it was time for a warning. "Remember one thing, Mike: You weren't the only one in that car today. Others could have been hurt."

Mike fell into a dark depression. He spent most of the

next three days sleeping, or wandering aimlessly through the house. I made tea and ordered pizza.

While he was sleeping, I sat looking out over the sea. It was remarkable how many people came to the Kaokoveld to escape from something. I could list them. There was Pieter du Preez on the Kunene River, an ex-soldier trying to make sense of the bush war. Gert van der Linde, the policeman at Sesfontein, who still had nightmares about the Soweto riots. Horace McAllistair and his failed marriage, his estrangement from his sons. Me, with my Kruger Park baggage.

We were all loners, outsiders, exiles. We all bore scars. In a way we had been living through Mike. He was the undamaged one, the one who was here because he wanted to be here, without any dark secrets. The golden boy.

How wrong we had been. Mike was one of us after all.

I met Emsie. One evening Mike and I went to Rafters to drink; Emsie had come to dance. Somewhere in the clamour we met.

That night I walked her back to her flat. Later I walked back home alone. She was also in search of something. In search of adventure. I gave her a name and a number to call.

After three years at the Skeleton Coast, I was ready for a fresh challenge. It came in the form of a new safari camp in the foothills of the Etendekas, in the Uniab River valley. A wilderness of half a million hectares in the heart of black rhino country. There were misgivings about the wisdom of a safari camp in rhino territory. Our competition was sceptical: A permanent undertaking would disturb the rhinos. We would frighten them away.

In some respects it was no more than jealousy because we had been given the concession, but some of the arguments were valid. Mike and I met under the mopanes at Rooiplaat.

"Mike, how do we approach this thing the right way?"

We formulated a strategy. The entire focus of our safaris would be rhino conservation, as opposed to rhino viewing by tourists. A policy of minimum interference would be followed. The black rhinos would be approached on foot. Safari groups would maintain their distance downwind, so that the rhinos would remain unaware of them. Every rhino viewing would be assessed for its disturbance factor. We would account for every rhino we encountered.

The safari guides would help the rangers of the Save the Rhino Trust to collect data. The safari camp would serve as a rangers' station, from where guides and game rangers would patrol the area together. Mike would be given a tent in the camp and would remain involved as far as possible. The initial plan had simply been to make money out of rhino conservation, but it was finally decided that the safari undertaking would be an integral part of the conservation project.

Our plan was submitted to our respective directors. It was accepted unanimously. I went back to the Skeleton Coast one last time to conclude my business there. When I returned to the safari camp at Rooiplaat, my fellow manager had arrived. It was Emsie. Emsie Verwey from Swakop.

During this time Mike and I were closer than ever. Zealously we tackled our new project. Emsie took over the management of the camp. She created order and atmosphere. She trained chefs, waiters and housekeepers. Mike and I spent our days in the veld, tracking black rhino. We trained guides and game rangers. We collected data. Which rhino bull was dominant in which area? This cow is pregnant and that one in season.

Mike was worried: there were equal numbers of male and female calves. It meant that the population was stagnant. Rhinos would have to be exported to other parts of the Kaoko where they had occurred naturally in earlier times. It would stimulate growth around here.

I realised again how completely dedicated Mike was. After eleven years of research he *knew* his subject. This knowledge was partnered with a genuine love of rhinos. He knew which calf belonged to which cow. He knew the individual temperaments of the various animals. This bull is old and docile, we can approach. No, look out for that one. It's not that he's about to charge, he's just getting ready for a high-speed investigation. To me it looked like exactly the same thing.

Back at camp we'd sit around the fire, glass in hand, chatting. Inspired by our dreams for this place. Emsie would sit down beside me and listen. We became a tight-knit group. In time Emsie became my love.

The Rhino Safari quickly made a name for itself. Our guests felt honoured to be part of a conservation project. Reporters came to visit. Mike, Emsie and I appeared on British, German and South African television.

To Mike the camp became an escape. The Save the Rhino Trust often needed him elsewhere. His studies took him back to England. There was his busy social life at Swakop. He came to the safari camp to relax with Emsie and me. Emsie and he prepared meals in the kitchen and joked and exchanged banter.

When there were guests, Mike shared his rhino conservation philosophy with them. A safari came alive in Mike's presence. After a while he would leave, and Emsie and I would stay behind.

From time to time rumours reached us in his absence: Mike had passed his exams with honours. Mike had fallen with his mountain bike. Mike had befriended the Swakop surfers; he was learning to surf. Then, weeks or months later, he would put in an appearance.

On 22 November 2003 England played Australia in the Rugby World Cup final. We drove from Rhino Camp to Palmwag to watch the game on satellite TV. There were a lot of people. Dennis Liebenberg of Etendeka Mountain Camp. Duncan Gilchrist of Kamanjab. Travellers and tourists. A jolly atmosphere prevailed. Mike was ecstatic about England's victory and partied the night away.

At breakfast the next morning we were all rather fragile. Mike didn't look well. He was sitting next to me. He turned to me. I could see something was wrong.

"Chris, stay with me," was all he said before his body

went into a spasm. I took hold of him firmly and laid him down on the floor. I moved the tables and chairs out of the way so that he wouldn't hurt himself. I assured the holiday-makers that everything was in order and asked them to leave the room; it would be over shortly. I closed the door and sat down next to Mike until he had recovered.

Life went on.

One day Mike arrived at camp. "Chris."

"Yes?"

"Let's celebrate Christmas and New Year in the desert."

"What a good idea, Mike. Where did you have in mind this time?"

"Right here in our own camp. Just you, me, Emsie, the game rangers, guides and staff."

It became a quiet, peaceful Christmas. Mike beat me at chess and remained unbeaten at boules. Emsie and he con-cocted meals in the kitchen. There was laughter around the fire in the evenings. By day we went in search of black rhino. New Year was livelier. Guests and staff members arrived. At midnight we drank a toast with champagne. We drank to Rhino Camp and black rhinos – may they live for ever. We drank to love and friendship and Mike's doctorate in the new year.

A week later Mike had to return to Swakop. He kissed Emsie and she hugged him for a long time. Then he and I embraced each other with love. The true love between two men who had gone through the mill together. A love that could only come into being in the wilderness.

Breaking stone in the basalt of the Etendekas was hard work. Fortunately twenty Damaras had volunteered to help. I had learned how to wield a pickaxe with one hand and a shor-tened arm. Actually it was easy: gravity did the work. Nevertheless, the Damaras wouldn't allow me inside the hole for long. They fell over each other to relieve me.

We sweated and bled. Once again I admired these people's

ability to work. It's a hard country. It took us three days to complete our task.

I drove to the safari camp, showered, dressed in clean clothes and said goodbye to Emsie. Then I got into the Land Rover and drove to Wêreldsend to meet Mike's parents; they had arrived earlier in the day. Mike had relocated the base of the Save the Rhino Trust from Kowareb to Wêreldsend a few years before, to be closer to the rhinos.

I found Mike's parents in his room, looking through his photos. They got into my Land Rover and we drove back to the safari camp. Emsie was waiting with tea and cake. Mike's father was old and frail. His mother put up a cheerful front; I could see Mike had been his mother's son.

Mike's elder brother was a banker and his younger brother a businessman. They had never been in Mike's world before. In his tent at our camp they selected a few of his books and photos. No, his eldest brother said, we should keep the chess set and the boules.

We left the camp and drove through the veld. We saw springbok and giraffe. As we passed through the neck at Koabesfontein a figure appeared. Etched against the blue sky, the massive rhino bull watched our passing.

At sunset we reached the place. It was a rocky ridge in the Uniab River valley with a view across the foothills of the Etendekas. Mike's rhino fields. Mike had lived here. His parents and brothers agreed: it was a good place.

The next day it was Mike's funeral. He had been on his surfboard in the sea at Swakop when he'd suffered the attack.

It was late afternoon when the procession arrived. Hundreds of people gathered around Mike's grave. In the distance the coffin bearers appeared, frequently relieving one another.

The Himbas, with assegais and kieries, followed behind, doing the rhino dance. "Ongava, huu. Ongava, huu." Their feet sent up a cloud of red dust.

I stood next to Mike's two brothers. "Go and fetch your brother," I said.

With their arms around each other they went to take over from the game rangers at the head of the procession. I fell in behind them with some of Mike's friends from Swakop and England, and we carried the coffin to its final destination.

Earlier that afternoon Mike's body had been flown in from Swakop. We had left the coffin uncovered, and Damaras, Hereros, Himbas and Riemvasmakers had filed past in their Sunday best. Game rangers and guides in uniform, immaculately turned out. There were heart-rending moments beside the coffin.

When everyone had left, I sat with him for a long time. Waited for him to regain consciousness. To me he was still alive. I waited for his bright green eyes to open and for him to say: "Chris. Let's celebrate Christmas in the desert." Finally I closed the coffin.

At the graveside the Himbas fell silent. The Anglican priest delivered a sermon. He read from John 14, verses 1 to 6. Emsie and I stood close together next to Mike's relatives. His parents had insisted that he be buried in his beloved renosterveld. They had flown from England to Namibia with his brothers, his professor and numerous friends.

King Eustace Garoëb addressed Mike's family. He thanked them for allowing Mike to rest in Damaraland. The Damara nation considered him a son of Damaraland. On a canvas chair at the graveside sat Mike's elderly father. He was deeply moved. Beside him stood his wife, brave and resolute.

Neil McGregor was there too, dumbstruck in his best faded khaki uniform. Horace McAllistair stepped forward to say a few words. He was overcome by emotion.

Then it was my turn. I walked up to Mike's coffin and tried to speak. Blinded by tears, I struggled to find words.

Then the words came. They rolled across the hills and plains of the desert. I bellowed in a loud voice. I was unaware of anyone around me. Only of the sun's rays on the red rocks and the smell of dust.

The lads in their hundreds to Ludlow came in for the fair,
There's men from the barn and the forge and the mill and the fold,
The lads for the girls and the lads for the liquor are there,
And there with the rest are the lads that will never be old.
There's chaps from the town and the field and the till and the cart,
And many to count are the stalwart and many the brave,
And many the handsome of face and the handsome of heart,
And few that will carry their looks or their truth to the grave.
I wish one could know them, I wish there were tokens to tell
The fortunate fellows that now you can never discern;
And then one could talk with them friendly and wish them farewell
And watch them depart on the way they will not return.
But now you may stare as you like and there's nothing to scan,
And brushing your elbow unguessed at and not to be told
They carry back bright to the coiner the mintage of man,
The lads that will die in their glory – and never be old. ★

Mike was in time.

★ Alfred E. Housman, "The lads that will never be old".

No-man's-land

In the glow of the lamplight we studied the map. We were bent over the table in the tent. Neil McGregor drew a circle with his calloused forefinger.

"Here. This part bothers me. I have no idea what goes on there." His finger lingered on the map. "At the moment we're not using that area. If we don't begin to do it, *they* will. We have to stop them. Beat them to it." Neil spoke heatedly. Theuns and I looked at each other.

Neil bent over the map again. "I've never been there myself. You'll have to take a look." With his finger he drew a line along a contour.

"This is where the old patrol road used to run. We used it in the early '80s. It's an alternative route between Groot Agab and Swartmodderfontein. That's as far as I've been, I have no idea what lies further south. I think it'll be a good idea to open up that patrol road again."

He stared at the open space on the map for a long time. The lamplight played over the wrinkles around his eyes. The frown cut deeply into his forehead. I could see a plan taking shape in his mind. He looked up, first at Theuns, then at me.

"Just like us, they're also studying the map. This part is no-man's-land. They're going to claim it. If we can't prove that it's an integral part of our operation, we're going to lose it. It'll be too late then. All the conservation that we've been doing here over the years will have been to no avail."

The older he grew, the more Neil McGregor tended to overdramatise, but I thought he was right.

Some months ago the Namibian government had announced that a number of conservation areas were going to be opened up to professional hunters. The rhino concession was one of those. Our director in Windhoek had immediately protested to the minister: Our company's product was irreconcilable with professional hunting. We specialised in wilderness expeditions and photographic safaris. They couldn't be undertaken in an area where hunting took place.

Neil McGregor of Nature Conservation had also expressed his concern immediately. How would hunting affect the black rhino? This last population had to be looked after like a treasure. The rhinos shouldn't be disturbed.

Mike and I agreed: Professional hunting was in conflict with the approach of our safaris. We sold a conservation project – the safaris were all about rhino conservation. We raised funds for the Save the Rhino Trust. When we followed the rhinos on foot, we tried not to disturb them. The data collection and research project were explained to our guests. They appreciated being able to take part in the conservation effort. How would we explain shots being fired by hunters?

Our director had convened a meeting in Windhoek. In the boardroom he had spoken earnestly: "I was in contact with the permanent secretary this morning. According to him, the hunting will carry on. In Etosha, Hobatere, Etendeka and in our own area. The quota includes six black rhino. He suggests we get used to the idea.

"I said no. Our company is the largest provider of employment in the Northwest. During the past five years we have employed and trained hundreds of people. We are actively involved with the local communities and with black empowerment organisations. We pay millions to the government in annual concession fees. No. We are entitled to fight this decision. Fight we will fight."

All day we had wrestled with the problem in the boardroom. The director, Neil McGregor, two members of empowerment organisations that have ties with the central government, various concession managers, Mike and I. We decided on a strategy. A management plan was drafted. We ordered takeaway pizza and studied maps of the area. By early evening we reached concensus.

The director summed it up: "We have a concession area of half a million hectares. Seventy per cent of Namibia's free-ranging black rhino can be found there. The only way we are going to keep the hunters out is by using the area optimally for our own purposes. Here are the ways in which we will be doing it."

Since the meeting in Windhoek quite a few things had happened. Neil McGregor had resigned from the Ministry of Nature Conservation and accepted a post as a consultant in our company. Shortly afterwards Mike had died. We had to try and fill the gap left by him. Theuns Kotze had offered his services. Now the two of us and Neil were standing around a map, on the eve of an adventure.

It was early morning when Theuns and I pulled up at Swart-modderfontein in the Land Rover. We had left the safari camp an hour before sunrise. The double-track road had taken us across the rocky plains of the Uniab River. In those parts you drove slowly. It was rugged terrain. We had to cross the rocky river bed a few times. There had been good rains around our camp that year; west of the camp the rain had been sparser. Here at Swartmodder it was dry.

Now we had to find the old patrol road. With map, compass and GPS we began to explore the area on foot. We found the drainage line that Neil McGregor had told us to look for. We returned to the Land Rover and began to drive along the river bed. We went up a slight rise and crossed a watershed. A rocky expanse stretched ahead of us. No sign of the old patrol road. Just keep going south, Neil had said. We headed south across the rocky surface and joined up with another stream bed. We descended into an undulating valley. In the east a prominent hill came into view. The stream bed snaked up to its foot.

"Theuns, let's climb that hill. Let's see what we can discover from up there."

It was a long climb. When we reached the top, we were soaked in sweat. From there we had a panoramic view over the renosterveld. Far to the east lay the Grootberg, hazy and colossal. Like a gigantic Hadrian's Wall, it isolates this region from the rest of the land. Beneath it, in folds, lay the flat tops of its foothills – the Etendekas. Then the countryside began to even out in undulating valleys. By the bright yellow grass and the green ribbon that was the Salvadora River we recognised the valley where our camp lay.

At our feet the Uniab valley lay to the north. The Agab River joined up with it from the east. The wooded stream bed of the Uniab snaked westward; on its banks Swartmodderfontein was visible as a green speck. We turned and faced south. Theuns and I looked at each other and smiled. We both felt the thrill of the unknown. To the south lay no-man's-land. I felt my spirit starting to soar.

This was unexplored territory. The explorers Anderson and Galton did not pass this way. Neither did Eriksson. Gert Alberts came down the Hoarusib River during his 1879 expedition, two hundred kilometres north of here. The Uniab was charted only in 1900 – Hauptman von Estorff explored the Uniab River as part of the Hartmann expedition. His journal was filled with descriptions of the desolation of these parts.

Where the Uniab mouths into the Atlantic Ocean, Von Estdorff found a colony of thirty Strandlopers. They had been there for centuries. At the Groot Agab fountain a small rock engraving is hidden among the rocks – someone chiselled out a spiral thousands of years ago. People survived there – *lived* there. They hunted; on the beach west of there white mussels were dug up. In the dunes they picked narras. To the south, at the mouth of the Kuiseb, people farmed with cattle. I looked down and in my mind's eye I saw a small band of people criss-crossing the plains.

After the Second World War farms were marked out east of there and made available to war veterans. Rooiplaat, where our safari camp stands today, was one of them. The

farmers kept karakul sheep. In 1968 the farms were expro-
priated and Damaraland was created. In the 1970s and '80s
illegal hunting flourished. Opportunists took advantage of the
border war to poach in the area. People like Neil McGregor
and Horace McAllistair stepped in. The Save the Rhino
Trust was established. The battle against rhino poaching was
on. The local Damara and Nama people were employed as
game rangers. That was the sum total of the European in-
fluence there.

Theuns and I walked back to the Land Rover. We drove
further south, into the unknown. We crossed another watershed. The valleys had steeper sides now. We joined up with a
well-trodden zebra path. An indistinct trail snaked alongside
it – years ago a bakkie wheel had moved rocks out of the way
there. We had found the patrol road.

It was difficult to stay on the track; in most places the
road had disappeared completely. I drove, while Theuns sat
with the map and compass on his lap. The road snaked east-
ward in the direction of Groot Agab.

Between navigating and driving, Theuns and I talked. He
was a qualified exploration geologist. Mike had introduced
me to him ten years before in the Springbok River. He was
working for the Save the Rhino Trust then.

He got to know this desert when he worked for the mining companies before that time. The desert cast its spell on
him, as it did on us. He realised that the destruction caused
by his employers was in conflict with his beliefs. He gave up
his highly paid job and began to work for the Save the Rhino
Trust for a pittance.

It was not sustainable, however. To survive, he left to do
contract exploration in the Khomas Highland. "It's close to
Windhoek. I don't feel so guilty about pushing a drill through
a rock there."

Theuns was a drifter. Sometimes he would disappear for
months, even years, on end. Time and again the desert called
him back. With his round spectacles and goatee he was
something between Adolf Lüderitz and Emin Pasha. After

271

Mike's death he came forward and offered his services. Now his function was to maintain roads in the concession areas – and open up new routes with me.

It became easier to follow the patrol road. It headed due east. Familiar peaks became visible. It led in the direction of Groot Agab. Our view to the south was restricted by a range of ridges. Far behind the ridges a mountain top was visible in the haze. I stopped the Land Rover. "Let's take a look."

With backpack, map and compass, Theuns and I walked south. One range of ridges made way for the next. We saw no game at all. We got into a rhythm. Except for the crunching of our boots, absolute silence reigned. Both of us delighted in the uniqueness of the wilderness. There is no greater, purer feeling.

We crossed another ridge and the earth fell away at our feet. Silently we stared out across the horizon. Vaguely defined drainage lines disappeared to the southwest. The mountain top that we had seen turned out to be part of a red basalt range. Monumentally it watched over the emptiness.

Excitement gripped me once again. I looked at Theuns. He shared my feelings. We knew: no man had been here before.

I tried to sum up my feelings. Ecstasy, fear, anticipation, humility. I had been in many godforsaken places. I had crossed the Kaokoveld. I had been on top of hills where I'd felt sure no one had been before me. This was different. Here desolation stretched into nothingness. I tried to imagine how our predecessors must have felt. Did Gert Alberts feel the same? Georg Hartmann? Fernando da Costa Leal?

I turned to Theuns. "We have to go in here."

In the Land Rover we made our way across the ridges. Then we reached a place where there was a gap. We tackled the descent down a small gorge. Theuns lit his pipe.

"Koos du Plessis must be turning in his grave now," he said out of the blue.

"What are you on about?" Theuns lived on his own planet most of the time.

272

He drew deeply at his pipe, coughed and looked at me. "Kyk, daar lê reeds spore op die maan – Look, there are footprints even on the moon."

In silence we drove on. The wheels trod on virgin soil – rocks were nudged aside. The basalt peaks kept watch over us. The sun moved across the sky to the west. The peaks became a deeper red. Something a client once said around a campfire came to my mind: "A road is a dagger in the heart of the wilderness."

All of a sudden we reached a moringa forest. The trees with their bright green leaves just appeared in front of us. In the shade of a big tree we ate the lunch Emsie had packed for us. We drank coffee. Had this tree with its gigantic trunk ever provided shade for anyone else?

Opposite us stood a single witgat tree. A gemsbok stood under it as if he had taken root there.

After we had eaten, we drove on. South of the mountain top were three round koppies. We got out of the Land Rover, took the map and compass and walked up the highest of the three. Each lost in his own thoughts.

On top of the koppie we spread out the map, placing stones on the corners. Below us the emptiness stretched in every direction. In a valley a herd of zebra walked in single file. According to the map Groot Tafelberg lay south of us, where the veterinary line meets the Skeleton Coast Park, but we could not see it from where we were standing. It felt as if we were off the map.

All of a sudden I wondered: What are we doing here? Are we busy with conservation or destruction? After decades the old patrol road is still visible. We drove the Land Rover here with very little difficulty. We have already made a road.

If we don't do it, someone else will.

But that's not the point. We are inextricably part of the epidemic. Where we set foot, we infect.

If we don't do it, someone else will.

That is the point entirely. Miner, hunter, nature conservationist – we are all people. Nothing stops our advance. We will penetrate the remotest corners of the earth. To use them for our own ends. Optimally.

The zebras disappeared through a neck in the mountain. Around us lay the unknown plains, valleys and mountains. They extended as far as the eye could see. Unnamed. Untouched.

For a long time we stood there. The sun moved closer to the horizon. A cold southwester came up. I drank in the scene for a while longer. Then I turned to Theuns.

"Are we going on, or are we turning back?"

Tier

I have a bad record with dogs. My first dog was Tonka, a labrador bitch. She died of a broken heart when I left for the army. Baloo, the dog I had in the Kaokoveld, also died because I had deserted him. In spite of this, I decided it was time to get another dog. This time I would try harder to look after him.

When Duncan Gilchrist's Jack Russell bitch had puppies, he sent word. Emsie and I drove from Rooiplaat to Kamanjab to take a look. In a small room behind the bar of the guest house we found Bonnie and her litter.

Bonnie was a darling dog. There was a gentleness in her that put a slight damper on the typical Jack Russell boldness and liveliness. Her tail wagged when she saw Emsie and me. She allowed us to look at her babies; she knew us, after all.

I spotted him immediately: the runt of the litter. With reddish brown and white patches and a white tuft on his forehead. Fine black hairs mingled with the brown along his spine. There were dark blotches on his pink tummy and willie. The first name I came up with was Spikkeltril. Emsie vetoed it straightaway.

I picked him up. Barely bigger than a field mouse. I held him against my cheek. He found my earlobe and sucked. I knew then he would be *my* dog.

We left him behind. He still had to be weaned. At sunset we crossed the Grootberg Pass. We stopped to admire the view. It was dark when we drove through the rocky drift in the Karkapi River.

"What's that?" Emsie asked.

In the bakkie's headlights I saw a head disappear behind a rock.

"Aardwolf," was my first reaction.

"No, it's not," Emsie said.

I went closer. Behind the rock a leopard rose to its feet. It narrowed its eyes against the light. It was a large male with a thick neck. He stood motionless for a few seconds. Then he disappeared behind a brosdoring.

I reversed the Land Rover so that the lights shone at an angle. We caught the leopard in the headlights. He came out from behind the brosdoring – a beautiful creature. This time he allowed us to admire him for longer. As always, we were enchanted. We stared at him in silence. Then he decided we had seen enough. He turned and walked away through the undergrowth.

As he disappeared from the circle of light, I realised the meeting had taken place for a reason.

"We'll call him Tier," I told Emsie. "We'll call the puppy Tier."

A month later Duncan came to Palmwag. I met him there to receive the puppy. On the way back, the little fellow curled up in my leather jacket on the passenger's seat of the Land Rover. He slept all the way.

It was the end of June and cold at night. Tier found a spot for himself under the blankets between Emsie and me. A territorial struggle ensued between Emsie's two cats and the puppy. The grey cat took one look at the dog and moved back to her hide-out in the river bank. Emsie was upset. The grey cat had finally begun to adapt – crawled into bed on Emsie's side late at night and sometimes stayed in the tent all day; now she was aloof again.

The white cat couldn't care less. She stayed on the bed with the puppy. When he was a bit too eager to acquaint himself with her, she gave him a few painful clips on the nose. He had to know his place.

When I wasn't on safari, I walked in the veld with the dog. Clumsily he stumbled over stones. He smelled every bush and dunghill. When we encountered springbok or zebra, I picked him up. As soon as he noticed them, he pricked up his ears and stared after them with his gentle young eyes.

To keep a dog in a safari camp is against company policy. I soon realised that Tier couldn't come to the veld when I had clients. Yet I wanted him to have as much veld experience as possible.

The safari season got underway and I was seldom at camp. Emsie was upset about her grey cat. The cat came in only to eat; she wanted nothing to do with anyone. The nights were cold. The puppy pissed and shat in the tent. It didn't improve his relationship with Emsie.

Because of my regular absences, I was also struggling to bond with the dog. I began to wonder whether it had been a good idea to get him after all. The puppy could sense this.

Our tent was some distance from the safari camp. In the evenings, while we were seated at the table or around the fire with our guests, the dog had to stay in the tent. He was desperate to follow us. We had to shut him in the bathroom tent, the only place with a door that closed properly. When we left, he whined pitifully.

One night, when I returned earlier than usual, the wails sounded intense. Our shower was sunk about half a metre into the stone floor of the bathroom. The puppy had fallen in. I lifted him out and held him against me. He pressed his little face into my neck and howled uncontrollably. I smelled his puppy body and lay down on the bed with him. He was cold and wet. I warmed him. Grunting, he fell asleep in my neck. What was I going to do with the dog?

Our leave came round. Emsie has a comfortable flat in Swakop, over the garage of a German couple. When she left for the wilderness two and a half years ago, she kept it on. The two of us share the rent now. It's a nice place – thatched roof with heavy rafters and whitewashed walls. The Germans have a beautiful garden, lush green and full of palm trees. From the bathroom window we overlook the Swakop River and the duneveld of its southern bank.

The flat is a lovely place to recuperate after a busy safari season. We relax in the cool sea air. We sleep late and watch videos and DVDs. The scent of thatch reminds me of the veld; it makes me feel at home. In the late afternoon I walk in the dunes on the opposite side of the river. Sometimes I'm alone, sometimes groups of people pass me on four-wheel motorbikes.

Emsie's cats usually accompany us on leave. We catch them early in the morning and put them in their wooden cage. Then we load them into the back of Steppenwolf, my Land Rover. They kick up a racket all the way. This time Tier came along too.

It's a long trip. Sometimes we drive past Twyfelfontein, via Brandberg, but our usual route is through Wêreldsend, and then down the Skeleton Coast.

The Germans whose flat we rent at Swakop have a boerboel bitch. A dumb, friendly animal. Yet I have always felt uneasy about her; there's a coldness in her eyes. She came charging up to welcome us when the Land Rover pulled in. Carefully I put the puppy down in front of her. They had to become friends; we were all going to live together.

Tier flattened his ears. He tucked his tail between his legs, trying to wag it at the same time. He displayed submissive behaviour. The boerboel bitch began to sniff him. Tentatively he raised his head and gave her small licks on the nose. She allowed him to carry on. I relaxed.

While Tier was scampering about between the boerboel's large paws and jumping up and down to lick her, Emsie and I unloaded our luggage. We carried everything up the stone steps to the flat. Emsie unlocked the door. Our arms full, we walked into the cool, dark flat. The door slammed shut behind us. I put my backpack on the sofa. It was good to be back.

A fierce growl came from outside the closed door, followed by pitiful yelping. Emsie and I dropped everything and rushed to the door. I jerked it open. The boerboel looked up guiltily from the small puppy. I shooed her away.

Tier sat at my feet on the small landing in a pool of his

own blood. His right eyeball was protruding from the socket. I gathered him up and held him close. He made choking sounds. His blood spattered over my shirt and pants and left a smear across my cheek.

I turned to Emsie. "Vet!" was all I could get out.

She swung round to grab the keys of the Land Rover. Down the steps. To the car. With Tier in my arms, I jumped in.

Emsie raced through the quiet Saturday afternoon streets of Swakop. I held the trembling, bleeding puppy against me. He pushed his head into my neck. Pathetically, grotesquely, the staring eye dangled outside its socket. The three minutes it took us to reach the vet felt like an eternity. Thank goodness Emsie knew the town.

At the surgery, she pressed the emergency button. Silence. She pressed it again. A figure appeared behind the safety door. The door was opened. "Can you help us?" Emsie asked.

"Bring him in," was all the vet said. In the theatre he examined the puppy while I held the small body.

"His jaw is broken too. I'll have to give him an anaesthetic."

While Tier was falling asleep in my arms, I whispered in his ear: "Nothing will ever hurt you again. I'll see to it."

The vet told us to come back at half past five. For the rest of the day I sat in the flat, blaming myself. My disappointment knew no end. What was wrong with me? Why couldn't I look after my dogs? Why would a bitch attack a seven-week-old puppy? Poor little Tier. Barely seven weeks old.

Emsie kept me busy. She put on the Jethro Tull DVD she had bought for me a while ago. She asked about the group. The original members were Mick Abrahams, Ian Anderson, Glenn Cornick and Clive Bunker. Mick Abrahams later formed his own group; he wanted to concentrate on the blues. The name of his group was Blodwyn Pig. They fared well. Martin Barre replaced Abrahams on lead guitar. Jeffrey Hammond and Barrymore Barlow replaced Cornick and Bunker. John Evan joined them on keys. Personally I consider it Tull's best

line-up. Today only Anderson and Barre are left of the original members of Jethro Tull.

The vet reported: the boerboel's tooth had penetrated the
puppy's soft skull; it had made the eye pop out. He had put
the eye back in the socket; the broken lower jaw had been
attached with wire. Now we'd have to see. Bring him back in
a week's time, he said.

That night the puppy slept between Emsie and me. It
looked as if the cats had calmed down. They came to lie on
the bed. Perhaps they realised he was in pain.

The next day Tier seemed to have forgotten about his
run-in with the boerboel. The bitch knew she had misbe-
haved; she fled as soon as she saw us. I walked in the dunes
and on the beach with Tier. True to the way Jack Russells
have been bred over the years, all he wanted to do was dig.
Sand stuck to his injured eye. We rinsed it with salt water.
The little eye looked lifeless.

A week later the vet confirmed our suspicions: There was
no reflex. He surgically removed the eye and sewed the eyelids together. One-eyed Jack.

We returned to Rooiplaat. There was a slight lull before
the safaris would start in all earnest. Tier and I walked long
distances in the veld. He came face to face with springbok,
guinea fowl and zebra. He chased after them excitedly. I
taught him to return when I whistled. His short legs got
stronger by the day.

I showed him his first desert elephants. Quietly he sat
beside me on a rock, staring at them attentively. It was as if
he knew: Chasing them would be looking for trouble. The
bond between Tier and me was growing.

An old kudu bull got entangled in the veterinary fence.
Emsie, Fly, Tier and I drove there to set him free. The dog
danced around me while I struggled to disentangle the
kudu's paws. At last we had him free. But he was too weak
and couldn't get up. With a single shot to the head I put him
out of his misery. Tier drank deeply of the blood that flowed
over the parched earth.

Then the safari season began. Tier had to stay behind at camp. Now there was a new development: Emsie and he were becoming friends. He was with her all the time. He helped her with stocktaking and administration. The kitchen tent was out of bounds, but he waited excitedly outside. Emsie usually brought him a surprise.

When her duties were over, they took long walks in the veld. He became a lively, eager little dog. His coat was glossy and his muscles began to fill out. His eye was lively and cheerful.

The night he caught his first gerbil in the tent, we knew: the loss of the eye was not going to hold him back. Even the cats looked at him in awe.

Leave time came round again. My friend Simon and I were going to the Caprivi. Tier came along. He went for long walks with us up the omurambas. When it became too hot, I put him on my shoulder. He sat there like a parrot. One night our camp site was surrounded by a herd of elephants. They moved around us like ships in the moonlight. Now and again the sound of a branch snapping. From my bedroll, Tier gave short, growling barks.

Back in Damaraland a routine was established. When I was not on safari, Tier and I were in the veld. His instincts were developing well. Nose to the ground, he ran on the spoor of gemsbok. At camp he was Emsie's friend. He watched over her while the cats slept.

Tier and I became comrades. Travellers heading across the rocky plains in the direction of Rooiplaat might come across a one-armed man and a one-eyed dog walking in the veld. We have worked out a thing between us.

Reunion

As part of our nostalgic trip to the Western Caprivi, Simon and I had scheduled a visit to the Bushman camp at Mashambo. The Bushmen had first been my troops, and then game rangers in my anti-poaching unit. I found four of them at the camp. Pa was the oldest and the yellowest; Duwonga, Dwasha and Ben Kupinga were also there.

Since my stint in the Caprivi sixteen years earlier, I had seen them from time to time when my work had taken me there for short periods. Ben, especially – he had been Simon's game ranger. Eight years had passed since our last meeting. Today was a happy reunion. They were still Bushmen, though nowadays they are called Barakwena or Kwhe. They could usually be found somewhere in the veld, hunting or searching for veldkos. But today I was lucky to find four of my old veld crew there.

"Chris, we miss you every day," said Pa. He looked the same, only considerably more wrinkled.

Duwonga walked to his hut and brought out two sturdy traditional axes as gifts for Simon and me – on his previous visit Simon had told them the two of us would be coming. I was moved. Their wizened parents came out to greet us. Their children had grown unrecognisably.

"The year in the bush with you was the best year of my life. You're all still in my heart," I said.

We laughed and joked about our younger days in the bush. It was a sunny, fine spring morning. There was a glow inside me. Absence makes you forget how much you can grow to love others.

"Simon and I will be coming back this way in a week's

time," I said. "I'll buy food and tobacco and sweets at Kongola."

"Get some Surf too," Duwonga said.

"I'll do that."

Before we said goodbye, we took photos. The Bushman children found the mood contagious and danced around us while we were talking. We said a warm farewell – until next week, then.

Simon and I camped in the omurambas and on the banks of the Kwando River. Between elephants and braaivleis, hippos, AC/DC and Jack Daniel's he agreed to be my best man when Emsie and I got married in a few months' time.

While we were walking or driving or leaning with our backs against a termite hill, we discussed the Bushmen. During a conflict they always landed in the line of fire. Before Angolan independence they sided with the Portuguese. Before Namibia's independence they were on the South African side. Always on the losing side. When the Caprivians wanted to secede and there was unrest, they were persecuted again. Many fled to Botswana.

"It's good to see that most of them are back and able to resume their traditional existence in relative peace and quiet," Simon said. Through his work he continued to have contact with the Caprivi Bushmen.

The day before our return we crossed the Kwando River to Kongola to buy supplies from the Portuguese smuggler.

It was Sunday morning when Simon and I drove into Mashambo. I was looking forward to seeing my old comrades again. Under a large false mopane beside the road a church service was being held – a preacher in a tie stood beside a white bakkie. He had a Bible in his hand. His finger was in the air. It was chiefly women, children and old people attending the service.

A few hundred metres further along we saw a red bakkie. A group of Bushmen crowded around it. On the back of the bakkie stood a man, handing them wares.

"Seems the pensions have been paid out," Simon said.

"The government pays the Bushmen a monthly pension. The officials come from Rundu. As soon as they leave, the preachers move in – they know there'll be collection money. The hawkers are usually hot on their heels."

We stopped at the cluster of huts. Ben Kupinga came out to meet us. His greeting was subdued and formal. He seemed embarrassed.

Dwasha lay under a tree with his face in the sand. Pa came stumbling along, babbling unintelligibly. Holding on to my hand, he laughed raucously at his own joke, his eyes disappearing into the wrinkles on his face. Duwonga staggered by with staring eyes, bottle in hand. He didn't notice us at all and kept going.

We left the supplies with Ben Kupinga and drove on.

Moments

The Damaraland rhino are the last viable rhino population surviving and thriving outside a national park or proclaimed conservation area. They are one of the last original rhino populations in the world. For thousands of years they have survived in this forbidding landscape, undisturbed by man.

Apart from being hunted relentlessly, black rhino are by nature highly-strung, antisocial creatures. Where they have been relocated in game reserves after spending time in holding pens, they have become more or less habituated. Still, many black rhino have died of stress and fear in wooden cages and crates during such operations.

The black rhino here on the rocky plains of Northwestern Namibia have never been handled by man. Their contact with people is so infrequent that there is no possibility of habituation. Before we opened the safari camp here, the only people the rhino had ever been exposed to were the staff of the Save the Rhino Trust on patrol. And a rare safari convoy.

When a desert rhinoceros becomes aware of human presence, he reacts negatively. Usually he will flee. In the heat of the day a cow and her calf will race across boulder-strewn mountains and valleys until they grow small on the horizon – the type of disturbance that runs counter to the conservation principles we uphold.

In certain cases, a rhino will charge. It wants to find out what is bothering it. When this happens, you can almost see the stress in its small eyes and bearing. While such a charge is certainly frightening, it is easily defused by making your presence known. Get up, wave your arms, call out to the animal in a loud voice. Usually it will swerve and charge past you.

However, that is not the way we like to introduce people to the black rhino of the desert. When rhinos are unaware of your presence, you'll see them doing their rhino thing. They'll amble from milk bush to brosdoring, browsing contentedly. They'll gobble down welwitschia leaves like macaroni. A big bull will trample his own dung with his hind legs. Occasionally he'll spray urine against a rock. A calf will drink from its mother. This is the behaviour we want to show our guests.

The way our company feels about rhino safaris can be summed up as follows: In less than two hundred years man has managed to destroy the wildernesses of Southern Africa. Everything has been displaced and chased off and exterminated. Today the wilderness is being kept alive artificially in fenced reserves. Closed systems, under human management. Damaraland is one of the last true wilderness areas; its god-forsaken setting has thus far protected it and its rhino population. As long as we had anything to do with it, there would be no further intrusion.

In my personal capacity I have also undergone a transformation over the years. In my early days as a game ranger I relished close encounters with big game. In my boat on the Kwando I would shave past a herd of hippo. In the Kruger Park I would lean quietly against a tree trunk downwind, while the white rhino grazed a hand's breadth away. It was awesome to walk among a herd of a thousand buffalo. As a wilderness trail guide, I shot two charging elephants – because there was no other way of stopping them. One bull I dropped at seven metres. In both cases the chief ranger found that I had been dangerously close.

It was my way of living on the edge. It was why I had lost my arm.

In later years I began to find fulfilment of a different kind. It was after I had come to the desert. Here I have experienced moments of tangible peace. It's not the thrill, but the tranquillity of the wilderness that I crave now.

To sit on top of Otjitheta, surrounded by the Hoarusib River, the Ohorondanomanga mountains to the north and

Ototora to the southwest. A herd of eleven elephant in the sandy river bed among the palms. Dwarfed by the majestic landscape.

A fogless moonlit night at False Cape Frio on the Skeleton Coast, the phosphorus in the surf more brilliant than any laser show. A flock of Damara terns in a soundless fly-past along the beach. Black-backed jackal calling from the ganna dunes. The distant bleating of the fur seals. Bliss.

Late afternoon on the rocky plain beside the Agab River. In the east, flat-topped hills changing from red to purple in the setting sun. A black rhino cow and her calf, browsing from one milk bush to the next, heading towards Gaigamsfontein. A herd of springbok here, a lone giraffe there. Sublime desolation.

It's moments like these that bring peace. It's the wilderness saying to you: you have nothing more to prove – you belong to me now.

There are other moments: To lie awake in the small hours, listening to the crunching of stones as the mountain zebra cavort around the camp. To hear a desert lion roar as he walks through camp. To know that all is well.

The first cup of coffee. The stuttering roar of the diesel engines at daybreak. The promise of a new day in the wilderness. The promise of adventure. Platonic adventure – no longer a blood sport. A mature relationship with the wilderness, where nothing is disturbed or upset. It feels right.

At Rooiplaat we are unarmed during the day. In camp at night I keep my 8x57 hunting rifle at the ready. The tents are far apart and the lions have lately been showing more interest after dark. Kapoi knows how to handle a rifle and I've trained Emsie to use one too – we accompany our guests at night.

On safari drives, however, I leave my rifle behind. The lions around here are timid by day and we usually see them only from a distance. Sometimes we come across them at the fountains; then they flee into the abiekwas thickets or the rushes. We don't pursue them.

With rhino and elephant, we keep our distance. We don't want to be forced to shoot a rare desert elephant or an endangered black rhino. I carry my revolver in my backpack, for use in emergencies only – if I have to walk back to camp after dark, for instance, when a vehicle has broken down.

It's against this background that the trackers and I noticed the rhino cow and calf in the valley below us early one August morning. I had gone to the veld in high spirits that morning. A week before I had turned forty. Three weeks before that Emsie and I had become engaged in a Chinese restaurant in Swakop. Life lay wide open in front of me. Sunny – like the desert valley on this beautiful morning.

With me were the trackers, as well as the newly appointed Ernest Machengeti. He was a Shona from Zimbabwe. Conditions were so bad there that their safari guides were approaching us for work. We appointed them temporarily to supplement our own shortage of guides. I liked Ernest. He was hard-working and helpful. His general knowledge was good and he understood elephants. He was currently in training; he had to familiarise himself with our approach and get to know the area.

We gathered together our group of safari-goers. Our clients were a jovial family of Germans – male and female cousins – and a young American couple. I checked the contents of my backpack: My revolver was there. As well as a first-aid kit and extra drinking water.

As I had done the previous night around the campfire, I explained again the purpose and approach of our rhino safaris. Then I gave a detailed safety talk. In the unlikely event of a confrontation with a rhino, the guests should never act independently, but should follow the guide's instructions to the letter. The best advice was to remain with the group.

With my sandalled foot, I kicked up some dust. A light easterly breeze was blowing. Today's trackers were Elio Ganuseb and Andries Jager. They entered the valley downwind of the rhino cow and calf. Ernest and I followed with the rest of the group.

On the valley floor the trackers gave the rhinos a wide berth. The river bed was rocky. We wound through the mopanes. The rhinos were out of sight now. The light easterly breeze was still blowing. We were well downwind.

We climbed up the opposite bank of the river. Now we were on higher ground. We ventured closer to the rhino. They came in sight, about eighty metres further along. Unaware of us. I identified the cow as Tina. Her bull calf of seven months had been born earlier in the year.

For several minutes we watched them. I signalled to the guests: they had a chance to take photos. As the shutters clicked, the calf walked to his mother's flank and began to suckle. Unique photos were taken. The guests were amazed. Everyone relaxed a little.

The eastwind began to swirl. The trackers signalled for us to change our position. We moved along the southern bank in an easterly direction. We were aiming for a crosswind position until the wind had decided what to do.

We reached a tributary joining up with the river from the mountains. We tiptoed through it cautiously. Ahead of us lay a level patch dotted with milk bush. Behind it was the mountainside – where I wanted to place the guests. We moved up the bank and onto level terrain. Now we were back on higher ground. The rhinos came into view. They were still unaware of us. I motioned to the guests that there was another photo opportunity. Shutters clicked. Elio and Andries joined us.

Without warning a southwesterly wind sprang up. I took hardly any notice of it. It was the prevailing wind; I had half expected it all along. We were in a crosswind position – the rhinos wouldn't pick up our scent.

Suddenly the rhino cow froze. She raised her head. The calf began to pace nervously. I motioned to the guests to freeze. The trackers looked at each other and then at me. I realised what was happening: the cow was picking up the scent from our previous position.

In an instant the cow turned and fled. The calf followed hard on her heels. They were running away from the place where the wind had picked up our scent – a place where we no longer were.

They raced along the river bed. The next minute they came charging up the bank and emerged on the plain. Fleeing blindly away from our scent – heading straight towards our present position.

It had happened before. Elio and Andries took up their positions on either side of me, each with a rock in his hand. We advanced on the fleeing rhino. I glanced back quickly and motioned to Ernest to keep the guests together.

Elio and Andries waved their arms and made noise. We made our presence known. Usually it worked. But today was different.

At twenty metres the cow became aware of us. Her maternal instinct kicked in: she had to protect her calf. It was too late to swerve or turn round. She lowered her head with its gigantic, lethal horns. At full speed, she launched her attack.

I knew that moment: the moment of truth – when a line had been crossed. I had known such moments before. With buffaloes. With elephants. With crocodiles. With poachers. I recalled all those moments clearly. It was make or break now. Life or death.

At incredible speed the rhino cow covered the distance between us. Elio and Andries flung their stones and broke away. The next minute she was on top of me.

The line of defence had crumbled. If the rhino got past me, the guests would be exposed. It didn't fall to Elio or Andries to protect the guests; the guests were *my* responsibility. All that stood between them and the rhino cow was I.

A certain presence of mind took over. As it had with the buffaloes. And the elephants. With the crocodiles and the poachers too. It had all been so long ago. Somewhere I registered gratitude that I hadn't lost it; that it was still with me. The cow was two metres away. I surrendered to my fate.

Face down, I hurled myself in the rhino's path. With one arm I protected my head. Her nose struck my neck a mighty blow. I skidded across the earth, but stayed down. I felt her hot, snorting breath. Mucus in my neck. I smelled the dust. The earth around me rumbled and thundered under her stomping feet. I waited for her to trample me.

Then she stopped short and stood over me. I was relieved; at least she hadn't gone over me and charged the guests. She moved around me. Snorting, she investigated my backpack. I peered through my eyelashes. Between the rim of my hat and the ground a gigantic big toe was dancing about, just a few centimetres from my nose.

I heard Elio and Andries shout: "Voertsek! Voertsek!" I heard stones striking rhino hide, then thudding onto the ground.

And then she was gone. The red dust of Damaraland settled around me.

I raised my head. The veld was dead quiet. I stood up, covered with dust. I looked around me. Elio and Andries were making sure the rhinos were underway. The animals were racing along the river bank.

The guests stared at me incredulously. Ernest had managed to keep them together, but two women had taken a fall.

"Are you hurt?" a girl asked as I walked up to them.

I took off my backpack and began to disinfect the bloody knee of one of the women. Elio and Andries rejoined us and shook my hand.

"Thank you, sir," was all Elio said.

In silence we walked up the hill to where we had left the Land Rover. When I reached the top, the adrenaline had subsided. An overpowering weariness came over me. I wanted to stretch out right there beside the Land Rover and sleep. But I couldn't – there was a safari to complete. I was considerably less talkative as we continued through the wilderness.

Later we saw the rhino cow and her calf again, high against the mountainside above Wêreldsendfontein. They stood calmly in the shade of a witgat tree. They had crossed a great distance to get there. I watched them through my binoculars. At first glance they seemed peaceful and unharmed.

It's not right, I thought. It's not right for a seven-month-old calf to be frightened like that. And then to have to flee across rocks and mountains over such a great distance. It's not right.

Even if we do our best to intrude as little as possible, we will always have an impact on the wilderness. It's part of us. The primitive fear we inspire in other earthly creatures will always be there. As long as man walks the earth, there will never be harmony.

It's not right. That calf is much too young.

And I? Well, I'm getting too old for moments like these.

Glossary

ABIEKWAS YELLOWWOOD: wild tamarisk

ASSEGAI: sharp light spear

BITTEREINDER: Boer commando member in the South African War who refused to surrender but instead fought to the bitter end

BOEKENHOUT: South African (or Cape) beech

BOERBOEL: crossbred mastiff

BOERE-OOM: typical elderly Afrikaans man of farming stock

BROSDORING: *Phaeoptilum spinosum*

CUCA SHOP: a small shop selling beer and other things like candles, biscuits and sweets; Cuca was a beer sold in colonial Angola

DASSIE: rock rabbit, Cape hyrax

DONNER: wallop

DOOS: twat

DORSLAND TREKKER: member of Thirstland Trek

FLETCHA: a unit of Bushman guerillas fighting for the Portuguese in colonial Angola; from the Portuguese for "arrow"

GANNA: lye bush

GATVOL: extremely fed up

GHWARRIE: guarri

GOEIE BLIKSEM!: Good grief!

INDUNA: military commander; here loosely used to mean "headman"

JA, WRAGTAG!: Well, I'll be damned!

KHAKI: British soldier in South African War

KIERIE: walking stick, fighting stick

KIERIEKLAPPER: russet bushwillow

KLIPSPRINGER: African chamois
KOPPIE: hill
KUTA: tribal council
LAPA: unroofed enclosure for cooking and eating
LEKKERRUIKPEUL: scented thorn tree
MANGETI: *Schinziopython rautanenae*
MATUMI: *Adina microcephala*
MEALIE: maize
MOER: beat up
MOFFIE: homosexual man
MORENA: Sir, Mister
MORINGA: *Moringa ovalifolia*
MUHANGO: millet
NARRA: butterpips
OMBONGORU: necklace worn by a married Himba man
OMBUKU: back part of a Himba loin cloth
OMURAMBA: depression along which water drains away in the rainy season
ONDUMBU: headdress worn by a married Himba man
ONGANDA: Himba homestead
OTJITATI: front part of a Himba loin cloth
PANGA: broad, heavy knife, used as a tool or weapon
PIET-MY-VROU: red-chested cuckoo
POORT: defile
POTBROOD: bread baked in a large cast-iron pot over an open fire
POTJIEKOS: meat and vegetables prepared in a large cast-iron pot over an open fire
RAASBLAAR: large-fruited bushwillow
RENOSTERVELD: rocky desert where rhinos live
RV: SA Defence Force lingo for "rendezvous"
SAMIL: heavy military truck
SANDVAALBOS: silver cluster leaf
SCHLUCHT: ravine
SPRUIT: stream
STAALDAK: SA Defence Force lingo for "steel helmet"

TORRAS: rounded basalt boulders common to Damaraland
VELDKOS: "veld food", such as roots, tubers, bulbs, berries
and wild fruits
VLEI: low-lying marshy area
VOERTSEK!: Bugger off!
WITGAT: shepherd's tree